Political Corruption and Governance

Series Editors
Dan Hough
University of Sussex
Brighton, UK

Paul M. Heywood
University of Nottingham
Nottingham, UK

This series aims to analyse the nature and scope of, as well as possible remedies for, political corruption. The rise to prominence over the last 20 years of corruption-related problems and of the 'good governance' agenda as the principal means to tackle them has led to the development of a plethora of (national and international) policy proposals, international agreements and anti-corruption programmes and initiatives. National governments, international organisations and NGOs all now claim to take very seriously the need to tackle issues of corruption. It is thus unsurprising that over couple of decades, a significant body of work with a wide and varied focus has been published in academic journals and in international discussion papers. This series seeks to provide a forum through which to address this growing body of literature. It invites not just in-depth single country analyses of corruption and attempts to combat it, but also comparative studies that explore the experiences of different states (or regions) in dealing with different types of corruption. We also invite monographs that take an overtly thematic focus, analysing trends and developments in one type of corruption across either time or space, as well as theoretically informed analysis of discrete events.

More information about this series at
http://www.palgrave.com/gp/series/14545

Elitza Katzarova

The Social Construction of Global Corruption

From Utopia to Neoliberalism

palgrave
macmillan

Elitza Katzarova
Braunschweig University
of Technology
Braunschweig, Germany

Political Corruption and Governance
ISBN 978-3-319-98568-8 ISBN 978-3-319-98569-5 (eBook)
https://doi.org/10.1007/978-3-319-98569-5

Library of Congress Control Number: 2018951567

Cover image: © Daniel Day/Photodisc/Getty Images
Cover design by Akihiro Nakayama

This Palgrave Macmillan imprint is published by the registered company Springer Nature Switzerland AG
The registered company address is: Gewerbestrasse 11, 6330 Cham, Switzerland

Preface and Acknowledgements

When my interest in corruption studies first developed about nine years ago, I had no interest in writing about global corruption. I started with an interest in two corrupt countries Bulgaria and Italy. I was, at the time, a Bulgarian living in Italy, so that made a lot of sense. The more I read about corruption however, the more I realized that there was an aspect of how corruption became a global governance issue that had not been properly accounted for. How corruption became a global problem has a lot to tell us not just about corruption but also about how international affairs work, how are problems defined and how is the regulatory response to them globalized.

The Latin root of the word 'corruption' means 'to break.' Our current preoccupation with global corruption can be seen to imply that the world is broken. Arguably, the exponentially increasing demand for global solutions to complex problems encounters one insurmountable difficulty, which is that the world itself is also broken: it is broken into nation states. The attempt to tackle global problems that exhibit ever-increasing sophistication has to overcome the broken landscape of international affairs. The world is broken also by conditions that necessitate collective definitions and collective responses. This study brought all of these elements together in accounting for how governments constructed and negotiated a global corruption problem, and how the resulting global governance structures shaped our thinking not just on what corruption is, but also on what government—business relations ought to look like.

Much of this story is about the United States and the Foreign Corrupt Practices Act (FCPA). The story of the internationalization of the FCPA is fascinating, and it was what attracted me to this study in the first place. A world without bribery would be a better world and definitely one that is better for developing countries. The point that this book tries to make is that maybe the US-sponsored issue of bribery is not the epitome of corruption. Corruption can be seen to operate at a much grander scale in the way in which business engulfed politics under the neoliberal transformation of governments and societies. Perhaps the task of the anti-corruption scholar is to start studying the potential conflicts of interest in well-established (and often legal) practices, such as the revolving door in politics, legal corporate campaign financing, corporate welfare, as well as the socialization of losses and privatization of profits that has become the new normal with the latest financial crisis. If we are to reconsider some of the early claims on corrupt influence, launched by developing nations, there might be something much more fundamentally broken with the world than brown envelopes slipped under tables.

There are many people who have helped me in my journey of completing this book. I would like to thank Paul Heywood, Vincent della Sala, Steven Sampson, Anja Jakobi, Jasmine Haunschild, Bastian Loges, Giorgio Fodor, Silvia Tomaselli, Rosaria Astarita, Jan-Anno Schuur from the Organization for Economic Co-operation and Development (OECD) Archives in Paris and Marvin Córdova from the United Nations (UN) Archives in New York. Finally, I would like to thank my mother and my husband for their love and support. I would like to dedicate this book to the family that I lost over the last years, my father Elko, and my grandparents Atanas and Liliana.

Sozopol, Bulgaria
June 2018

Elitza Katzarova

Contents

Abbreviations

ACRN	Anti-Corruption Research Network
BAE	British Aerospace
BIAC	Business and Industry Advisory Committee
CCL	Corporate Criminal Liability
CIME	Committee on International Investment and Multinational Enterprises
CIPE	Center of International Private Enterprise
CoE	Council of Europe
CPI	Corruption Perceptions Index
DAFFE	Directorate for Financial, Fiscal and Enterprise Affairs
ECOSOC	United Nations Economic and Social Council
EU	European Union
FATF	Financial Action Task Force
FCPA	Foreign Corrupt Practices Act
FDI	Foreign Direct Investment
FIDIC	Business Integrity Management Clearing House of the International Federation of Consulting Engineers
G7	Group of 7
G20	Group of 20
G77	Group of 77
GATT	General Agreement on Tariffs and Trade
GFC	Global Financial Crisis
GIACC	Global Infrastructure Anti-Corruption Centre
ICC	International Chamber of Commerce
IFIs	International Financial Institutions

IME	Committee on International Investment and Multinational Enterprises
IMF	International Monetary Fund
ITT	International Telephone & Telegraph
NIE	New Institutional Economics
OAS	Organization of American States
OECD	Organization for Economic Co-operation and Development
PACI	Partnering Against Corruption Initiative
PPP	Public–Private Partnership
RBIBT	Recommendation on Bribery in International Business Transactions
SEC	Securities and Exchange Commission
SME	Small and Medium Enterprises
TI	Transparency International
TI USA	Transparency International United States of America
TNC	Trans-National Corporation
TUAC	Trade Union Advisory Committee
UK	United Kingdom
UN	United Nations
UNCAC	United Nations Convention Against Corruption
UNCTAD	United Nations Conference on Trade and Development
UNICORN	Unions Anti-Corruption Network
UNODC	United Nations Office on Drugs and Crime
UNTERM	United Nations Terminated Missions
UNTOC	United Nations Convention against Transnational Organized Crime
US	United States
WGI	Worldwide Governance Indicators
WTO	World Trade Organization

List of Tables

CHAPTER 1

Introduction: The Origin Story of Global Anti-Corruption Governance

The origin story of global anti-corruption governance reads like a heroic quest for justice and transparency. It is a reassuring story of liberal triumphalism. It is a cautionary tale for corrupt public officials and governments. It is a shameful reminder for the corrupt countries of the Global South to upend their ways and join the peaceful yellow of the North on Transparency International's (TI) world map. It is also a story that in most academic literature occupies an introductory paragraph. It is a story that, albeit uplifting, deserves little thought.

This book looks into an aspect of the global governance of corruption that was previously considered unworthy of scholarly attention. To the extent that global anti-corruption efforts prior to the mid-1990s were mentioned, it was usually as a brief note on a 'false start'. The lack of attention to the intergovernmental talks, that by the mid-1990s were ongoing for 25 years, has led to some persistent myths in the origin story of global anti-corruption governance. One of these myths is that TI and the World Bank were pioneers in the process. The founding of TI in the early 1990s and the acclaimed Wolfensohn speech on the 'cancer of corruption' in 1996 were events much more visible than the workings of ad hoc groups and confidential intergovernmental talks, and it was the former, rather than the latter, that came to symbolize the new era of global anti-corruption efforts.

E. Katzarova, *The Social Construction of Global Corruption*, Political Corruption and Governance, https://doi.org/10.1007/978-3-319-98569-5_1

In addition to the 'founding fathers' myth, another persistent myth in the origin story of global corruption is that there was no conflict on the definition of a global corruption problem. On the contrary, the social construction of a global corruption problem was ridden with strife, and in the process of contention, corruption became subject to a radical metamorphosis. Corruption was transformed from corporate abuse of power in the 1970s to government abuse of power in the 1990s. The trope of the corrupt corporation came to be supplanted by the tropes of the corrupt politician, corrupt public official and corrupt country. In the process, the blame for corruption was shifted from developed countries (and their corporations) to the developing countries (and their governments). As the current study aims to show, the nature of global problems is not devoid of power struggles and battles for meaning. Shaping governance responses to global problems also means shaping the world.

What makes this study distinctive is that it is the first International Relations (IR) monograph to systematically examine the rise of corruption as a global governance problem from the 1970s onward. While many articles and studies tackle the question tangentially (Naim 1995; Elliott 1997; McCoy and Heckel 2001; Bukovansky 2002; Krastev 2004; Pieth 2007; Jakobi 2013), this book puts the question of how corruption rose and developed as a global governance issue in the center of investigation. As the book argues, this gap in the literature is due to a significant extent to the lack of theoretical and methodological tools in IR that can trace the development of global social problems. In sociological research on the contrary, the study of the emergence of (national) social problems has a long research pedigree (Spector and Kitsuse 2009). The book offers a sociological approach for the study of problems in IR and makes a contribution to the constructivist agenda in IR by showing how sociological models for the study of social problems are applicable to international politics. Using the case of corruption, the book shows how global problems are negotiated and constructed and how global governance structures have emerged from them. The findings presented in the book are based on previously unexamined archival sources from the Organization for Economic Co-operation and Development (OECD) and the United Nations (UN) which would be of interest to academics and anti-corruption practitioners but also to a wider audience of readers to which it would also provide a glimpse into the work of international organizations that usually appear as black boxes to the general public.

Since the mid-1990s, the topic of corruption has started to dominate the global policy agenda; corruption has increasingly been understood as a global policy problem that cannot be adequately tackled within the jurisdictional boundaries of the nation state. In the period 1994–1997, corruption as a global problem entered a stage of institutionalization after the formal introduction of the subject in a number of regional organizations such as the Organization of American States (OAS), the Council of Europe (CoE) and the European Union (EU). Yet, the formal agreements produced by these organizations as well as the OECD and the UN appear to have failed at ameliorating corruption across the globe. In academic research, this post-institutionalization phase is also referred to as a 'legitimacy crisis' stage and has produced a shift from the study of corruption to the study of anti-corruption work across different fields, in particular political science, sociology and social anthropology (Krastev 2004; Haller and Shore 2005; Sampson 2005; Bracking 2007; Roden 2010; Brown and Cloke 2011). The legitimacy crisis that counter-corruption measures have entered has led scholars in these disciplines to question the definition, scope and ways to tackle corruption internationally and has paradoxically revived issues that were hotly debated at international organizations prior to institutionalization.

The book offers new ways of thinking about corruption by examining the two distinct ways in which policy approaches and discourse on corruption developed in the UN and the OECD. One of these approaches extrapolated bribery as the main form of corrupt practices and advocated a single-actor, limited scope offense, while the other approach tackled the broader structure of the global economic system and the increasing power of transnational corporations. One offered a ban on bribery—the other international regulation of transnational corporations. This study traces how these two interpretations of corruption as bribery and corruption as undue power of big corporations emerged from different state sponsors and how these two versions of what business–state relations should look like evolved over two decades of pre-negotiation talks at the UN and the OECD (as well as other organizations) until the understanding of corruption as bribery prevailed in the mid-1990s. The book concludes that the outcome of these debates has to a significant extent shaped the global economy as we know it today and that the discussed issues still resonate powerfully with current debates about the power of global economic actors and corporations that are 'too big to fail.'

Chapter 2 provides a roadmap through the complex landscape of the global governance of corruption and an introduction to the implicit and explicit hypotheses that have been generated by the academic literature on the factors and agents responsible for the global anti-corruption eruption in the 1990s. The first part of the chapter presents an outline of the major global anti-corruption initiatives and introduces the main actors in five different groups. The second part of the chapter starts to analyze the question as to why there has been a global anti-corruption eruption and who are the major actors responsible for this development. This section starts to problematize corruption as a global issue by introducing the six factors that have contributed to the rise of corruption as a global policy problem: the end of the Cold War, the good governance agenda of the World Bank, the coalition building of TI, the quantification of corruption through the publication of international perception-based indices, the instrumental use of the issue of corruption as a smoke screen for policies of liberalization and finally, the role of the United States in raising corrupt payments on the global agenda. The third part of the chapter then proceeds to examine four major ways of conceptualizing global anti-corruption work: anti-corruption as an issue for global governance, as an international regime or regimes, as a movement and as an industry.

Chapter 3 argues for the relevance of sociological approach to social problem to the study of global problems and IR. To account for the social construction of a problem means to provide for historical contingencies and to understand problems as evolving products of collective definition that are in a dynamic relation to the condition they refer to. This book studies the process of definition through claims-making and other discursive strategies and practices that are presented in this chapter and are applied in the empirical chapters. In order to clarify what is meant by construction of a global problem, the chapter proceeds in three steps. First, the concept of social construction and different types of social constructs are examined in order to show that the social construction of problems provides a useful analytical vehicle in relation to factual relativism. Second, the long tradition of the study of social problems in sociology is briefly introduced, and the theory of Spector and Kitsuse on claims-making is given further attention and is adapted to IR and the cast of actors that are present on the global arena. Third, other theoretical and conceptual issues are tackled before the presentation of the cases and the data sources. The chapter concludes that the application of the Spector and Kitsuse approach to IR can help elucidate the role of power, contestation and conflict in the social construction of global issues, and in this way, it can counteract what some scholars consider to be an implicit liberal bias in much of constructivist IR scholarship.

Chapter 4 examines the first anti-corruption discussions at global venues and the first instances of global institutional legitimation. Since the 1970s, claims on corruption within international organizations developed in two major directions. The chapter argues that these clashing interpretations of the same condition can be called the Chilean and the American (US) legacies. The major difference between these two approaches was that the Chilean legacy developed at the UN and defined corruption as corporate influence on politics, while the American legacy developed predominantly at the OECD and defined corruption as bribery. The chapter examines the content of global claims at the OECD and the UN in the 1970s and argues that the successful campaign to establish corruption as a global governance problem in the 1990s can only be understood as the legacy of the 1970s. By showing that nation states pioneered the process of global social construction, the chapter lays the groundwork for the argument that state power is essential in the creation of global problems and that powerful states can be proactive participants in this process.

Chapter 5 traces the steps that led to the re-launch of global claims-making in 1989 and shows how the US concern with illicit/corrupt payments emerged in the first place. The main reason for the US initiative of 1989 was the Foreign Corrupt Practices Act (FCPA), which can be seen as a product of Watergate, as much as a product of the International Telephone & Telegraph (ITT) aftermath. While the ITT affair triggered debates in the United States on the foreign policy repercussions of corporate misconduct, Watergate made these debates more domestically oriented. It was the combined work of the Subcommittee on Multinational Corporations, the Watergate Special Prosecution Force, the Securities and Exchange Commission (SEC) and a number of follow-up Senate committees that shed light on the illicit payments problem and informed much of the thinking behind the FCPA. Furthermore, the US Congressional hearings after the ITT affair were the main source of information for other governments to start their own investigations into corporate and government misconduct. As such, these testimonies provide information on the putative condition out of which global claims on corruption emerged. This is why this chapter discusses the content of the US

Congress hearings on multinational corporations and foreign corporate payments. The chapter further establishes the re-emergence of claims after the 1988 Amendment to the FCPA, when the United States chose the OECD as the most appropriate international forum in which to achieve consensus on corrupt practices.

Chapter 6 accounts for the 1980s as the 'middle years.' In the 1980s, a counterrevolution that re-configured the relationship between state and market took place. The idea that the free market provides the best governance mechanism, of course, delegitimized the role of the state as defender of the public interest against the excesses of global corporate profit maximization. If in the 1970s anti-corruption debates in international organizations were dominated by the problem of corporations as political agents, in the 1990s the role of the state as economic agent came center stage. The Global South lost its strategic importance with the end of the Cold War, but also much changed with the Third-World foreign debt crisis. Yet, the UN venues dominated by developing countries, such as the United Nations Conference on Trade and Development (UNCTAD), the Group of 77 (G77) and the United Nations Center on Transnational Corporations (UNCTC), continued to argue for regulatory activism in the developing world and that the US-sponsored issue of bribery should be understood within the broader agenda of international regulation of multinationals. When the United States re-introduced the issue of bribery at the OECD in 1989, other major competitors from the Global North seemed largely uninterested in the appeal to ban transnational bribery. This chapter traces the position of OECD member states, as well as the work of the OECD Working Group in controversy management. The chapter further discusses the anti-corruption debates at the UN after 1980, and the different take that developing nations had on the good governance agenda, which emerged in the early 1990s.

Chapter 7 accounts for the making of the global anti-corruption eruption in the 1990s. In the period 1994–1997, the foundation of the global anti-corruption governance was laid out. As this chapter shows, the success of the anti-corruption endeavor was to a large extent determined by a systematic approach of state-sponsored coalition building. The advancement of talks at the OECD and the adoption of the Recommendation on Bribery in International Business Transactions (RBIBT) led OECD member states to introduce the topic of corrupt practices in the OAS, the CoE, the EU, the UN and the G7/8. Non-state actors contributed to the process of coalition building, but much of what they achieved was shaped by previous efforts of state actors, in particular the United States, and the ongoing intergovernmental dynamics. The instrumental use of publicity and the change of venues contributed to the success of the OECD initiative to outlaw transnational corrupt payments and led to the spread of talks in a number of regional organizations. The formal agreements reached at organizations such as the OAS, the CoE, the EU, the OECD and the World Bank then provided the legal and discursive underpinnings for the re-introduction of the subject at the UN. Building on Chapter 6, the first part of this chapter zooms closer in on the way in which the decision for the RBIBT was reached and discursively shaped. The second part then goes on to zoom out and shows the bigger picture of how, in relation to progress at the OECD, the subject of corruption was introduced in regional organizations. In this way, this chapter works toward striking a balance between showing how the social construction of problems is negotiated within organizations and how the interconnection and overlaps between organizations also shape the processes of collective definition and the formulation of an official plan of action.

Chapter 8 compares global anti-corruption debates in the 1970s and 1990s in order to provide the big picture in the development of a global corruption problem. The chapter analyzes the main differences in terms of problem content, venues and external events, as well as the strategy of the US executive and the level of uncertainty within which this strategy operated. The chapter argues that anti-corruption rhetoric was indeed neoliberalized in the 1990s, but the link between anti-corruption, as part of a broader agenda to regulate multinationals, and neoliberalism, as an agenda for deregulation, could be more complex than previously thought. The chapter suggests that, rather than being used as neoliberal window-dressing, the question of corruption in global venues was to some extent constitutive of a neoliberal agenda; anti-corruption policies were about the making of neoliberalism itself. The diachronic comparison shows that depending on their membership base different venues, such as the UNCTAD, the G77 and the UNCTC on the one hand and the G7, the OECD and the World Bank on the other, have offered two distinctive competing versions of how is corruption to be understood and how it should be tackled. These competing narratives are indicative of two different projects of world building proposed by the Global South and the Global North, and their convergence in the 1990s is what made the institutionalization of corruption as a global governance issue possible.

References

Bracking, Sarah, ed. 2007. *Corruption and Development: The Anti-corruption Campaigns*. New York: Palgrave Macmillan.

Brown, Ed, and Jonathan Cloke. 2011. "Critical Perspectives on Corruption: An Overview." *Critical Perspectives on International Business* 7 (2): 116–124.

Bukovansky, Mlada. 2002. "Corruption Is Bad: Normative Dimensions of the Anti-corruption Movement." Working Paper 2002/5, Department of International Relations, Australian National University. Accessed October 20, 2017. https://digitalcollections.anu.edu.au/bitstream/1885/40136/3/02-5.pdf.

Elliott, Kimberly Ann. 1997. "Corruption as an International Policy Problem: Overview and Recommendations." In *Corruption and the Global Economy*, edited by Kimberley A. Elliott, 175–233. Washington, DC: Peterson Institute for International Economics.

Haller, Dieter, and Cris Shore, eds. 2005. *Corruption: Anthropological Perspectives*. London: Pluto Press.

Jakobi, Anja P. 2013. "The Changing Global Norm of Anti-corruption: From Bad Business to Bad Government." *Zeitschrift Für Vergleichende Politikwissenschaft* 7 (1): 243–264.

Krastev, Ivan. 2004. *Shifting Obsessions: Three Essays on the Politics of Anticorruption*. Budapest: Central European University Press.

McCoy, Jennifer L., and Heather Heckel. 2001. "The Emergence of a Global Anti-corruption Norm." *International Politics* 38 (1): 65–90.

Naim, Moses. 1995. "Corruption Eruption." *Brown Journal of World Affairs* 2 (2): 245–261.

Pieth, Mark. 2007. "Introduction." In *The OECD Convention on Bribery: A Commentary*, edited by Mark Pieth, Lucinda A. Low, and Peter J. Cullen, 3–42. Cambridge: Cambridge University Press.

Roden J. 2010. "The International Anti-corruption Crusade: Neo-Liberal Institutional Structures, Moralization, and Social Capital." *Undercurrent Journal* 7 (1): 12–22.

Sampson, Steven. 2005. "Integrity Warriors: Global Morality and the Anti-corruption Movement in the Balkans." In *Corruption: Anthropological Perspectives*, edited by Cris Shore and Dieter Haller, 103–131. London and Ann Arbor, MI: Pluto Press.

Spector, Malcolm, and John Kitsuse. 2009. *Constructing Social Problems*. 4th ed. Rutgers, NJ: Transaction Publishers.

CHAPTER 2

Corruption and Its Discontents

Corruption appears to be one of the most pressing global problems at the beginning of the twenty-first century. A global survey conducted for the BBC in 2010 and 2011 ranked corruption as the second most serious global problem. Since the mid-1990s, corruption has also become the center of an impressive global governance architecture. International organizations, global business associations and international non-governmental organizations (INGOs) have all taken a tough stance against corruption. The fairy-tale version of how this collective global governance response took shape usually features TI. The setting of the fairy tale is the end of the Cold War when non-partisan, non-governmental organizations (NGOs) could finally get down to the business of fixing global problems. While TI definitely played a catalytic role in the mid-1990s, the fairy-tale version of anti-corruption governance exaggerates the INGOs impact. It does so, perhaps, in an idealistic attempt to carve a place for solving global problems outside of politics. This is where the setting of the fairy tale comes into place. After the end of the Cold War, we woke up in a crisp new world beyond politics, a world in which technical problems could finally be solved pragmatically and without generating controversy. Corruption, however, is not a technical or natural problem. What came to be defined as global corruption was dependent on the ideas and interests of a number of collective and individual actors. Anti-corruption discourse and practice are not neutral, technocratic and devoid of struggles for power. In a similar way, the process through which

E. Katzarova, *The Social Construction of Global Corruption*,
Political Corruption and Governance,
https://doi.org/10.1007/978-3-319-98569-5_2

the problem rose on the global agenda was laden with power struggles and controversies over the future direction of the global economy. An understanding of global problems as natural phenomena, which come clearly defined and pre-packaged, obscures the power and ideational struggles of collective definitions. This chapter systematizes the state of the art of global anti-corruption governance before setting on to analyze the social construction of a global corruption problem.

The expansion of global anti-corruption initiatives has been so impressive in the past two decades (1996–2018) that enumerating and systematizing its manifestations across the globe have become a daunting task. The purpose of this chapter is, firstly, to present a map of the 'anti-corruption eruption' that has swept the globe; secondly, to frame the anti-corruption initiatives conceptually and tackle the reasons for their rapid emergence and expansion according to the existing literature; and thirdly, to delineate the main actors involved in the process. To this purpose, the first part of the chapter presents an outline of the major global anti-corruption initiatives and introduces the main actors in five different groups. The second part of the chapter starts to analyze the question as to why there has been a global anti-corruption eruption and who are the major actors responsible for this development. This section starts to problematize corruption as a global issue by introducing the six factors that have contributed to the rise of corruption as a global policy problem: the end of the Cold War, the good governance agenda of the World Bank, the coalition building of TI, the quantification of corruption through the publication of international perception-based indices, the instrumental use of the issue of corruption as a smoke screen for policies of liberalization and finally, the role of the United States in raising corrupt payments on the global agenda.

The third part of the chapter then proceeds to examine four major ways of conceptualizing global anti-corruption work: anti-corruption as an issue for global governance (Rosenau and Wang 2001; Eigen 2013; Kirton et al. 2013), as an international regime or regimes (Bukovanvsky 2002; von Rosenvinge 2009; Wolf and Schmidt-Pfister 2010), as a 'movement' (Yao 1997; Sampson 2005; Hough 2013) and as an industry (Sampson 2010). Two of the four concepts and their compatibility are given further consideration—that is the existence of an international anti-corruption regime and its relation to the theoretical framework of global governance. Regimes in the context of global governance literature can be seen as specific 'governance systems,' providing governance in specific issue area (Ba and Hoffmann 2006; Stokke 2012). This book is based on the premise that global governance structures, in particular issue areas, emerge from problems. These global problems are not natural, but have to be constructed, and despite the recent focus on the role of non-state actors in international affairs, state agency remains essential to the process of social construction.

In a short period of time in the mid-1990s, the question of corruption emerged in a number of venues and was addressed with a wide range of instruments. It seemed like a new issue had exploded onto the international scene after the end of the Cold War. The famous reference of Naim (1995) to a 'corruption eruption' was met with an equally imposing anti-corruption eruption that took over the major international organizations and financial institutions and involved the business community and civil society actors. A number of international legal treaties have been adopted since the mid-1990s that tackle the subject of corruption. The only legal anti-corruption instrument that is truly global in scope is the United Nations Convention Against Corruption (UNCAC) adopted in 2003. A number of international conventions with regional scope precede the UNCAC. These are the Inter-American Convention Against Corruption (1996), the Convention on the Fight Against Corruption Involving Officials of the European Communities or Officials of Member States of the European Union (1997), the Council of Europe Criminal and Civil Law Conventions (1999a, b) and the African Union Convention on Preventing and Combating Corruption (2003). Even though the OECD Convention is not a global instrument, it cannot properly be placed in the regional profile. This is primarily because the membership base of the OECD is not regional, but also because the Convention for Combating Bribery of Foreign Public Officials in International Business Transactions (1997) involves a strong transnational element with its focus on transnational bribery which has been incorporated into almost all of the above conventions.

A complementary, albeit 'national,' side of the global governance of corruption that further developed as a consequence of the OECD Convention is the application of domestic acts with extraterritorial reach such as the UK Bribery Act from 2010 and the US FCPA from 1977. While other national legal acts targeting the curbing of corruption exist, these two pieces of legislation enjoy an extensive extraterritorial application. The extraterritorial reach of the Bribery Act and the FCPA is partly due to their legal provisions, but also to the special position that both the United Kingdom and the United States hold in the global economy. The jurisdictional reach of the Bribery Act, for example, is extended to all companies that have a 'presence' in the United Kingdom, which may be an office, operations or subsidiary (Bribery Act 2010). The UK jurisdiction applies even to acts committed in a third country that do not bear connection to the operations of the liable company in the United Kingdom (Dunst et al. 2011). In this respect, Article 12 of the Bribery Act comes close to the provisions of the FCPA which came into effect after the amendments of 1998. The extended US jurisdiction was possible because the OECD Convention, adopted the previous year, allowed for amendments to the FCPA, so that all companies listed on a US stock exchange would be liable even for corrupt acts committed in a third country (Ashe 2005). The prosecution of companies under these two powerful extraterritorial acts and under other anti-corruption national laws with similar reach are an important part of the global governance of corruption because of the broad extraterritoriality they enjoy. Since the application of the Bribery Act has been significantly postponed, for the time being only the FCPA provides robust proof that on behalf of the United States, this national legislation is vigorously employed in the fight against corrupt practices internationally, and the Siemens and BAE cases constitute point in case (Lord 2014). Both cases were brought to the Court of Columbia (U.S. v. Siemens Aktiengesellschaft and U.S. v. BAE Systems PLC). In the case of the BAE, the British government chose to close the case and evoked issues of national security as justification for the decision, but yet it had to concede to an investigation under the FCPA in which it pleaded guilty (US Department of Justice 2018).

A trans-governmental element in the global governance of corruption has developed as a consequence of the need for enforcement of the international conventions and the extraterritorial national laws. Delaney (2005) explains the trans-governmental twist in the anti-corruption effort as a network that has developed from the necessity for cooperation between national agencies, entrusted with the power to implement national anti-corruption laws and to comply with international obligations.

Both private- and public-sector initiatives have developed to counteract corruption internationally and have led to attempts to combine business and governmental approaches to anti-corruption work in a comprehensive framework. Global business actors have adopted anti-corruption practices as part of general strategies for corporate responsibility, or specific attempts to address national and international legislation on the subject. The International Chamber of Commerce (ICC), the leading business organization worldwide, was the first international non-government organization that addressed the issue of corruption internationally in 1977 with the ICC's Rules on Extortion and Bribery in International Business Transactions.

Business actors continue to be actively involved in curbing corruption. The scope of the OECD Convention, for example, focuses on the 'supply side' of bribery. While addressed at states, the Convention concentrates on the role of global business as the provider of bribes and does not scrutinize the 'demand,' or recipient side of the corrupt transaction. Abiding to formal legal restrictions, however, is not the only way in which business actors contribute to the global anti-corruption campaign. Voluntary action, as in the case of the ICC Rules on Extortion and Bribery, remains at the forefront of business attempts to curb corruption internationally.

Anti-corruption policies have become an integral ingredient of corporate social responsibility. An example of how this was achieved at a global scale is provided by the Global Compact. The Compact is the most significant 'voluntary corporate responsibility initiative in the world,' and it involves close to 9000 corporate actors from 130 countries. In light of the UNCAC, in June 2004, a 10th Principle was added to the Global Compact which states that 'Businesses should work against corruption in all its forms, including extortion and bribery' (UN Global Compact 2018). Stressing the importance of voluntary action, the Compact aims at complementing international regulation and mainstreaming the ten principles of corporate responsibility and sustainability worldwide.

While the endorsement of self-regulating mechanisms could be an effective preventive mechanism against corruption for big companies, Small and Medium Enterprises (SME) may find it more challenging to build internal integrity systems that ensure compliance. The Business Anti-Corruption Portal (Portal), an Internet tool, is tailored for SMEs that are less often placed in the media limelight, but face as many challenges, especially when investing abroad, as big companies do. The Portal provides tools, free training and information tailored to SMEs and stresses the importance of the involvement of the private sector in the global fight against corruption (Business Anti-Corruption Portal 2018).

Another notable business portal with a global scope is the Resource Center for Business 'Business Fighting Corruption' of the World Bank Institute (World Bank 2018). While these initiatives remain business oriented, they reach toward wider civil society and therefore provide a good platform for interaction between INGOs and global business actors.

The Business and Industry Advisory Committee (BIAC), which represents business interests to the OECD, also takes an active stance against corruption and bribery and structures the plethora of formal and informal initiatives on the subject in the BIAC Anti-Bribery Resource Guide (BIAC 2018). Membership associations, such as TRACE International and Center of International Private Enterprise (CIPE), specialize in consulting multinational corporations on compliance with international anti-corruption regulation (CIPE 2018). The Partnering Against Corruption Initiative (PACI) of the World Economic Forum is another 'global anti-corruption initiative, developed by companies for companies' (World Economic Forum 2018). Notable initiatives by industry include the Extractive Industries Transparency Initiative, the Global Infrastructure Anti-Corruption Centre (GIACC), and the Business Integrity Management Clearing House of the International Federation of Consulting Engineers (FIDIC). The Global Unions Anti-Corruption Network (UNICORN) is an international trade union network, sponsored among others by TUAC (the Trade Union Advisory Committee to the OECD) which specializes in trade union anti-corruption work at the international level (UNODC 2018).

The G20 Anti-Corruption Action Plan, first adopted in 2010, constitutes an attempt at a comprehensive reform and harmonization of the global governance of corruption. The Action Plan also provides an example of the existing synergies between government and business actors and reveals the dense web of communication and collaboration between a number of international organizations on the subject of anti-corruption. The current resurgence of interest in the international fight against corruption can be partially attributed to fears that the global financial crisis (GFC) would undermine standards in business transactions. It was in relation to the GFC that the G20 Anti-Corruption Action Plan was adopted at the Seoul Summit in November 2010. Strengthening the existing 'international anti-corruption regime' appears at the front of the reform effort with the two pillars of the regime being the UNCAC and OECD Conventions (Action Plan G20 Annex III 2010).

The driving force behind efforts, such as the G20 Action Plan, is a fear that, especially in Western Europe, the fight against corruption in the interaction between business and the public sector could become subordinated to the pursuit of profit, thus jeopardizing the implementation of the OECD Convention as the most effective insurance against this development (Wolf and Schmidt-Pfister 2010). At the same time, Wolf and Schmidt-Pfister (2010) argue, the challenges posed by the GFC may provide impetus for the future development of the anti-corruption regime and become a robust 'example of politics in an era of fragmented statehood' in a field as politically sensitive and multi-dimensional as corruption (16).

The OECD and G20 are cooperating for the successful implementation of the Anti-Corruption Action Plan. Together with the UN Office on Drugs and Crime in Vienna, which is the agency responsible for tackling the implementation of the UNCAC, the OECD and G20 organize common events for strengthening coordination between business and government (OECD 2018). Currently, momentum appears to have been built for improving the consistency of the anti-corruption effort through the annual review of the action plan which aims to develop a dense network of interlocutors beyond the G20 membership to tackle foreign bribery in particular (Action Plan G20 2015–2016).

The World Bank, the International Monetary Fund (IMF) and the World Trade Organization (WTO) have addressed corruption in the broader framework of good governance and transparency since the mid-1990s. The oldest provision on anti-corruption measures, Article X, was passed to the WTO from General Agreement on Tariffs and Trade (GATT) in 1994 and has remained virtually unchanged since 1947 (Ala'i 2008). The WTO has therefore been addressing the issue of transparency and (indirectly) corruption since its creation in 1995. The IMF has tackled corruption directly in the overall framework of good governance promotion since 1997. Corruption, defined as 'the abuse of public authority or trust for private benefit,' undermines the legitimacy of government and 'market integrity' and is therefore a focal point of the IMF efforts to address poor governance globally. 'The Partnership for Sustainable Global Growth' (1996) and 'Good Governance: The IMF's Role' (1997) are the two essential publications which laid the foundations for the IMF's anti-corruption policies (IMF 2018).

Although other regional and development banks have also developed anti-corruption policies in the last twenty years, the World Bank retains a central position on the anti-corruption frontier. The World Bank's anti-corruption strategy was first made public in September 1997 and it evolved into a comprehensive program by 2007, when the Governance and Anticorruption Strategy of the World Bank Working Group was approved. The successful implementation of the strategy would see 'the emergence of a shared vision in which countries recognize the links between governance, corruption, growth and poverty reduction' (GAC 2007, 2). Another anti-corruption instrument with global magnitude is the World Bank's Listing of Ineligible Firms and Individuals, which sanctions companies for a limited amount of time and can be used as a global reference for firms that breach anti-corruption regulation (World Bank 2018).

TI is undoubtedly the most significant civil society organization, operating at the global level in the field of anti-corruption. Its work is so visible that very often it has become synonymous with the global campaign against corruption itself. The founder of TI, Peter Eigen, left the World Bank at the beginning of the 1990s in order to begin a journey of coalition building that would lead to the foundation of the Berlin-based INGO and subsequently aid significantly the rise of corruption to the global agenda (Rosenau and Wang 2001). TI is credited with providing the missing ingredient in the global attempt to curb corruption—that is, establishing the role of civil society and breaking down the intergovernmental veto on corruption as an issue amenable to global regulation (Galtung and Pope 1999).

Founded in 1993, TI has become a dense network of over a hundred national chapters. It has pioneered innovative tools for raising awareness about the detrimental effects of corruption, and since 1995, it publishes the annual Corruption Perceptions Index (CPI), which receives extensive media coverage (TI 2018). It also coordinates the Anti-Corruption Research Network, an Internet hub for anti-corruption research. Galtung and Pope (1999) argue that TI has acquired a leading role in the global anti-corruption debate within a few years of its establishment. The strength of TI is that while it deals with corporate responsibility and works in cooperation with global business and governments, it can also serve as an opposition, as an independent watchdog that holds other actors accountable and represents the interests of unorganized civil society.

Another global anti-corruption watchdog is Global Integrity. Employing a methodology that developed from field research over the years to capture the opinion of local experts and citizens, Global Integrity started publishing the Global Integrity Index in mid-2000

(Global Integrity 2018). Global Witness is another INGO which addresses in particular the so-called Dutch disease or resource curse—the fact that countries rich in resources face more problems of corruption and development because of rent-seeking governments and elites (Global Witness 2018).

Understanding the Global Anti-Corruption Eruption

The major task of a social constructivist agenda is not to study the evident, but to show how what is now evident came to be. This book investigates the question of how corruption was constructed as a global problem, and the following sections present the main arguments for the process of social construction. The factors and agents discussed in the literature can be essentially broken down into six groups. The first, and most commonsensical, explanation is that corruption became a global problem with the end of the Cold War and the subsequent increase in capital movement due to the opening of new markets. This explanation presents the emergence of global problems as an automatic response to changed conditions. Other studies part with this structural explanation, introducing the agents responsible for the rise of corruption to the global agenda. Two of these agents are the World Bank and TI. The 'measurement revolution' initiated by these two organizations through the publication of corruption indices is also credited for the de-politicization of corruption and its rise to the global policy agenda. Critical studies then present this de-politicization of corruption and the anti-corruption work of the World Bank in particular as a neoliberal window-dressing, an analytical position which argues that corruption's rise to the global agenda was meant to provide a smoke screen for policies of liberalization and privatization. Lastly, the role of the United States in pushing corruption within the policy priorities of a number of international organization, in particular the OECD, presents another route through which corruption became a global problem.

The first set of explanations as to why corruption emerged on the global agenda is that there has been an objective increase in levels of corruption throughout the world. The 'corruption eruption' was a name initially given by Naim (1995) to signify a number of successive corruption scandals that broke out in the mid-1990s throughout Europe, the United States, Latin America and other parts of the world. The phrase came to represent the argument that there has been a significant increase in the occurrences of corruption throughout the globe. The original article by Naim argued, however, that the corruption eruption from the mid-1990s was not due to an objective increase in corruption, because no reliable data existed to support this argument. It would be difficult to conclude whether in the 1990s there has been any significant increase in actual rather than perceived levels of corruption worldwide, but such an increase can be inferred indirectly from the rise in capital flows to emerging markets, which according to TI representative Frank Vogl has triggered a boom in grand corruption across the globe (Rosenau and Wang 2001).

According to Naim (1995), the real change occurred not in the objective number of corrupt cases, but at the level of public perception that no longer rendered corrupt practices dismissible. The perception of a 'corruption eruption' was due to the spread of democratic ideals around the globe, which abolished the once tacit acceptance of illicit practices. A 'legitimation crisis,' which has taken power away from the leaders and brought it to the public in a progressive global trend toward more open and democratic governance, was the essential ingredient to the public concern with corruption (Glynn et al. 1997). The end of the Cold War according to this argument was catalytic in speeding up and intensifying these revolutionary structural processes. With the Soviet Union removed as a security threat and the increased economic interdependence spreading toward new markets, the problem of corruption could potentially be exacerbated, but the above structural changes have also provided the solution in terms of a historical opportunity for more transparent and democratic governance worldwide. This argument of interdependence due to the process of globalization and the end of the Cold War as a challenge and opportunity to democratization, despite being much more nuanced and explanatorily rich, provides the conventional view of how corruption rose to global prominence in the mid-1990s. The relationship between the Cold War and the corruption eruption is more complicated, however, and can be understood in two major ways. One is that the end of the Cold War and the spread of democracy led to higher expectations toward accountability and ethics in politics, which, in turn, alerted public opinion to resurfacing instances of corrupt behavior, as Naim argues. The second is to understand corruption as a legacy of the Cold War, during which illicit payments were used by both government and business to buy influence necessary to secure the loyalty of foreign governments and provide access to resources (Neild 2002).

The conventional story goes that in the mid-1990s, due to the increased level of capital movement and the entrance into the world economy of new national markets, corruption rose to the attention of international policy makers and became an issue for global governance. This book argues that the end of the Cold War and events in the 1990s provided a window of opportunity rather than the source of corruption as a global agenda item since processes of establishing the problem of corruption internationally were already in place since the 1970s. Structural explanations, such as the end of the Cold War, obscure agency and entail a degree of automaticity and determinism, which is detrimental to elucidating the concrete mechanisms through which national troubles become global problems. Structural explanations that do not delve into how certain issues acquire the status of global policy problems, therefore, contribute to the 'naturalization' of problems and preclude critical examination that has theoretical and practical advantages—theoretical because it brings to light the agents and processes through which issues become policy problems; practical because it can map future directions in the redefinition of problems through the establishment of phases and patterns in the trajectory of otherwise disparate global issues.

The following two sub-sections highlight the role of agency in global affairs and start the de-naturalization of corruption as a global issue, by presenting the major actors that have contributed to the emergence of corruption as a global problem in the existing literature—international organizations such as the World Bank, global NGOs such as TI and state actors. These explanations attribute the rise of corruption as a global policy problem to the influence of these actors and the processes of de-politicization and quantification of corruption that they started.

The Measurement Revolution of the World Bank and TI: The Advent of Global Corruption Indices

The World Bank is largely perceived to be one of the first international actors to start addressing corruption within the broader framework of good governance. Following the famous Wolfensohn speech in 1996, the first formal reference to corruption appeared the following year in the World Development Report. Weaver (2010) explains that the attempt to tangentially tackle the issue of corruption within the broader framework of institutional development dated back to the 1970s. During this decade, staff within the African branch of the World Bank started promoting the idea that in order to accomplish the goals of development, the international financial institution had to address problems of political character. Weaver traces the process through which this small group of what would later become 'governance advocates' managed to convince upper management of the importance of public institutions for the purposes of development, at first with limited success. With a mandate from then President McNamara, a task force, managed by Arturo Israel, was created in 1979 and in 1983 a brief reference to 'good government' was included in the annual World Development Report. Weaver explains that it was only later, in 1989, that the more neutral term of 'good governance' was adopted in order to depoliticize the issue and make it part of a technocratic discourse (55).

Corruption only later gained a central position as an impediment to development in the good governance agenda of the World Bank. Corruption as a World Bank development prerogative can be understood only within the broader framework of debates about the role of the state or what Israel (1990) calls the 'quality of the state' or the 'quality of politics' in development. In this context, corruption becomes just one symptom of the illegitimate interaction of public and private interests that is peculiar to 'bad government.' The lack of corruption, however, cannot be equated with quality of government as Rothstein (2011) observes. Rothstein employs 'quality of government,' understood foremost as the impartial application of public authority, as a more precise concept than the term 'good governance' which has become overstretched. Stressing the role of government in these conceptualizations brings them closer to a political, rather than an economic, reading of the exercise of public authority.

Weaver (2010) captures this opposition between politics and economics within debates in the World Bank by stressing that the change of terminology from 'government' to 'governance' was ultimately one of the changes from political to economic development prerogatives. As Polzer (2001) argues, the World Bank has economized the concept of corruption and placed politics as inferior to economics. Questioning whether the pendulum between the dichotomies of politics and economics has slung too far, Israel (1990) comments on the World Development Report from 1988 that 'balancing the arguments of both the public interest and private interest views and concentrating on the benefits and costs of government intervention' is essential for changing the views on how development works (5). Israel's argument that the prescription to dismantle the state has probably gone too far was relevant for the search of improved 'quality of politics' that would inform partly what was to become the good governance agenda of the World Bank. In the mid-1990s, in particular, much of the thinking between World Bank policies shifted from the premises of the so-called Washington Consensus to New Institutional Economics (NIE) and the importance of sound regulative institutions for economic development (Cameron 2004). The impact of the broader institutional framework on economic performance argued by Israel's team since the late 1970s was solidified by the influence of NIE at the World Bank in the 1990s and, also starting in the 1990s, corruption took central stage in the good governance debate.

Currently, corruption has an almost omnipotent explanatory power in the development debate and questions of development are seen to have established corruption as a problem of global concern. Within the framework of the Bank's good governance agenda, corruption emerges as an impediment to development and growth, but also as a symptom of 'bad government.' From the point of view of the World Bank, as one of the most visible actors in the anti-corruption field, corruption emerged as a global problem because it was an impediment to development for the Bank's borrowers and, therefore, a substantive hindrance for the effectiveness of the financial institution. The attempt to address issues of corruption within the broader framework of 'good government' spanned for a few decades until it finally received central stage status in the mid-1990s with the change of the Bank's leadership in 1995 and the influence of NIE on policy thinking, but also with developments at major intergovernmental organizations such as the OECD and other regional venues, as well as the emergence of non-state actors such as TI.

The founding of TI in 1993 was intertwined with the African Section of the World Bank through the NGO's founder Peter Eigen, who worked as manager in World Bank programs in Africa and Latin America. After a pivotal meeting in Swaziland in 1990 and extensive discussions with his colleagues, Eigen designed a comprehensive plan for action against corruption (Galtung and Pope 1999). The reception in the World Bank was hesitant because anti-corruption work involved going beyond the Bank's mandate, which was to deal with economic issues only (Eigen 1996). Eigen set out to find a solution outside the World Bank, leading him to leave the financial institution; after a series of meetings around the world, he founded the Advisory Council of TI (Galtung and Pope 1999). Since then, TI has expanded into a global NGO with over a hundred national chapters.

As discussed previously, Rosenau and Wang (2001) provide an analysis of how corruption rose as an issue for global governance by concentrating on the role of TI. NGOs and transnational advocacy groups, however, are only one of a number of actors, including intergovernmental organizations and national governments, who have contributed to the emergence of corruption as a global problem. As Rosenau and Wang note, TI is not the main actor or source of change but is acting as an important 'intervening variable.' TI is credited for building a non-confrontational coalition model between government, business and civil society actors (Galtung and Pope 1999). Raising media and public awareness through the annual CPI and other publications makes TI a catalyst in the process of constructing corruption as a global problem, but that process remained largely intergovernmental. As later chapters show, TI became part of the attempt of state actors to create an international policy response that began 20 years prior to the foundation of the civil society organization.

The design and publication of the CPI and the Worldwide Governance Indicators (WGI) changed the idea that international corruption was unquantifiable and this development is credited for raising the issue to the global policy agenda (TI 2018).[1] The measurement revolution that these subjective indices started contributed significantly to the visibility of corruption worldwide, whether it was by convincing policy makers that quantifiable ultimately means manageable or by promoting an exponential growth in academic papers on the subject. The CPI, in particular, has served its purpose as a powerful public relations tool for raising awareness of corruption by making headlines across the globe with its annual publications. Both the WGI and the CPI have promoted a boom of academic papers, which have contributed to a rising consensus on how corruption relates to other development issues such as Foreign Direct Investment (FDI) and growth. According to Galtung (2006), the positive view of corruption has become part of the past with the help of studies using corruption indices. A foreign investor in a country burdened with inefficient bureaucracy and incomprehensible procedures

[1] There are business-oriented data sets (such as Business International and the World Competitiveness Report) which predate the CPI (Ades and di Tella 1997). The indices of TI (CPI) and the World Bank (Control of Corruption as part of the WGI) were developed by Lambsdorff and Kaufmann, respectively, and cover the period from 1995 and 1996, respectively (TI 2018; World Bank 2018).

can find an efficient and inexpensive shortcut in the form of bribing a public official, the general argument went (Leff 1964; Huntington 1968). The high cost of corruption and its negative effect on growth, FDI and development have only recently been broadly accepted and the debate whether corruption is 'grease' or 'sand' in the wheels of development and trade has taken on a life of its own (Ades and di Tella 1997; Kaufman and Wei 1999; Meon and Weill 2010).

The academic studies and debates prompted by the corruption indices promoted the view that corruption can be studied internationally as an objective fact, although indirectly through the quantification of expert and lay perception (Treisman 2000; Connors et al. 2006). At the same time, the 'measurement revolution' has attracted criticism that what is being measured are perceived levels of corruption or quantified perception. Some authors go as far as to argue that the limited 'Western-style' definition used in the indices is a form of 'neo-colonialism through measurement' (De Maria 2008, 184). As much as the indices of the World Bank and TI were turning points in the study of corruption worldwide, their connection to the 'objective fact' of corrupt exchanges remains ambivalent. Firstly, since what is being measured is perception, some amount of bias and stereotyping can occur, such as the 'poor is bad effect' which considers countries with lower economic performance to be inherently more corrupt (Søreide 2006). The tendency to gather data from business surveys and therefore capture mainly the opinions of Western businessmen is another point of criticism toward the CPI (Lambsdorff 2006). As Andersson and Heywood (2009) argue, taking into consideration business transactions and understanding the corrupt exchange predominantly as bribery preclude a more nuanced and deeper quantitative understanding of the forms and impact of corruption. Furthermore, proxies, such as overall economic performance and the stability of the political system, affect the estimation of corruption levels. Secondly, on their own turn, corruption indices affect investment decisions and can turn into a self-fulfilling prophecy (Warren and Laufer 2009).

Philip (2006) observes that corruption indices do not include 'hard data' about actual occurrences of corruption in 'soft' perception-based data, but it is usually the latter that is used in academic studies.[2] Lambsdorff (2006) addresses the problem that the perception indices

[2]This is due to comparability issues and discrepancies in the legal procedures of countries from which the data are collected (Philip 2006).

do not relate directly to real phenomena, but yet these subjective indices remain the most comprehensive way of estimating the levels of corruption worldwide. The bias in the sample of respondents is tackled by including data that consist of both residents (who may also be employees of multinational companies) and expatriates, according to the designer of the CPI.[3] This attempt to balance the sample of respondents, however, does not provide a solution to generalized bias that can be common to both residents and expatriates. The question remains to what extent the perception is based on empirical evidence or on personal preconceptions and reproduction of media and social biases (Miller 2006). Most of this criticism is targeted toward the CPI as a perception-based index, but as Heywood and Rose (2014) show, non-perceptual measurement of corruption remains a distinct possibility, yet one less likely to generate comparable results and as a consequence make newspaper headlines. Despite these problems with studying international corruption quantitatively, the publication of corruption perception indices has contributed significantly to the global visibility of corruption in the media and has helped solidify consensus on the negative impact that corruption has on development objectives.

A growing amount of literature places the explanation of the origin of anti-corruption policies and discourse within the context of neoliberal reforms and usually adopts a critical stance toward the politics of anti-corruption (Brown and Cloke 2004; Krastev 2004; Whyte 2007; Bracking 2009; Roden 2010). Brown and Cloke (2011) offer a comprehensive analysis of critical studies and, despite the nuances, a common trend appears to be that anti-corruption work is or at least has become a program, providing legitimacy to a neoliberal 'economistic' and anti-state paradigm. The conventional understanding of corruption presents the role of politics as a source of rents and promotes deregulation as the only way to reduce opportunities for rent-seeking (Bracking 2007).

[3]The CPI is a composite index of 13 data sources: the African Development Bank Governance Ratings, the Bertelsmann Foundation Sustainable Governance Indicators, the Bertelsmann Foundation Transformation Index, the Economist Intelligence Unit Country Risk Ratings, the Freedom House Nations in Transit, the Global Insight Country Risk Ratings, the IMD World Competitiveness Yearbook, the Political and Economic Risk Consultancy Asian Intelligence, the Political Risk Services International Country Risk Guide, the Transparency International Bribe Payers Survey, the World Bank—Country Policy and Institutional Assessment, the World Economic Forum Executive Opinion Survey (EOS) and the World Justice Project Rule of Law Index (TI 2018).

The neoliberal charge inherent to the anti-corruption movement is criticized as being biased and a-historical; it is also business centered and privileges the interests of market actors. Civil society actors, such as TI, have also contributed to a program of 'normalization' by trying to bring diverging political and economic institutions in line with neoliberal criteria (Hindess 2005). The anti-corruption crusade (Brown and Cloke 2004; Roden 2010) can therefore be seen to employ a 'hollowed out' discourse (Bukovansky 2006) as a window-dressing technique for policies of sometimes aggressive liberalization.

The actual implementation of World Bank anti-corruption policies has also been placed under scrutiny (Harrison 2004; Carroll 2009; Brown and Cloke 2011). The Bank has been seen to support, through its governance program, an 'American-led liberal capitalist globalism' which has been ascending steadily after the Second World War (Harrison 2004, 9). Anti-corruption policies, seen from this critical perspective, provide a smoke screen for neoliberal policies of deregulation, privatization and the withdrawal of the state from the economy. In particular, through the work of the World Bank, a new type of 'governance-state' has emerged which has to limit its steering activities to a minimum and allow free market reforms to work properly (Harrison 2004). Sociologists and anthropologists have equally criticized the occupation of the anti-corruption discourse by economics, the establishment of quantified perception through the CPI and the WGI as a standard measurement for corruption, which has allowed the transformation of anti-corruption debates into a 'one-size fits all' scientific enterprise (Krastev 2004).

The critical strand of the anti-corruption literature provides a lot of valuable insights into the politics of anti-corruption, but could be criticized for making a straw man out of neoliberalism. Even the so-called Washington Consensus is not such a coherent body of thought as is usually assumed (Williamson 2008). The term 'Washington Consensus' initially developed as a response to questions about the development of Latin America and Williamson, who coined the term in 1989 was the first to engage conceptually with what was to become the new embodiment of neoliberalism. Williamson (2008) explains that as part of a conference paper he wrote a list of ten policies that he 'thought more or less everyone in Washington would agree were needed more or less everywhere in Latin America, and labeled this the "Washington Consensus."' (Williamson 2008, 14). The conference in 1989 was meant to capture the way in which development ideas that have dominated economic thinking in Latin America for decades 'were being swept aside by the set of ideas that had long been accepted as appropriate within the OECD' (Williamson 2008, 14). Williamson (2008) stated that the term he coined had become 'the center of fierce ideological controversy' (14), and that it has come to signify 'a set of neoliberal policies that have been imposed on hapless countries by the Washington-based International Financial Institutions (IFIs) and have led them to crisis and misery' (Williamson 2002, 11). At the same time, the World Bank good governance agenda is supposed to be part of a post-Washington Consensus era since the very goal of good governance policies was to address the limited view on development as dependent on economic factors alone (Jayasuriya 2002). Rodrik (2006) calls the inclusion of anti-corruption and other more politically and socially oriented objectives 'augmented' Washington Consensus, while Naim (2000) stresses the incoherence of the 'Washington confusion.'

Krastev (2004) has argued that the World Bank and the IMF have in practice redesigned the elements of the 'Washington Consensus' as anti-corruption strategies in order to silence opposition to reforms. This argument pertains to the improper instrumentalization of policies to serve other objectives, but also to the rationale behind anti-corruption strategies. Understood as neoliberal window-dressing, anti-corruption policies rose to prominence as a way to promote the interests of major developed states in the rest of the world.

In the Shadow of Global Hierarchies: The Role of the United States

Another argument for the rise of the problem of corruption to global prominence is the attempt of the United States to level the playing field in relation to the FCPA. The argument that the breakthrough of corruption as a global agenda item was due to US interests in leveling the playing field, however, only offers a procedural explanation; it does not address the more substantive question as to why the United States would put itself in a disadvantaged position by adopting the Act in the first place. The FCPA was essentially the first anti-corruption tool with potentially global reach. The 'procedural' explanation of why corruption rose as an issue for global governance points to the US attempt to overcome the competitive disadvantage that the adoption of the anti-bribery law was creating for American companies since 1977. Pieth (2007) argues that the reasons why the United States adopted the FCPA in the first place can be seen as threefold: (1) in order to manage publicity; (2) in order to keep corporate (defense) actors under check; and (3) in order to preserve the integrity of the free market system.

From the ITT affair to Watergate and the Lockheed scandal, the 1970s were seen by the American public as a venal age. Under the investigation of Senator Frank Church, an increasing number of illicit deals were resurfacing both within and outside the borders of the United States. The uncovering of a chain of corporate scandals established corporate bribery as a common practice (Cragg and Woof 2002). To manage the public outrage over the findings was one reason why the United States adopted the FCPA. Pieth (2007) argues that a second more covert agenda pursued by the US government was to prevent private defense interests from interfering with US security objectives during the Cold War. The danger of US defense companies bribing their way into crucial arms markets, especially in the Middle East, can be seen as another reason for the adoption of a law that would proscribe the practice of foreign bribery and it is given further attention in the fifth chapter. The Watergate affair had long-lasting effects on the American public and on American domestic and foreign policy. As Pieth (2007) observes, based on case law and other evidence, the US legislator post-Watergate was trying to protect the 'free market system against the erosion of public confidence' (8). The question was not one simply of bribery but of much more subtle and often legal instances of private interests exerting disproportionate influence over the direction of public affairs. In particular, Watergate led to the 'public integrity war' at the center of which was the debate about the role of government in the agendas of new progressives and movement conservatives (North and Doss 1997).

The focal point of the 'integrity war' was the interaction between government and corporate actors. The defenders of 'big government' tried to portray corruption scandals as the consequence of the power of 'special interests' over the democratic process. According to these new progressives, the Industrial Revolution changed American politics irretrievably by placing powerful corporate actors in the political landscape of the country and allowing them to exhibit strong influence over the political system. The movement conservatives tried to portray the corruption scandals since Watergate, as a natural consequence of the 'moral bankruptcy of big government' (xii). The new progressives' preoccupation with the ability of private actors to exert disproportionate influence (both legally and illegally) over the outcomes of the national political process influenced the 'good government' reform model in American politics. This model was also central to the initial development of the good governance agenda within the framework of the World Bank. In particular, the 'good government' model shaped the conviction that in order to reinstate 'public trust in government…citizens must demand that special interests and public officials comply with strict codes of conduct and fully disclose their attempt to influence public officials' (North and Doss 1997, 9). Protecting the legitimacy and integrity of the free market meant also to prove that the system could work within a political context according to clear and ethical rules that did not compromise the public's confidence in the integrity of private companies and public officials alike. At stake was the very legitimacy of the free market, because the perceived venality of public power under the pressure and financial resources of big business fell under the scrutiny of the American public. The fifth chapter elaborates on the historical and ideational climate of the 1970s and further traces the causal link between the FCPA and the establishment of corruption as an international agenda item.

Conceptualizing the Global Anti-Corruption Eruption: From International Regimes to Global Movements and Industries

Scholars have tried to make sense of the rapidly expanding global anti-corruption work through the prism of different conceptual tools. The anti-corruption eruption has been conceptualized in the existing literature in four major categories: (1) anti-corruption as an issue of global governance (Rosenau and Wang 2001; Eigen 2013; Kirton et al. 2013); (2) as an international regime or regimes (Bukovanvsky 2002; von Rosenvinge 2009; Wolf and Schmidt-Pfister 2010); (3) as a movement referring either to the work of TI or as a loose term addressing both regional and global efforts to tackle corruption (Yao 1997; Sampson 2005; Hough 2013); and (4) as an industry in anthropological studies (Sampson 2010).

These four conceptualizations are neither clear-cut nor mutually exclusive but they all come with different insights about the global anti-corruption resurgence. The 'industry' debate portrays anti-corruption work as 'anti-corruptionism' (Sampson 2010) and is critical of the effectiveness of implementing anti-corruption projects (Haller and Shore 2005).

The practitioners of anti-corruptionism refer to it as a 'movement' but some of them are simply drawn to the 'marketplace' of anti-corruption programs, the success of which is difficult to establish. The industry debate offers another notable insight: Anti-corruption is not 'innocent' (Sampson 2005). The recent consensus on the high cost of corruption and the necessity to tackle it has mobilized support from groups with diverging agendas: from anti-globalization activists to liberalization reformers, and potentially offers a new platform for consensus on global governance. At the same time, this branch of the literature warns that global anti-corruption has been transformed into an industry that cohabits with the phenomenon of corruption it was intended to fight.

Studies on the global governance of corruption have stressed the role of non-state actors in the anti-corruption eruption. Rosenau and Wang (2001) set two criteria in order for an issue to qualify as the subject of global governance—the existence of emerging norms and the higher visibility and sensitivity on behalf of the public. The role of TI as a norm entrepreneur is the explanation they put forward for the rise of corruption on the global agenda. A global anti-corruption norm (McCoy and Heckel 2001) has emerged, and the importance of TI lies in framing corruption as an issue of development and accountability while translating it from a highly sensitive political problem into legal and economic terms.

Some academic literature poses the existence as well as the taxonomic characteristics of an international anti-corruption regime or regimes at the center of scholarly investigation (von Rosenvinge 2009; Wolf and Schmidt-Pfister 2010). This work tends to mix a definition of international regimes coming from the field of IR with a legal conceptualization of regimes in which a single treaty can represent an international legal regime; a given issue area can therefore be covered by a number of intersecting legal regimes. In anti-corruption studies, both 'anti-corruption regime' and 'global governance of corruption' are used (Rosenau and Wang 2001; Bukovanvsky 2002; von Rosenvinge 2009; Wolf and Schmidt-Pfister 2010; Eigen 2013; Kirton et al. 2013). The two concepts are sometimes used interchangeably and this is due partly to the broadly perceived compatibility between international regimes and global governance. This book conceptualizes of global anti-corruption policies and initiatives as a specific issue area of global governance and therefore tries to clarify the conceptual overlap between international regimes and global governance of corruption since the classic definition of international regimes posed by Krasner (1982) could also be interpreted as the governance of a specific issue area.

In the development of IR as a discipline, research agendas have continuously been abandoned in favor of new ones, which offer a new perspective and focus on different elements of international politics. Older research agendas with their respective conceptual tools remain in use, and even though they are compatible with the new conceptual tools, their explicit link is rarely specified. One example of two such concepts, which pertain to two different, yet connected, research agendas, is international regimes and global governance. On the one hand, the difference between the two concepts is strictly historical. The work on international regimes, from the 1980s and 1990s, paved the road for the ideational and normative turn in the field of IR. Regime theorists developed sensibility toward the 'normative superstructures' underlying international cooperation and did not conceive of regime formation simply as useful vehicles for solving collective action problems and reducing transaction costs (Puchala and Hopkins 1982).

The concept of governance was already implicitly and sometimes explicitly present within the theory of international regimes, and as global governance became an independent research agenda, the concept of international regimes continued within this framework. Regimes in the context of the global governance literature can be seen as specific 'governance systems' providing governance in a specific issue area (Stokke 1997; Ba and Hoffmann 2006). Regimes are therefore more limited issue areas in the broader landscape of global governance. Keohane (1993) posited the question of discerning the existence of an international regime as the task of finding 'the existence of explicit rules that are referred to in an affirmative manner by governments, even if they are not necessarily scrupulously observed' (28).

The rules, referred to by Keohane, guide the behavior of actors at the international level or at least generate a sense of obligation toward appropriate behavior. This sense of obligation can also be referred to as an anti-corruption norm (McCoy and Heckel 2001). McCoy and Heckel argue that the institutionalization of the global norm took place in the 1990s with the adoption of a number of international legal instruments. As discussed previously, the legal backbone of the anti-corruption regime consists of regional conventions adopted by the OAS, CoE, the EU and the African Union, as well as the UNCAC and the OECD Convention.

These 'rules written on a piece of paper' testify for the intergovernmental agreement that there is a problem with corrupt practices that has to be addressed collectively. Agreeing on the existence of a harmful condition and arriving at a definition of what is problematic about it is essential, since in the framework of social constructivism, the problem is not an objective fact out there, but a product of social construction. As Blyth (2002) observed 'controlling the definition…is inherently political' because it helps the reinterpretation of reality (105). This intersubjective component of the regime refers to the way in which corruption rose onto the global agenda and how state and non-state actors collectively defined a putative condition as a global problem, a definitional process which constituted a necessary step for the emergence of formal agreements.

The global anti-corruption resurgence can also be seen as a case of a global prohibition regime (Nadelmann 1990). In their study of criminalization through global prohibitions, Andreas and Nadelmann (2006) identify five phases of prohibition regime development. During the first phase of non-regime, the issue is seen as a tolerable or legitimate part of the global landscape. During the second phase, a redefinition of the condition as a problem happens, which is followed by a third phase, during which active agitation for prohibition occurs leading to the establishment of a global regime during the fourth phase. In some cases, a fifth phase ultimately witnesses the suppression of the prohibited activity. Spector and Kitsuse (2009) coming from a long tradition of social problems studies in sociology are even less optimistic about the eradication of social problems. They capture the development of social problems in four stages: (1) debate and publicity prompted by claims-making groups; (2) recognition of legitimacy leading to official plan for reform; (3) critical stage of dissatisfaction with official plan; and (4) rejection of official plan, attempt to create alternative solutions.

Work already done on the history of international anti-corruption regimes identifies five similar phases (Wolf and Schmidt-Pfister 2010). The first phase of non-regime lasts until the 1970s and is characterized by the complete absence of the issue of corruption from the global agenda. The second phase, which spans from the mid-1970s to the mid-1990s, features unilateral US measures and the third one starting from the mid-1990s (referred to as the 'global corruption eruption') spans until 2005. Since the late 1990s, increased compliance efforts have marked a fourth implementation phase. Simultaneously, as early as the mid-2000 evidence suggests that insufficient performance and compliance have led to a legitimacy crisis, which characterizes the current fifth phase of regime development (15–16). This chronological evolution can be simplified into three main non-overlapping phases of the development of corruption as a global problem. The first phase starts in the early 1970s (1971–1976) from virtually no formal or informal recognition of the legitimacy of the issue as anything else, but a national concern and spans for approximately 20 years. From the early-1970s to the mid-1990s, the discussion of the issue gained international momentum, but intergovernmental accord led to limited institutionalization. The second phase started in 1994 and marked the institutionalization of the issue and the development of an official plan. Within a decade (1995–2005), a plethora of formal international legal arrangements, a boom of codes of conduct and vast media coverage brought the problem of corruption to the top of the international public, media and policy agenda.

The third phase started in 2005 and is ongoing. It can be described as a new phase of normalization. Corruption has been transformed into a legitimate issue of concern for global governance. Spector and Kitsuse (2009) have established that the phase of institutionalization of a social problem is always followed by a legitimacy crisis. Based on decades of sociological research, they argue that the development of social problems follows a pattern in which the implementation phase leads to a loss of credibility and legitimacy, because the expected results are not seen. As a consequence, during the last phase competing definitions of the issue start to emerge. The attempt to strengthen the governance of the issue area during the legitimacy crisis stage goes in two major directions: attempts to consolidate efforts in order to ensure better compliance with the existing course of action and/or calls to re-formulate the definition of the issue and the objectives of the plan of action. In the anti-corruption case, both trends are evident. The G20 Anti-Corruption Action Plan, for example, aims at the consolidation of the regime and the implementation of the already existing instruments. At the same time, the G20 Plan relates the implementation effort to the exigencies of the post-crisis economic recovery without questioning the usefulness of their rationale (Action Plan G20 Annex III 2010). Daniel Kaufmann, former director at the World Bank Institute, sees the financial crisis as one of the symptoms of what he calls 'legal corruption' (Kaufmann 2010; Vicente and Kaufmann 2005). Kaufmann (2010) calls for a re-formulation of the problem and redefines corruption as a form of collusion between government officials and business actors which has remained outside the grip of the law. This collusion may start with legal forms of influence peddling and lead to a subtle form of state capture in developing and developed countries alike. Kaufmann's argument presents a point in case of how the last phase of regime development generates claims over the expansive redefinition of the problem. Similarly, following the publicity of the 'Panama Papers,' former British Prime Minster David Cameron proposed the establishment of an international anti-corruption body targeting tax havens (Wintour 2016) that would significantly expand the anti-corruption mandate of the OECD and broaden current definitions of corrupt practices.

This chapter presented the main aspects of the global anti-corruption eruption from the mid-1990s to the mid-2000s. It further offered an overview of the main ways to think about the rapid anti-corruption expansion, as well as the main agents that brought forward this change. The existing literature is already laden with implicit or explicit hypotheses about the rise of corruption as a global problem, and the second part of the chapter outlined the main routes through which corruption arose as an international agenda item by presenting structural arguments and explanations providing for the role of agency. A number of studies have placed the emergence of corruption as a global concern at the center of investigation (McCoy and Heckel 2001; Bukovansky 2002; Krastev 2004; Jakobi 2013). These studies offer valuable insights into the emergence of corruption as an issue for global governance and allow to varying degrees for the role of state actors in the process. By presenting the concepts and the main actors, involved in anti-corruption work, this chapter laid the ground for the contextualization of the empirical chapters and the elaboration of the conceptual tools that are used in this book and which inform the content of the next chapter.

This introduction to the intellectual puzzle sets the ground for the elaboration of the mechanism through which corruption was constructed as a global problem in the empirical chapters and for supporting the argument that the construction of corruption as a global problem was a predominantly intergovernmental endeavor in which power and interests had a strong impact on the shared construction of meaning. This approach to the construction of global problems can help us better understand the way in which specific governance issue areas emerge and develop.

References

Action Plan G20 Annex III. 2010. "G20 Agenda for Action on Combating Corruption, Promoting Market Integrity, and Supporting a Clean Business Environment." Accessed April 22, 2018. http://www.oecd.org/daf/anti-bribery/G20_Anti-Corruption_Action_Plan.pdf.

Ades, Alberto, and Rafael di Tella. 1997. "The New Economics of Corruption: A Survey and Some New Results." *Political Studies* 45 (3): 496–515.

African Union. 2003. *African Union Convention on Preventing and Combating Corruption*. Addis Ababa: Secretariat, African Union.

Ala'i, Padideh. 2008. "The WTO and the Anti-Corruption Movement." *Loyola University Chicago International Law Review* 6 (1): 17–54.

Andersson, Staffan, and Paul Heywood. 2009. "The Politics of Perception: Use and Abuse of Transparency International's Approach to Measuring Corruption." *Political Studies* 57 (4): 746–767.

Andreas, Peter, and Ethan Nadelmann. 2006. *Policing the Globe: Criminalization and Crime Control in International Relations*. New York: Oxford University Press.

Ashe, Daniel Patrick. 2005. "The Lengthening Anti-Bribery Lasso of the United States: The Recent Extraterritorial Application of the U.S. Foreign Corrupt Practices Act." *The Fordham Law Review* 73 (6): 2897.

Ba, Alice D., and Matthew J. Hoffmann. 2006. *Contending Perspectives on Global Governance: Coherence and Contestation*. London: Routledge.

BBC World Service. "Global Poll: Corruption Is World's Most Talked About Problem." Accessed May 29, 2017. http://www.bbc.co.uk/pressoffice/pressreleases/stories/2010/12_december/09/corruption.html.

BIAC. 2018. "The Fight Against Corruption." Accessed April 17. http://biac.org/focus-areas/the-fight-against-corruption/.

Blyth, Mark. 2002. *Great Transformations: Economic Ideas and Institutional Change in the Twentieth Century*. Cambridge: Cambridge University Press.

Bracking, Sarah, ed. 2007. *Corruption and Development: The Anti-Corruption Campaigns*. New York: Palgrave Macmillan.

———. 2009. "Political Economies of Corruption Beyond Liberalism: An Interpretative View of Zimbabwe." *Singapore Journal of Tropical Geography* 30 (1): 35–51.

"Bribery Act 2010—Ministry of Justice." Home—Ministry of Justice. N.p., 8 April, 2010. Web. 12 December, 2012.

Brown, Ed, and Jonathan Cloke. 2004. "Neoliberal Reform, Governance and Corruption in the South: Assessing the International Anti-Corruption Crusade." *Antipode* 36 (2): 272–294.

———. 2011. "Critical Perspectives on Corruption: An Overview." *Critical Perspectives on International Business* 7 (2): 116–124.

Brown, Chris, and Kirsten Ainley. 2009. *Understanding International Relations.* New York: Palgrave Macmillan.

Brytting, Tomas, Richard Minogue, and Veronica Morino. 2012. *The Anatomy of Fraud and Corruption: Organizational Causes and Remedies.* Farnham: Gower Publishing.

Bukovansky, Mlada. 2002. "Corruption Is Bad: Normative Dimensions of the Anti-Corruption Movement." Working Paper 2002/5, Department of International Relations, Australian National University. Accessed October 22, 2017. https://digitalcollections.anu.edu.au/bitstream/1885/40136/3/02-5.pdf.

———. 2006. "The Hollowness of Anti-Corruption Discourse." *Review of International Political Economy* 13 (2): 181–209.

Business Anti-Corruption Portal. 2018. "Compliance Resources." Accessed April 22. http://www.business-anti-corruption.com/.

Cameron, John D. 2004. "The World Bank and the New Institutional Economics: Contradictions and Implications for Development Policy in Latin America." *Latin American Perspectives* 31 (4): 97–103.

Carroll, Toby. 2009. "'Social Development' as Neoliberal Trojan Horse: The World Bank and the Kecamatan Development Program in Indonesia." *Development and Change* 40 (3): 447–466.

CIPE. 2018. "Anti-Corruption Compliance." Accessed April 23. http://www.cipe.org/.

Connors, Carmel, Arthur Shacklock, Fredrik Galtung, and Charles Sampford, eds. 2006. *Measuring Corruption.* Aldershot: Ashgate.

Council of Europe. 1999a. *Criminal Law Convention on Corruption = Convention Pénale Sur La Corruption.* Strasbourg: Council of Europe Publishing.

———. 1999b. *Civil Law Convention on Corruption: And Explanatory Report.* Strasbourg: Council of Europe Publising.

Cragg, Wesley, and William Woof. 2002. "The U.S. Foreign Corrupt Practices Act: A Study of Its Effectiveness." *Business and Society Review* 107 (1): 98–144.

Delaney, Patrick. 2005. *Transnational Corruption: Regulation Across Borders.* Canberra: Australian National University Press.

De Maria, William. 2008. "Neo-Colonialism Through Measurement: A Critique of the Corruption Perception Index." *Critical Perspectives on International Business* 4 (2/3): 184–202.

de Sousa, Luís, Peter Larmour, and Barry Hindess. 2009. *Governments, NGOs and Anti-Corruption: The New Integrity Warriors.* London: Routledge.

Dunst, Lee G., Michael S. Diamant, and Teresa R. Kung. 2011. "Hot off the Press: Resetting the Global Anti-Corruption Thermostat to the UK Bribery Act." *Business Law International* 12: 257.

Eigen, Peter. 1996. "Combatting Corruption Around the World." *Journal of Democracy* 7 (1): 158–168.

———. 2013. "International Corruption: Organized Civil Society for Better Global Governance." *Social Research: An International Quarterly* 80 (4): 1287–1308.

European Union. 1997. "Convention Drawn Up on the Basis of Article K. 3 (2) (C) of the Treaty on European Union on the Fight Against Corruption Involving Officials of the European Communities or Officials of Member States of the European Union: [May 26, 1997]." *International Legal Materials: Current Documents* 37: 12–21.

Foreign Corrupt Practices Act (amendments), Pub.L.No. 100–418, 102 Stat. 1415 (1988).

Foreign Corrupt Practices Act of 1977, Pub.L.No. 95–23–, 91 Stat. 1494 (Codified as amended at 15 U.S.C. 78 m, 78dd-1 to 78dd-2, 78ff (1994) [Hereinafter FCPA] as amended by International Anti-bribery and Fair Competition Act of 1998, 15 U.S.C.A. 78dd–1 to 78dd–3, 78ff (1999) [IAFCA].

GAC. 2007. "World Bank Country-Level Engagement on Governance and Anticorruption." Accessed April 17, 2016. http://ieg.worldbankgroup.org/evaluations/world-bank-country-level-engagement-governance-and-anticorruption.

Galtung, Fredrik. 2006. "Measuring the Immesurable: Boundaries and Functions of (Macro) Corruption Indices." In *Measuring Corruption*, edited by Carmel Connors, Arthur Shacklock, Fredrik Galtung, and Charles Sampford, 101–131. Aldershot: Ashgate.

Galtung, Fredrik, and Jeremy Pope. 1999. "The Global Coalition Against Corruption: Evaluating Transparency International." In *The Self-Restraining State: Power and Accountability in New Democracies*, edited by Andreas Schedler, Marc Plattner, and Larry Jay Diamond, 257–285. Boulder, CO: Lynne Rienner.

Global Integirty. 2018. "Global Integirty Report." Accessed April 17. https://www.globalintegrity.org/global-report/what-is-gi-report/.

Global Witness. 2018. "Twenty Years of Global Impact." Accessed April 7. http://new.globalwitness.org/aboutus.php.

Glynn, Patrick, Stephen Kobrin, and Moises Naim. 1997. "The Globalization of Corruption." In *Corruption and the Global Economy*, edited by Kimberly Ann Elliott, 7–31. Washington, DC: Peterson Institute.

Haller, Dieter, and Cris Shore, eds. 2005. Corruption: Anthropological Perspectives. London: Pluto Press.

Harrison, Graham. 2004. *World Bank and Africa: The Construction of Governance States*. London: Routledge.

Heywood, Paul M., and Jonathan Rose. 2014. "'Close But No Cigar': The Measurement of Corruption." *Journal of Public Policy* 34 (3): 507–529.

Hindess, Barry. 2005. "Investigating International Anti-Corruption." *Third World Quarterly* 26 (8): 1389–1398.

Hough, Dan. 2013. *Corruption, Anti-Corruption and Governance*. New York: Palgrave Macmillan.

Huntington, Samuel P. 1968. "Modernisation and Corruption." In *Political Corruption: Concepts and Contexts*, edited by A. J. Heidenheimer and M. Johnston, 253–263. Rutgers, NJ: Transaction Publishers.

ICC, Rules of Conduct to Combat Extortion and Bribery in International Business Transactions, 26 March 1996, reprinted in 35 International Legal Materials 1306, 1996.

IMF. 2018. "Good Governance: The IMF's Role." Accessed April 17. https://www.imf.org/external/pubs/ft/exrp/govern/govindex.htm.

International Chamber of Commerce. 1977. *Extortion and Bribery in Business Transactions: Report Adopted by the 131st Session of the Council of the ICC, 29 November 1977*. Paris: International Chamber of Commerce.

Israel, Arturo. 1990. *The Changing Role of the State: Institutional Dimensions*. Washington, DC: World Bank Publications.

Jakobi, Anja P. 2013. "The Changing Global Norm of Anti-Corruption: From Bad Business to Bad Government." *Zeitschrift Für Vergleichende Politikwissenschaft* 7 (1): 243–264.

Jayasuriya, Kanishka. 2002. "Governance, Post-Washington Consensus and the New Anti-politics." In *Corruption in East Asia: Rethinking the Governance Paradigm*, edited by T. Lindsey and H. Dick, 24–36. Sidney: Federation Press.

Kaufmann, Daniel. 2010. "Daniel Kaufmann on State Capture." *World Policy Journal* 27 (1): 3–4.

Kaufmann, Daniel, and Shang-Jin Wei. 1999. "Does 'Grease Money' Speed Up the Wheels of Commerce?" Policy Research Working Paper, Series 2254, The World Bank, Washington. Accessed October 22, 2014. http://elibrary.worldbank.org/doi/book/10.1596/1813-9450-2254.

Keohane, Robert. 1993. "The Analysis of International Regimes: Towards a European-American Research Programme." In *Regime Theory and International Relations*, edited by Volker Rittberger, 23–45. Oxford: Clarendon Press.

Kirton, John J., Michele Fratianni, and Paolo Savona. 2013. *Corporate, Public and Global Governance: The G8 Contribution*. Aldershot: Ashgate.

Krasner, Stephen D. 1982. "Structural Causes and Regime Consequences: Regimes as Intervening Variables." *International Organization* 36 (02): 185–205.

Krastev, Ivan. 2004. *Shifting Obsessions: Three Essays on the Politics of Anticorruption*. Budapest: Central European University Press.

Lambsdorff, Johann Graf. 2006. "Measuring Corruption—The Validity and Precision of Subjective Indicators (CPI)." In *Measuring Corruption*, edited by Carmel Connors, Arthur Shacklock, Fredrik Galtung, and Charles Sampford, 89–101. Aldershot: Ashgate.

Leff, Nathaniel H. 1964. "Economic Development Through Bureaucratic Corruption." *American Behavioral Scientist* 8 (3): 8–14.
Lord, Nicholas. 2014. *Regulating Corporate Bribery in International Business: Anti-Corruption in the UK and Germany*. Aldershot: Ashgate Publishing.
McCoy, Jennifer L., and Heather Heckel. 2001. "The Emergence of a Global Anti-Corruption Norm." *International Politics* 38 (1): 65–90.
Méon, Pierre-Guillaume, and Laurent Weill. 2010. "Is Corruption an Efficient Grease?" *World Development* 38 (3): 244–259.
Miller, William. 2006. "Perception, Experience and Lies: What Measures Corruption and What Do Corruption Measures Measure?" In *Measuring Corruption*, edited by Carmel Connors, Arthur Shacklock, Fredrik Galtung, and Charles Sampford, 163–189. Aldershot: Ashgate.
Nadelmann, Ethan. 1990. "Global Prohibition Regimes: The Evolution of Norms in International Society." *International Organization* 44 (4): 479–526.
Naim, Moses. 1995. "Corruption Eruption." *Brown Journal of World Affairs* 2 (2): 245–261.
———. 2000. "Washington Consensus or Washington Confusion?" *Foreign Policy* 118 (86): 86–104.
Neild, R. R. 2002. *Public Corruption: The Dark Side of Social Evolution*. London: Anthem Press.
North, Roberts, and Marion T. Doss. 1997. *From Watergate to Whitewater: The Public Integrity War*. Santa Barbara, CA: Greenwood Publishing Group.
OECD. 1998. OECD Convention for Combating Bribery of Foreign Public Officials in International Business Transactions (1997) Organisation for Economic Co-operation and Development. Convention on Combating Bribery of Foreign Public Officials in International Business Transactions: And Related Documents. Paris:
———. 2004. *Implementing the OECD Anti-Bribery Convention Implementing the OECD Anti-Bribery Convention: Report on the United States 2003*. Paris: OECD Publishing.
———. 2018. "G20-OECD Conference: 'Joining Forces Against Corruption: G20 Business and Government.'" Accessed April 17. http://www.oecd.org/daf/anti-bribery/g20-oecdconferencejoiningforcesagainstcorruptiong20businessandgovernment.htm.
Omnibus Trade and Competitiveness Act of 1988, Pub. L. No. 100–418, 3001–3604, 103 Stat. 1372 (1988) (codified as amended in scattered sections of U.S.C. (1988).
Organization of American States. 1996. *Convención Interamericana contra la Corrupción = Inter-American Convention against Corruption*. Washington, DC: Organización de los Estados Americanos, Secretaría General.

Philip, Mark. 2006. "Corruption Definition and Measurement." In *Measuring Corruption*, edited by Carmel Connors, Arthur Shacklock, Fredrik Galtung, and Charles Sampford, 45–57. Aldershot: Ashgate.

Pieth, Mark. 2007. "Introduction." In *The OECD Convention on Bribery: A Commentary*, edited by Mark Pieth, Lucinda A. Low, and Peter J. Cullen, 3–42. Cambridge: Cambridge University Press.

Polzer, Tara. 2001. "Corruption: Deconstructing the World Bank Discourse." Working Paper Series No. 1–18. London School of Economics. Accessed April 1, 2018. http://www.lse.ac.uk/internationalDevelopment/pdf/WP/WP18.pdf.

Puchala, Donald J., and Raymond F. Hopkins. 1982. "International Regimes: Lessons from Inductive Analysis." *International Organization* 36 (2): 245–275.

Roden J. 2010. "The International Anti-Corruption Crusade: Neo-Liberal Institutional Structures, Moralization, and Social Capital." *Undercurrent Journal* 7 (1): 12–22.

Rodrik, Dani. 2006. "Goodbye Washington Consensus, Hello Washington Confusion? A Review of the World Bank's Economic Growth in the 1990s: Learning from a Decade of Reform." *Journal of Economic Literature* 44 (4): 973–987.

Rosenau, James, and Hongying Wang. 2001. "Transparency International and Corruption as an Issue of Global Governance." *Global Governance* 7 (1): 25–49.

von Rosenvinge, Alison. 2009. "Global Anti-Corruption Regimes: Why Law Schools May Want to Take a Multi-Jurisdiction Approach." *German Law Journal* 10: 785–802.

Rothstein, Bo. 2011. *The Quality of Government: Corruption, Social Trust, and Inequality in International Perspective*. Chicago: University of Chicago Press.

Sampson, Steven. 2005. "Integrity Warriors: Global Morality and the Anti-Corruption Movement in the Balkans." In *Corruption: Anthropological Perspectives*, edited by Cris Shore and Dieter Haller, 103–131. London and Ann Arbor, MI: Pluto Press.

———. 2010. "The Anti-Corruption Industry: From Movement to Institution." *Global Crime* 11 (2): 261–278.

Søreide, Tina. 2006. "Is It Wrong to Rank? A Critical Assessment of Corruption Indices." CMI Working Paper WP 2006: 1. Accessed May 22, 2017. http://www.cmi.no/publications/publication/?2120=is-it-wrong-to-rank.

Spector, Malcolm, and John Kitsuse. 2009. *Constructing Social Problems*. 4th ed. Rutgers, NJ: Transaction Publishers.

Stokke, Olav Schram. 1997. "Regimes as Governance Systems." In *Global Governance: Drawing Insights from the Environmental Experience*, edited by Oran R. Young, 27–65. Cambridge, MA: MIT Press.

———. 2012. *Disaggregating International Regimes: A New Approach to Evaluation and Comparison*. Cambridge, MA: MIT Press.
TI. 2018. "Corruption Perceptions Index: Full Source Description." Accessed April 17. http://www.transparency.org/research/cpi/overview.
Treisman, Daniel. 2000. "The Causes of Corruption: A Cross-National Study." *Journal of Public Economics* 76 (3): 399–457.
United Nations Office on Drugs and Crime. 2004. *United Nations Convention Against Corruption*. Vienna: United Nations.
UN Global Compact. 2018. "Anti-Corruption." Accessed April 22. https://www.unglobalcompact.org/issues/transparency_anticorruption/.
UNODC. 2018. "Action Against Corruption and Economic Crime." Accessed April 17. http://www.unodc.org/unodc/en/corruption/.
US Department of Justice. 2018. "FCPA and Related Enforcement Actions." Accessed April 17. http://www.justice.gov/criminal/fraud/fcpa/cases/a.html.
Vicente, Pedro, and Daniel Kaufmann. 2011. "Legal Corruption." *Economics & Politics* 23 (2): 195–219.
Warren, Danielle E., and William S. Laufer. 2009. "Are Corruption Indices a Self-Fulfilling Prophecy? A Social Labeling Perspective of Corruption." *Journal of Business Ethics* 88 (4): 841–849.
Weaver, Catherine. 2010. "Constructing Development: The World Bank's Good Governance Agenda." In *Constructing the International Economy*, edited by Rawi Abdelal, Mark Blyth, and Craig Parsons, 47–67. Ithaca, NY: Cornell University Press.
Whyte, Dave. 2007. "The Crimes of Neo-Liberal Rule in Occupied Iraq." *British Journal of Criminology* 47 (2): 177–195.
Williamson, John. 2002. "Did the Washington Consensus Fail?" Outline of Speech, Center for Strategic and International Studies, Washington, DC, November 6.
———. 2008. "A Short History of the Washington Consensus." In *The Washington Consensus Reconsidered: Towards a New Global Governance*, edited by Narcís Serra and Joseph E. Stiglitz, 14–31. Oxford: Oxford University Press.
Wintour, Patrick. 2016. "Cameron to Propose Global Anti-Corruption Agency at Summit." *The Guardian*, May 4. Accessed May 5. http://www.theguardian.com/world/2016/may/04/cameron-to-propose-global-anti-corruption-agency-at-summit.
Wolf, Sebastian, and Diana Schmidt-Pfister, eds. 2010. *International Anti-Corruption Regimes in Europe: Between Corruption, Integration, and Culture*. Baden-Baden: Nomos.
World Bank. 2018. "WBI Governance and Anti-Corruption." Accessed April 23. http://web.worldbank.org/.

World Economic Forum. 2018. "Partnering Against Corruption Initiative." Accessed April 17. http://www.weforum.org/projects/partnering-against-corruption-initiative.

Yao, Shuntian. 1997. "Corruption and the Anti-Corruption Movement: The Modelling and Analysis of the Situation in China." *Australian Economic Papers* 36 (68): 156–165.

CHAPTER 3

The Social Construction of Global Problems

IR scholarship has studied the way in which global problems are managed across different issue areas (Avant et al. 2010; Biermann and Pattberg 2012; Hale et al. 2013; Harman and Williams 2013; Lesage et al. 2016). Both the scholarship on international regimes, which consolidated in the 1980s, and the scholarship on global governance, which followed it in the 1990s, to a large extent revolve around the management of global issues. Yet, despite the fact that problems are at the center of global governance structures, their social construction has not been seen as an analytical problem in itself. This gap is particularly obvious for constructivist IR, which has borrowed a lot from sociology, but not the long tradition on the study of social problems. This chapter argues for the usefulness of the social constructionist approach by Spector and Kitsuse for the study of global problems, and corruption in particular.

The central argument of this book is that corruption in particular and global problems in general are not 'natural' but constitute processes of collective definition and have to be constructed as problems to become focal points in issue-specific governance structures. As the previous chapter showed, in less than a decade (1994–2004) a number of binding and non-binding anti-corruption instruments cascaded and corruption was

E. Katzarova, *The Social Construction of Global Corruption*,
Political Corruption and Governance,
https://doi.org/10.1007/978-3-319-98569-5_3

brought forth as a serious problem and a legitimate topic for discussion at international organizations and financial institutions. This book enquires into the mechanism through which this change became possible. Conventional explanations of the puzzle attribute agency to global civil society organizations and argue that the reason for the emergence of anti-corruption initiatives is nested in the post-Cold War exigencies. In order to provide a systematic account of how corruption became a global problem, the book builds on the work of Spector and Kitsuse (1973, 2009) on the social construction of problems. The central research question of the book is: How was corruption constructed as a global problem? This chapter lays the conceptual and theoretical foundations of the social construction of corruption as a global problem by adapting the sociological approach of Spector and Kitsuse (2009) to the field of IR.

To account for the social construction of a problem means to provide for historical contingencies and to understand problems as evolving products of collective definition that are in a dynamic relation to the condition they refer to. This book studies the process of definition through claims-making and other discursive strategies and practices that are presented in this chapter and are applied in the empirical studies. In order to clarify what is meant by construction of a global problem, the following sections proceed in three steps. First, the concept of social construction and different types of social constructs are examined in order to show that the social construction of problems provides a useful analytical vehicle in relation to factual relativism. Second, the long tradition of the study of social problems in sociology is succinctly introduced, and the theory of Spector and Kitsuse on claims-making is given further attention and is adapted to IR and the cast of actors that are present on the global arena. Third, other theoretical and conceptual issues are tackled before the presentation of the cases and the data sources.

The chapter concludes that the application of the Spector and Kitsuse approach to IR can help elucidate the role of power, contestation and conflict in the social construction of global issues, and in this way, it can counteract what Barkin (2011) calls the implicit liberal bias of much of constructivist IR scholarship.

What Is Social Construction and the Social Construction of What?

The literature on global governance provides, to a large extent, an automated view of the process through which problems emerge and develop; problems are treated as natural. The way in which issue areas of global governance become densely institutionalized is well developed (Rosenau 1995; Barnett and Duvall 2005; Bernstein and Cashore 2007; Weiss and Wilkinson 2014), but the way in which problems are socially constructed has been given close to no attention in IR scholarship (Hülsse 2007). In order to provide a systematic account of how some conditions emerge as global problems, this book argues that the work of Spector and Kitsuse (1973, 2009) on the social construction of problems would make a valuable contribution to constructivist IR. The book lays the conceptual and theoretical foundations of the social construction of global problems by presenting and adapting the sociological approach of Spector and Kitsuse (2009) to the field of IR.

The literature on global governance developed to capture dramatic shifts in authority on the global stage (Rosenau 1995; Pierre 2000; Hall and Biersteker 2002; McGrew and Held 2002; Kahler and Lake 2003; Grande and Pauly 2007). Accounts of the changes in the way the world is governed and, in particular, the rise of private authority (Cutler et al. 1999; Ronit and Schneider 1999; Scherer et al. 2006) have been supplemented by the study of issue areas, such as environmental governance (Young 1997; Cashore 2002; Bernstein 2004; Levy and Newell 2005; Biermann and Pattberg 2008), energy governance (Florini and Sovacool 2009; Dubash and Florini 2011; Van de Graaf and Colgan 2016) and financial governance (Baker 2006; Underhill and Zhang 2008; Helleiner 2014). This fragmentation of the global governance literature into the study of broader and more specific issue areas is reminiscent of the study of international regimes (Krasner 1982) and makes the global governance literature revolve even more closely around the collective management of specific global problems. Constructivists in IR have contributed indirectly to the global governance literature through the study of norms, but norm research has neglected, according to Hofferberth and Weber (2015), the processes of social re-negotiation that drives normative transformations at the global level. One of the main objects of study in sociology, which is the social construction of problems, accounts for dynamic processes of social negotiations from which problems emerge as changing products of a collective definition. The study of global problems can contribute to the literature on global governance by accounting for both demand (Acharya 2016) and agency of state and non-state actors (Avant et al. 2010; Büthe and Mattli 2011) in the social construction of transnational and international issues. By denaturalizing problems that are at the center of global governance structures, the constructionist theory developed by Spector and Kitsuse also allows for the study of conflict and power—two essential elements of world politics.

The central argument of a constructivist reading of global problems is that they are not 'natural,' but constitute processes of collective definition. Conditions have to be socially constructed as problems to become focal points in issue-specific governance structures. 'Social construction' is one of the central concepts of social constructionism or as it has entered the field of IR—constructivism (Onuf 1989).[1] Constructivists in the social sciences are interested in the construction of (social) facts. The process of social construction entails that the human or collective intentionality of agents, which has led to the construction of a particular social fact or problem, is embedded in a social context within which specific beliefs, ideas and interests gain currency at a given time. Social construction, therefore, stresses the historical contingency of social facts and problems.

The treatment of social facts in the social sciences has, to a significant extent, softened the contestation that constructivism as an ontological and epistemological approach has received from scientific realists in other academic fields. The question—what it means for X to be socially constructed—cannot be adequately addressed without first answering the question about what is the X that is being constructed. Facts, or social facts, in general, are one of a number of 'things' being claimed as the products of social construction. Social constructs are potentially innumerable. In 'The Social Construction of What?' Hacking (1999) presents an extensive list of items that are claimed as social constructs: from 'quarks' to 'postmodernism.' The number of social constructs is continuously

[1] The term social constructionism is usually used in sociology and the sociology of science, while in the field of IR the term constructivism has become more widely accepted after the seminal article of Onuf (1989). This book uses the terms interchangeably.

growing in sociology and politics and includes the construction of social agency (Meyer and Jepperson 2000), leadership (Grint 2005), literacy (Cook-Gumperz 2006) and deviance (Goode and Ben-Yehuda 2009). European Studies and IR have produced their own list of social constructs: from Wendt's seminal publication (1992) on the social construction of power politics and anarchy through the construction of international politics (Wendt 1995; Hopf 2002), of pluralistic security communities (Barnett and Adler 1998), of ethnic identity (Fearon and Laitin 2000), to the 'moral' construction of power politics (Williams 2004) and the construction of the international economy (Abdelal et al. 2010).

These examples show that different *types* of things are claimed as social constructs. The social construction of facts (Latour and Woolgar 1979) or reality (Berger and Luckman 1966) provides the broader ontological framework for different products of social construction. Sociologists of science have challenged the absolute objectivity of the scientific enterprise of the natural sciences inserting elements of sociality and subjectivity in the study of how scientists produce knowledge (Boghossian 2006). In the field of politics and international affairs, however, the dynamics have been reversed because scientific principles coming from the natural sciences have 'naturalized' and reified social processes. While sociologists of science have tried to socialize the natural sciences, studying the process of social construction in the field of politics has the function to 'denaturalize' problems and reclaim the sociality of the discipline.

Within the social constructionist tradition of Spector and Kitsuse (2009), problems can be seen as claims that actors make about *social* reality and are, therefore, inseparable from value judgments and the normative beliefs of actors concerning what society should look like. The social constructionist agenda of Spector and Kitsuse does not concern itself with the sociology of science or the way in which scientists construct scientific knowledge, but with the way in which social problems are collectively negotiated through claims-making. In this perspective, social problems are transformed from self-evident objective realities into activities through which particular social groups identify certain conditions as harmful and in need of corrective action. The first analytical significance of this 'subjective turn' is that social problems become processes of social interaction. The second consequence is that the existence and the analytical importance of an actual social condition that triggers the claims-making process by the social participants are kept on a different analytical plane. Researchers can remain agnostic of the objective condition that gave rise to the claims (strict constructionism) or try to engage with or even evaluate the claims in relation to the putative condition (contextual constructionism). The analytical importance of the objective condition for the process of claims-making has been a debated issue (Holstein and Miller 1993), and the different relations between problem construction and an objective condition in the framework of contextual and strict constructionism within the discipline of sociology are given further attention in the following section.

Factual, rather than moral, relativism is at the center of contestation in debates on constructivism within the philosophy and sociology of science (Boghossian 2006). While only radical forms of constructionism deny the existence of objective facts, the social construction of global problems provides a useful shift of focus from 'fact fabrication,' as Goodman (1978) calls it, to the processes of social negotiation that construct conditions as problems. The concept of 'problem,' in the sense of 'bringing an issue forward,' can provide a useful conceptual vehicle of reconciliation when less radical forms of constructivism are employed.[2] Presenting the process of social construction as a problematization of a certain condition does not undermine the facts behind the socially constructed problem, but stresses that at a certain point in time these facts were brought forward by human agents and became problematic.[3] The object of construction, therefore, does not refer to an objective condition, but to its problematization, which, by definition, is involved in a mechanism of cultural and social production. Hence, the subjective turn does not challenge the existence of objective conditions, but argues that these conditions are not self-evident as social problems until they become the center of a process of social and definitional negotiation. The contribution of Spector and Kitsuse's subjective approach, in particular, was that it led to the systematization of the literature on social problems in sociology and to the delimitation of perspectives, which had, until then, been based on unspecified ontological and epistemological assumptions.

[2]The etymological root of the word problem comes from the Greek verb *προβάλλω, which means to highlight or to bring forward.* Oxford Dictionaries, s.v. 'problem,' accessed October 22, 2017, http://www.oxforddictionaries.com/definition/english/problem.

[3]Problematization has a long pedigree of scholarly interest with one of the most prominent examples coming from Foucault (1985).

The 'Subjective Turn': Sociological Perspectives on Social Problems

The 'subjective turn' to social problems was not invented with the establishment of social constructionism, but had a long evolution in the field of sociology, starting with the Theory of Social Disorganization. Mooney et al. (2011) single out the value-conflict and the symbolic interactionist perspectives as providing more sophisticated analytical tools for the study of social problems.[4] Drawing on the long pedigree of social problems studies in the field, the two schools started theorizing social problems by shifting attention to the process of social negotiation (value-conflict) or collective definition (symbolic interactionist) through which conditions become social problems.

The value judgments of the sociologist in assessing social conditions were first attacked by the value-conflict perspective, which argued that social organization is always imperfect and sociologists should not base their analysis on the expectation that a return to some nonexistent social equilibrium is possible (Spector and Kitsuse 2009). The Value-conflict perspective turned social problems into a subjectively defined condition that is selected from a number of social participants as harmful and deserving of corrective action. This definitional process is also called a 'negotiation' because it is inherently political, and also because social conditions become problems by being defined and negotiated by agents. As Spector and Kitsuse (2009) argue, agents also make their case through 'quasi theories' and causal inferences in order to explain, provide order and restore confidence that the situation can be successfully handled. The discovery of a 'cure' and the invention of causal inferences to support the quasi-theory become essential parts of the negotiation process. While this epistemological position is far from being broadly accepted, the argument that the value-conflict perspective promotes is that the sociologist should be, above all, interested in the process through which prescriptions and explanations are voiced and how some of them prevail rather than others. This change of analytical focus

[4] Mooney et al. (2011) single out three broader perspectives that have been the most influential on the study of social problems: (1) structural-functionalist; (2) value-conflict; and (3) symbolic interactionist perspectives. Other theories and approaches to the study of social problems can be taxonomically ordered around these three perspectives.

transforms the role of the social scientist from a diagnostician of social problems to an investigator of the process through which social problems are negotiated, defined and institutionalized.

Symbolic interactionism and, in particular, the social problems analysis of Blumer (1971) significantly influenced social constructionism. Work on the trajectory of social problems has been done since the 1930s, but one of the early models, which clearly tracks the career of social issues, belongs to Blumer (1971). Blumer argues that rather than positioning social problems in objective conditions, the sociologist should study problems as a process of collective definition because it is this socially negotiated mechanism that determines the career of the social problem rather than its objective makeup. Without challenging the objectivity of conditions, Blumer argues that sociologists have failed to answer why some problems come to public attention while others do not. Thus, the sociologically significant question—under which conditions societies come to recognize putative conditions as problematic and what is the mechanism through which the recognition and institutionalization come about—remains unanswered. The negligence of this process is not only of theoretical concern, but also of practical concern for the reason that: 'The societal definition and not the objective makeup of a given social condition, determines whether the condition exists as a social problem' (300). The social definition determines what is done at the policy level about the putative condition and thus, the mechanism through which society recognizes, defines and subsequently institutionalizes the governance of social problems appears as an intrinsic part of their practical resolution.

The Blumer model (1971) systematizes the career of a social problem in five generic stages: (1) emergence, (2) legitimation, (3) mobilization of action, (4) formation of an official plan and (5) transformation of the official plan in its empirical implementation (301). During the first phase, social awareness of a condition and, consequently, the selective process through which the public and media recognize social conditions constitute the main factors in the emergence of a social problem. If the bid for attention is successful, the second phase leads to legitimation. The popular recognition of the problematic situation is a necessary, but insufficient, condition for a certain 'degree of respectability' (Blumer 1971, 303) to be attached to the social problem so that it becomes a matter of debate in the public sphere. The problem could achieve some limited recognition in the first stage, but could be seen as an integral part of 'the way things are done' and can be judged as unworthy of reformative action. In this case, it becomes one of the many harmful conditions in society that are being ignored. As Blumer argues, the selectivity of the process through which only some harmful conditions emerge as problems cannot be adequately explained with some intrinsic urgency of the problem, but is quite often the product of influential interests that raise the problem on the public agenda.

Mobilization—the third stage in this process—is a controversial clash of competing interests and interpretations, during which the advocates for reform clash with the vested interests that want to bury the problem and exclude it from public policy. The media, at this stage, also becomes a hotbed for strategic moves, evaluation and falsification of claims and actively participates in the redefinition together with other interested actors who attempt to bend the definition according to their interests and power. This stage is characterized by intensification and, as Blumer notes, the mobilization stage is when the problem is radically redefined in order to accommodate conflicting interests, or it perishes. The fourth stage is when the problem enters the sphere of officialdom in the legislative process. At this stage, the bargaining and compromises lead to another redefinition of the problem: 'This is a defining and redefining process in a concentrated form – the forming, the re-working and the recasting of a collective picture' (304). This official definition may present the social problem in a completely different light than the popular sentiment. During the implementation phase, the problem is once again recast under the weight of practice with potential losers trying to undermine the implementation of the plan, and the public administration trying to sometimes adjust it subversively to their own, or somebody else's political agenda. Thus, according to Blumer, rather than constituting the end of the definitional process, the implementation phase prompts a new phase in the collective redefinition of the problem. The role of contingency is another of Blumer's contributions toward the study of social problems (Spector and Kitsuse 2009). Quite often, favorable or unfavorable events and social environments make or break the career of a social problem.

The Natural History of Social Problems and the Empirical Study of Claims

A variety of approaches analyze different aspects of social problem construction, such as the literature on framing and agenda-setting, but the sociological approach of Spector and Kitsuse (2009) offers the most comprehensive framework through which to examine the entire career of a global issue. It provides the advantage of tracing a collective definition process with a focus on how a putative condition is renegotiated rather than concentrating on external factors, such as policy windows and focus events (Kingdon 2010). By concentrating on the process of collective definition from the first emergence of claims, to the phases of post-institutionalization, Spector and Kitsuse's approach maps tendencies in the development of social problems. The Spector and Kitsuse approach to social problems offers some distinct benefits because of its comprehensive framework, which builds on a long pedigree of social problems studies in sociology. Spector and Kitsuse built on the 'subjective turn' in sociology in order to arrive at a theory of social problems and significantly expand the research agenda of symbolic interactionism and the value-conflict school on the social construction of problems.

In a series of publications dating back to the 1970s, Spector and Kitsuse (1973, 1975) made a pioneering attempt to systematize the existing literature on the study of social problems. They argued (2009) that the field has hitherto been 'dominated by textbooks that offer compilations of facts documenting the existence of the author(s) arbitrary selected assortment of what they conceive to be "social ills"' (ix). They offered a redefinition of social problems not as objective, self-evident conditions, but as processes in which the power of claims-making groups is the most crucial factor in the establishment of a putative condition as a problem. What Spector and Kitsuse contributed to the conventional study of social problems is that they shifted the sociological attention from the objective condition to the process through which claims-makers argue for and define a problem. The process of claims-making can be easily documented, as it is usually discursive and the 'claims-making activity itself can be empirically observed and documented without regard to the presence or 'reality' of the 'social condition,' which is conventionally asserted to be the basis of the claims' (xi).

The five stages proposed by Blumer have been modified by Spector and Kistuse (2009), who have considerably expanded the implementation phase. Their four-stage model of the natural history of social problems essentially merges all the five phases of Blumer into two (Stage 1: debate and publicity prompted by claims-making groups and Stage 2: recognition of legitimacy leading to an official plan for reform). They introduce the third and fourth stages (Stage 3: critical stage of dissatisfaction with official plan and Stage 4: rejection of official plan and an attempt to create an alternative solution) as 'a second generation' social problem, which study what happens after legislation has been enacted and plans of action have been put into place (142). Spector and Kitsuse argue that the third and fourth stages reveal that government legislation, as well as civil society plans of action, usually fails to ameliorate the harmful social conditions they aim to address. Furthermore, while Spector and Kitsuse delve substantially in the symbolic interactionist school's theorization of social problems, they dismiss the search for objective definitions of social problems (see below).[5]

The first stage of Spector and Kitsuse's natural history of social problems concentrates on the activities of groups that argue for the existence of a harmful social condition, by which they may or may not be directly affected. This stage is essentially the attempt to transform, in the famous formulation of Mills (1959), private problems into public concerns. This is the stage at which statistically significant occurrences of otherwise private troubles, such as unemployment or divorce, make a bid for public attention. Due to the fact that a lot of claims are discarded, the success of claims is dependent on the power of the pressing groups and their use of claims-making mechanisms. For Spector and Kitsuse, claims-making is a 'form of interaction' in which 'definitions of conditions as social problems are constructed by members of society who attempt to call attention to situations they find repugnant and who try to mobilize institutions to do something about them' (78).

[5] Blumer (1971) still considers, the study of the 'objective makeup' a valuable research agenda, but since the process of collective definition is ultimately politicized in his perspective, 'the knowledge of the objective makeup of the social problem is of significance only to the extent that the knowledge enters into the process of collective definition' and this is the process of 'being seen and defined' by society that ultimately determines the rise and demise of social problems in the public arena (305).

While the first stage can continue for an indefinite period of time, the beginning of the second stage is marked by the recognition of the claims-making group by an official agency. The success of the group may be achieved through mounting pressure, or the agency could recognize that it can gain dividends from assuming control over the problem.[6] Spector and Kitsuse (2009) remark that often 'commissions reform by public relations, in which the commissions to study the problem are taken to be the substance of reform itself' (150). In the long process of producing a final report, the putative problem may find its premature end or go to the next level of institutionalization. When staff and resources are attributed to the governing of a problem, this does not mark the end of its career, but rather, signifies a new stage of development. The institutionalization of the problem marks the moment when dealing with complaints, rather than mitigating the condition itself, may become a primary goal. Spector and Kitsuse mark the end of the second stage: 'when complaints about some condition have become domesticated and routinized by some agency that develops a vested interest in doing something about the complaints, though not necessarily in dealing with the conditions to which the complaints refer' (151).

Stage three further complicates the relationship between the problem and the proposed solution due to the inability of the plan of action to mitigate the condition. This lack of effectiveness could be planned, due to the fact that reforms by public relations aim to diffuse social tension and take control over the solution of the problem. In the third stage of social problem development, 'assertions about the inadequacy, inefficacy or injustice of the procedures may themselves become the conditions around which new activities' become organized, often by different groups than the ones that achieved initial recognition (Spector and Kitsuse 2009, 151–152). When the bureaucratic handling of the problem generates new

[6] Spector and Kitsuse adopt a grassroots approach in which groups try to get governmental recognition and push a putative condition as a 'formal part of an institutional agenda' (154). The authors, however, recognize that this is simply one route for agenda-setting in society and quite often the initiative comes from governmental institutions that want to raise a condition to the status of a social problem. The difference between 'initiator' and 'responder' can be hard to discern, but the initiative in the construction of social problems can come from both grassroots movements and governmental institutions. The major indicator of the successful career of a social problem in both cases, however, remains the raising of an issue as part of an official agenda and the enactment of legislation.

predicaments, and claims start to emerge about the procedures rather than the problem itself, these are 'second generation' claims. According to Spector and Kitsuse, after the routinization of claims is achieved at the previous stage, stage three concludes with a legitimacy crisis. At the fourth stage, interested groups contend that it is no longer viable 'to work within the system' (153). Since the legitimacy of institutions is compromised, either the organizations try to reform, or new methods to ameliorate the condition are established at the community level.

The transition from one stage to the next is highly volatile; at each stage, the career of the social problem can be interrupted, as not all problematic situations that come to public and media attention are taken seriously by the administration and the government, and not all situations that are discussed in official institutions manage to make it to legislation. Furthermore, the confrontation of positions and interests complicates the smooth development of any social problem no matter how urgent its resolution appears: 'A social problem is always a focal point for the operation of divergent and conflicting interests, intentions and objectives' (Blumer 1971, 301).

While Spector and Kitsuse built upon sociological scholarship on social problems, and in particular, the work of Blumer, they carried the research agenda one step further by presenting social problems as claims-making processes. There are different empirical questions that a social constructionist agenda on social problems can pursue at the different stages of the career of a social problem. Some examples at the primary stages of claims-making would be questions such as: Who are the claims-makers? What is the context of their interest in the claims? What type of evidence do they provide? Spector and Kitsuse (2009) provide a dynamic conceptualization of social problems—one that shifts the understanding of problems from a 'condition' to an 'activity.' Claims-making is an interactive process in which demands are made from one group or organization on another: A 'claim is a demand that one party makes upon another' (83). Spector and Kitsuse (2009) explain that before making a claim, claimants first construct an etiology of the putative problem, which conditions the way the claim is expressed. The empirical study of claims starts from isolating the first occurrence of claims-making and studying the background that provoked a particular group to start the process. As a first step, the researcher should: 'identify the beginning point of a particular group's interest and participation in the preliminary and preparatory stages of claims-making' and recognize that many cases of claims-making will be unsuccessful (128). After providing this background, the researcher should follow the thread of continuity in the redefinition of social problems as they become part of the agenda of different organizations. Spector and Kitsuse (2009) place the legitimation of the claims by a public institution as the first indicator that claims are being successful. The main research task in the first phase of the empirical analysis of claims, therefore, is to individualize the initial claims-makers.

Recognition by an official public institution is the usual method of seeding successful claims, even though public institutions themselves may be the generators of claims. If the claims are rendered legitimate, an ad hoc committee to study the issue is usually formed. The selection of the committee sheds light on what kind of experts are deemed authoritative, and what kind of definition is about to emerge, in light of sociologists, economists and legal experts having differing takes on the same objective condition. Whether a problem is of an economic, humanitarian or legal nature is not a self-evident aspect inherent to the objective condition itself, and the prism through which a problem is viewed becomes a strategic and, essentially, a political tool. Appeals to legal rhetoric, for example, can be used as a universalistic rationalization for self-interest: 'International talk is often moral and legal because the obligatory vocabulary of moral and legal dispute between individuals is also useful for purely amoral strategic interactions when cooperation and coordination are involved' (Posner and Goldsmith 2002, 115). The way an understanding of a condition is continuously shifted from the first occurrences of claims-making through the internal proceedings of the organizations that deem the claims legitimate is of high relevance to the social construction of problems: 'The data document the development of claims and issues as they are defined, redefined, and passed from one set of participants to another; this thread of continuity leads through a variety of institutions and casts of characters' (Spector and Kitsuse 2009, 125).

The processing of claims leads to a continuous redefinition of the problem and the inclusion of contributions from new participants in the definitional process. Excavating competing claims from the definitional process and contextualizing the emergence of claims-making provide potential clues as to what types of claims, and under which conditions, prevail over others, and show that other interpretations of putative conditions are possible, but are neglected or overruled by more successful claims. Shifting claims from 'localized' to 'globalized' changes the definition of the putative condition and is reflected in the negotiation of practical solutions. Spector and Kitsuse (2009) provide relevant empirical cases for how the expansion of the geographical and definitional scope of a problem may lead to a deadlock. Opening up the research to controversial questions and proposing solutions that are too radical, and potentially disconcerting in the public eye, is another route to an impasse. Nevertheless, the claims are still successful if they have received formal recognition and have become part of the agenda of international organizations. Claims-making activities might go through a number of cycles of recognition and failure before the institutionalization of the problem.

An important aspect in the empirical study of claims is the role of the researcher, who studies the social construction of problems. The core of the constructivist argument put forward by Spector and Kitsuse (2009) is that as individual agents and organizations promote a problem in the sphere of public recognition, they become an intrinsic part of the problem construction, and this includes the social scientists investigating the problem. This approach argues that the sociologist who promotes awareness of a social problem, or even simply studies it, is in a similar position to a lobbyist. Spector and Kitsuse, therefore, argue that claims-making activities should be at the center of investigation because any attempt to 'study the problem itself' is an act of promotion of a particular interpretation of the problematic situation in which the sociologist simply promotes her version of reality over others. The process of social interaction which constructs the problem is a more suitable approach to the study of society: 'how individuals and groups become engaged in collective activities that recognize putative conditions as problems, and attempt to establish institutional arrangements.' The claims-making activities of groups who promote a certain version of reality, and reject others, are placed at the center of sociological investigation shedding light on 'how methods of social control and treatment are institutionally established' (72).

The research agenda of Spector and Kitsuse has been very influential, but their early work has been contested on the grounds of 'ontological gerrymandering' (Woolgar and Pawluch 1985). This meant constructionist scholars pushed the boundary between what remained problematized and what remained fixed in the analytical process quite indiscriminately. The debate that came out of this critique led to the consolidation of strict and contextual constructionism (Best 2009). The epistemological differences between the two are elucidated in relation to the validity of objective conditions. While strict constructionism remains neutral toward the validity of claims, contextual constructionism can try to not only position claims within their socio-historical context, but also place the analyst in a position to evaluate their validity (Best 1993, 2009). In this sense, Best offers a middle ground in the objectivist-subjectivist debate by incorporating elements of both. Contextualizing the process of claims-making, however, does not necessarily entail that the analysts should expose 'erroneous' claims.

Best (1993) finds strict constructionism insufficient because in the quest for epistemological consistency and theoretical purity, Spector and Kitsuse are trying to fence off their research from the messy business of empirical analysis. A theory of social problem discourse, which studies only rhetoric and language, is more feasible, but it collides with the argument that constructionism is empirically grounded. Best is critical of this view because it renounces the sociological purpose of understanding and changing reality for the better, and relegates sociological studies down to the level of language games. The extremes of completely ignoring the initial condition or completely debunking the way the condition has been institutionalized are not the only two options—rather they are two points on a continuum. It is possible to contextualize discourse and to provide analysis for a variety of claims and counterclaims without making the final judgment on their validity. The study of social problems does offer practical clues to understanding the empirical realities 'behind' problems, but these clues remain implicit. By investigating who are the claims-makers and what are the interests that are fueling their activities, as well as what type of evidence they are providing for their claims, the constructionist researcher can present a variety of clues as to the possible validity of claims, but not the final judgment as to proving one group of claims erroneous and another group of claims valid. In order to reconstruct the unsuccessful claims, this book will show how two interpretations emerged from the same putative condition. While reconstructing and arguing for the enduring relevance of the unsuccessful claims, the book does not aim to prove that the unsuccessful claims were the accurate way to understand and define the problem. On the contrary, both the successful and unsuccessful claims were valid ways of interpreting the situation. At the same time, the reason why one set of claims prevailed over the other did not have to do with the validity of the claims, but rather with the power of the claims-making group. As the following section will show, the claims-making groups, especially in the context of international intergovernmental organizations, are nation states and groups of states.

The Social Construction of Global Problems: Agency and the 'Globalization' of Problems

Claims-making on global problems will differ on two major accounts. The first fundamental difference between global and national claims-making concerns the content of the claims. Global claims would not only assert that a problem exists, but they would be directed at proving that this problem is best addressed through coordinated action at the global level. The second major difference between global and national claims-making is that a different set of agents would be engaged in claims-making activities. These two major differences, between national and global claims-making, are given further attention and illustrated with relevant examples from IR scholarship in order to adapt the sociological approach to IR.

Spector and Kitsuse (2009) define social problems as 'the activities of individuals or groups making assertions of grievances and claims with respect to some putative condition' (75). This condition is in need of amelioration according to the etiology presented in the claims of these groups. Global problems are the claims-making activities of state and non-state actors who make assertions that some putative condition is a problem that can be ameliorated only through coordinated action at a global level. The claims as to why a problem is global, rather than national, are therefore an essential part of the claims-making process.

Global problems are, by definition, trans-sovereign because sovereign states are not able to deal with them on their own (Love 2010). The amelioration of global problems is often the prerogative of global governance structures, and global governance can indeed be defined as 'collective actions to establish international institutions and norms to cope with the causes and consequences of adverse supranational, transnational, or national problems' (Väyrynen 1999, 25). Demand for global governance is intensified through globalization, and global governance is to an extent a collective response to global problems. Claims-making activities that demand a global response are a necessary prerequisite for the social construction of global problems. While the term 'global' can be applied to a variety of problems that are encountered by nation states, as long as there are no demands for the creation of institutional structures with international, transnational or trans-sovereign character, we cannot speak of a global problem the way it is intended in this book. For example, unemployment is often referred to as a 'global problem' because a lot of nation states have undesirably high unemployment rates; however, unemployment is still not a global problem as intended in this book. Unemployment has indeed reached the status of a global fright in a period of just a few years with the International Labor Organization (ILO) estimating the global number of unemployed persons for 2017 to be over 201 million. The BBC World Service Survey showed that unemployment has joined corruption and poverty as the most talked about global problems. A six fold increase in public concern with unemployment has been marked just from 2009 to 2011 (GlobeScan 2011). Yet, no global claims have been made of unemployment being in need of a systematic global governance approach. The IMF has made appeals for international coordination of policies on aggregate demand to boost job creation indirectly, but has not recommended coordination of labor market policies (Blanchard and Gali 2010; Blanchard et al. 2013).

The 'non-problematicity' (Freudenburg 2000) of unemployment as an issue for global governance is in stark contrast with the highly institutionalized nature of corruption as a global governance issue (Rosenau and Wang 2001; McCoy and Heckel 2001). While unemployment rivals corruption in worldwide public concern, this concern is not yet matched by successful claims-making activities that will boost unemployment as a global agenda item. A global problem will start its career after claims are being made that the unemployment situation can be ameliorated only through coordinated international and global action, and not through more effective policies of national governments.[7] Therefore, the construction of unemployment as a global governance problem would begin with claims-making that the unemployment numbers can be tackled only through collective action at a global level and these claims can then be legitimated in the framework of different international forums. The subsequent attempt to govern the problem of unemployment globally, or at least through coordinated international action, will mark the beginning of a stage of institutionalization.

That a problem is a legitimate global governance issue can become a major point of contestation. The social construction of problems is studied as an intersubjective process characterized by claims and counterclaims and similar dynamic processes between actors have already been examined in IR. The process of claims-making in the

[7] Even the IMF calls for reform are limited to coordination not of labor market policies, but of fiscal and monetary policies to influence aggregate demand (Blanchard and Gali 2010).

context of global governance shows some similarity to the conceptualization of Abbott and Snidal (2000), who distinguish between 'demandeurs' and 'resisters' in the production of international legislation. Demandeurs are 'states (and other actors) that have worked to obtain commitments from others, often in the face of strong resistance' (431). In international law, legal regimes often become 'functions of demandeur preferences' (Gopalan 2008). The main difference between the claims-making process of Spector and Kitsuse and the demandeur approach of Abbott and Snidal is that in the conceptual framework of the former, both demandeurs and resisters will be considered claims-makers. When the construction of social problems becomes the product of a process of collective definition, the resisters stop being presented as simply being in opposition to the 'problem' and become contestant claims-makers in the construction of the problem. This shift is significant because it sheds new light on the production of global governance structures. If we take as an example the politics of contestation by developing countries on global environmental arrangements, the conventional perspective is that their opposition to solving the problem of environmental degradation has finally been overcome (Najam 2005). From a constructivist perspective, however, the same politics of contestation by the Global South becomes part of claims-making activities that are analyzed at the same level as the proactive politics of the demandeurs. A conventional understanding of social problems existing simply as an objective condition would assume that the resisters are against the 'problem,' but according to the constructionist reading of the same dynamic, this may not be the case. The resisters or the counterclaims-makers may have a different understanding of the putative condition, and their rejection of the demands could be justified by this differing interpretation. The claims-making activities of the demandeurs may not be given priority, their bid for attention may not be taken seriously, and the claims may lack legitimacy. In the global arena, state and non-state claims-makers make their bids for legitimacy in front of official organizations and in front of each other. The participants in the process of claims-making will differ in national and international environments (Table 3.1).

Table 3.1 National and global claims-makers

National claims-makers	*Global claims-makers*
1. Governmental and municipal bodies and agencies	1. States
2. Pressure groups: political activists and lobbyists	2. International organizations
3. Moral entrepreneurs	3. Global civil society/global business
4. Academic experts: academic and social researchers	4. Epistemic communities
5. The traditional and social media: newspaper columnists, media commentators	5. Global traditional and social media

Source on national claims-makers: Spector and Kitsuse (2009)

One of the major tasks in denaturalizing problems is to account for agency. If the etymological root of the word 'problem' is to be taken seriously, the process of problematization would 'bring forward' a condition now defined as a problem.[8] The process is not automatic because even if state, non-state actors or international policy makers 'spot' a problem out there, they still have to engage in ontological persuasion at the beginning of negotiations (Hülsse 2007).[9] When agency is accounted for, the emergence of the problem loses both its naturalness and its automaticity. Finnemore and Sikkink (1998) argue that international actors 'call attention to issues or even create issues' (893). Usually, these are assumed to be disinterested non-state actors, such as INGOs and epistemic communities, who call attention to issues and act as norm entrepreneurs.

International organizations constitute another global actor who can engage in claims-making activities or at least provide a venue for such activities. Hülsse (2007) calls for the study of global problems and adopts a radical constructivist approach to prove that actors who are in

[8]The notion that the emergence of problems is always triggered by some objectively measured increase or worsening of the condition has been challenged by constructivist scholars. Epstein (2005), for example, argues for the explanatory weakness of material-based factors in the emergence of an international whaling regime by showing the causal irrelevance of the levels of endangerment of whales to the formation of the regime.

[9]Hülsse (2007) places ontological persuasion as a prerequisite for normative persuasion. During the process of ontological persuasion, other actors with competing interpretations have to be convinced of the existence of the problem, its definitional parameters, as well as the causal connections between the claimed problem and other objectives on the agenda.

the business of managing global problems also create them. He argues for the agency of organizations, such as the Financial Action Task Force (FATF), in constructing global problems. The argument that global actors, who have an inherent interest in expanding their mandate, transform previously national prerogatives into global concerns does not, however, answer the question of why a particular problem emerges at a given time. FATF, for example, is an intergovernmental body at the OECD headquarters and was created with a mandate from the G7 to carry out work on money-laundering; that is, FATF may have an interest in creating global problems in general, but it was given a specific mandate to work on money-laundering by nation states. Hülsse, therefore, brackets the problem by taking money-laundering for a natural problem and accounts only for its instrumental use. This account in which money-laundering is taken for granted, but its instrumental use is 'problematized' may lead to relativism (as if the problem is chosen at random). As one of the basic premises of constructivism is that agents of social construction can act instrumentally (Ruggie 1998), it is in denaturalizing problems that the task of social construction lies. This entails asking questions such as: Why this particular issue? Who claimed it was a problem and why? How did they define it? In order to provide a systematic account of a research agenda with a methodology that can answer these types of questions, the work of Spector and Kitsuse (1973, 1975, 2009) on the construction of social problems could provide useful theoretical and conceptual tools for researchers in IR.

Another aspect of the theoretical approach of Spector and Kitsuse and the work of Blumer that make them particularly suitable for the study of IR is the treatment of the concept of power in the social construction of problems. Groups with higher membership, economic resources and more sophisticated organization are more likely to have their claims processed as legitimate. The power of a group to make claims is understood as the ability of a group to realize demands it makes on other groups, agencies and institutions. Therefore, the actual results that a claims-making group manages to produce are the measurement of its power. The agents of social construction at the global level are often identified as non-state actors or international organizations; but, the neglect of state agency can lead to a neglect of a significant factor for change in the social construction of global problems. Barkin (2003, 2011) has criticized the implicit liberalism of constructivist scholars in IR who have not provided for a satisfactory inclusion of state power into studies of social construction. Power in interstate relations is understood not solely as brute material force or violent coercion, since, as Dahl (1957) famously argued, it is the ability to make others do what otherwise they would not have done that is at the core of power relations. The greatest success of power, therefore, is to coerce without threatening: 'political power is ultimately about persuasion, about convincing others rather than forcing' (Barkin 2011, 19). To adapt this argument to the construction of global problems, power is convincing others that your national troubles are global problems. Persuasion can be seen as the opposite of power, understood as material force and is therefore seen as the weapon of the weak. Consequently, the agents of persuasion at the global level are often appointed as civil society actors, epistemic communities and other non-state actors who do not possess the same material capabilities as states. In the creation of global problems around which policy responses are built, however, state actors can be central players who embark on persuasion campaigns. Their material power is not irrelevant, but at the same time cannot completely account for the outcome and the methods they use. By taking into account the role of state (as well as non-state actors) in the social construction of global problems, constructivism can study how power shapes normative transformations at the global level, and show that even state-centered international relations are a battlefield of ideas.

This constructivist conceptual re-formulation of power as the power of claims-making groups to realize demands could be particularly robust when adapted to the field of IR, as it allows for the study of the role of power in establishing ideas and promoting versions of international reality. The construction of global problems as a perspective on global governance offers a potentially new interpretation of how ideational factors contribute to the establishment and institutionalization of power at the international level, and that this power can also be ideational. The ability of some agents to establish their version of reality is inseparable from their relative power. The struggle of ideas at the global level can be seen as a power struggle in which the stronger prevail not necessarily because of the validity of their argument. The ideas that are established as legitimate in this power struggle contribute to the social construction of one version of reality over another.

Definition and Data Sources

Different understandings of corruption saturate academic and policy debates. From an expansive definition of corruption as the permeation of the political sphere by the logic of the market (Girling 1997), to a more operational understanding of corruption as a monetized exchange, setting precise definitional boundaries is a difficult task. The most referenced and broadly accepted conceptualization is the operational definition used by TI: 'the abuse of entrusted power for private gain.' This definition is shared by the World Bank with a slight alteration—'the abuse of public office for private gain.' When the definition is not attributed to TI or the World Bank, it is mistakenly attributed to Joseph Nye, but it can actually be traced back to Senturia (1931). Senturia put forward the 'misuse of public power for private profit' as the definition of political corruption (448). The book preliminary understands corruption in the conventional (Senturia) sense, as the misuse of public power for private profit.

As discussed earlier, the book employs discourse and practice analysis methods in accordance with the strategies of Spector and Kitsuse (2009) for the empirical study of claims. These discursive strategies include the study of the definition of conditions, expression of claims and imputation of motives and values by the claims-makers, as well as practices and strategies of managing controversy and publicity. Spector and Kitsuse put forward library and archival research, analysis of documents, as well as unstructured elite interviews as the right methods to obtain the data for their definitional approach. The presentation of the data has to be highly detailed and includes excerpts of memos, faxes, letters, minutes of meetings, commentaries and dossiers in the media.

In the empirical chapters, within-case analysis of the discursive strategies of social construction of the problem of corruption in two international organizations—the OECD and the UN—is investigated in detail. In the process of data collection, the two discussions proved to be more entangled than expected. In particular, in 1977 the OECD discussion of a potential treaty on corrupt payments was made conditional upon the successful advancement of the same issue within the framework of the UN. Similarly, in the late 1990s, it was after the adoption of the OECD Convention on Combating Bribery of Foreign Public Officials in International Business Transactions that the discussions within the UN changed and allowed for the adoption of the most comprehensive global instrument against corruption. The interconnection between the two cases enhances the argument that problematizing global issues is an essential step in the adoption of international treaties within the framework of global governance. The successful legitimation of a global problem within one institutional framework may lead to a quick spillover to other international forums. Finnemore and Sikkink (1998) credit norms for this policy cascade, but as the empirical chapters show, the spillover effect can also be due to state agency.

The empirical within-case analysis of discursive strategies is based on primary data from three main sources—US Congressional and State Department archival data, as well as an extensive investigation of previously unexamined archival materials at the OECD Archives in Paris and the UN Archives in New York. The data analyzed are sensitive, and different declassification procedures apply within the different institutional frameworks. Congressional and State Department archival materials, in particular from the 1970s, are available to researchers due to the exhaustion of the 20-year period of disclosure. In the case of the OECD, the Council Resolution on the Classification and Declassification of Information (CES/CRC(97)16) provides access to all archival materials (including classified) after a period of maximum 6 years. The access to primary documents dating before 1997 is possible under the same conditions, but necessitates a special request. The OECD data provide the most abundant resource for the analysis with more than 20,000 documents. The review and reproduction of all types of data proved unproblematic during my research period at the OECD Headquarters and the UN Archives. The access to some preparatory documents and minutes of meetings also proved possible. Lastly, the compendium of primary archival sources is complemented with the examination of journalistic sources reproduced in the OECD press reviews in order to gain an understanding of the media and public perception of the talks and the wider societal context.[10]

[10]George and Bennett (2005), in a compendium of the same type of data sources, emphasize that classified sources require acquaintance with the wider social context through the reading of journalistic articles from the period corresponding to the archival material (97).

This chapter introduced the conceptual building blocks of the book by presenting the main elements of a research agenda on the social construction of problems. It did so in three steps: first by presenting the essentials of the concept of social construction and second by channeling it toward the more specific agenda of Spector and Kitsuse (1973, 2009) on the social construction of problems. Third, adapting this sociological approach to the field of IR entails the consideration of a different type of agents, such as state actors and non-state actors. This book argues that the social construction of a global corruption problem remained a largely intergovernmental process, driven by powerful states. Finally, with this examination of state power in the social construction of international reality, this book joins the approaches that aim for integrating realist insights into constructivism.

The secondary aim of this chapter was to show the broader relevance of social problems research to IR. From that vantage point, corruption is but one example of the social construction of global problems. Constructivism arrived in IR with the assertion that the world is of our own making (Onuf 1989). While studying the role of norms and rules, as well as the constitutive role of discourse in the making and remaking of the social world, IR constructivism has so far neglected to account for the social construction of global problems.

Problem construction enjoys a long research pedigree in sociology and has been very influential in the development of social constructionist thought in the field. IR constructivists can adapt the sociological approaches to the landscape of international affairs in order to understand better how global governance structures emerge, and what actors and factors drive demand for global governance. The special attention that the sociological constructionist approach pays to the concept of the power of claims-making groups, and the role of conflict in the claims-making activities can help IR constructivists better understand the ontological battles with which global governance structures are established. Analyzing the actors, who are successful at establishing their interpretation of a putative condition as a problem, facilitates the study of shifting authority at the global level and the deconstruction of ontological warfare. The study of the problematicity of certain issues and the non-problematicity of others shows how state and non-state actors make sense of the world, and it sheds light on who is successful at persuading or imposing on others their own views on global social ills. Therefore, the sociological approach to the social construction of problems exhibits a constructivist understanding of power as the power of claims-making groups to impose their understanding of a condition and shape the social world.

Spector and Kitsuse's approach is particularly well tailored for the empirical study of claims. A feasible working strategy for empirical research on claims is for the researcher to first look for institutional legitimation. The first occurrences of claims-making can be easily identified by the well-documented institutional legitimation of claims. The official recognition of a respondent is an essential tool in the isolation of specific claims. The response in most organizations is routinized, and the strategies for a successful recognition become part of the organization of claims. The organization and processing of claims-making activities become, therefore, an empirical question to be answered because there is 'no simple mechanical, causal relationship between a condition, and the activation of responses and complaints' (Spector and Kitsuse 2009, 84). Following the identification of such successful claims, a step back to the historical and political context of the claims can be made in order to identify the putative condition that gave rise to such claims. The search for the historical context of the claims or the objective definitions that gave rise to the claims in the first place would depend on the researcher's commitment to conventional or critical constructivism (similar to contextual and strict constructionism in sociology). Tracing the dynamic relation that claims-makers sustain with the putative condition they are addressing can then lead to the identification of the major claims and counterclaims, as well as the reconstruction of alternative routes for defining and addressing the problem. The careers of social problems follow similar patterns that can help the understanding of the impact of agents on the social construction of global issues, as well as help discern future trends in the development of a social problem past the legitimacy crisis phase and the emergence of second-generation claims.

The social construction of global problems constitutes a kaleidoscope of overlapping claims and definitions that accompany the understanding of the putative condition both theoretically and practically. The natural history or career of a social problem is a process—it is the trajectory through which a given society comes to recognize, legitimize and govern social issues. The process of social construction accommodates not simply scientific facts about the putative social condition, but also conflicting interpretations, diverging strategies, inequality of power and vested interests, as well as practical implementation predicaments. What type of transboundary problems remain contested as national, and for what reasons is one of the relevant empirical questions through which the power of claims-making groups can be assessed at a global level. The denaturalization of global problems and the political processes of negotiation and collective definition that determine the process of social construction can shed further light on how and by whom is meaning produced in this world of our making.

References

Abbott, Kenneth W., and Duncan Snidal. 2000. "Hard and Soft Law in International Governance." *International Organization* 54 (3): 421–456.

Abdelal, Rawi, Mark Blyth, and Craig Parsons, eds. 2010. *Constructing the International Economy*. Ithaca: Cornell University Press.

Acharya, Amitav, ed. 2016. *Why Govern? Rethinking Demand and Progress in Global Governance*. Cambridge: Cambridge University Press.

Avant, Deborah D., Martha Finnemore, and Susan K. Sell, eds. 2010. *Who Governs the Globe?* Cambridge: Cambridge University Press.

Baker, Andrew. 2006. *The Group of Seven: Finance Ministries, Central Banks and Global Financial Governance*. London and New York: Routledge.

Barkin, J. Samuel. 2003. "Realist Constructivism." *International Studies Review* 5 (3): 325–342.

———. 2011. *Realist Constructivism: Rethinking International Relations Theory*. Cambridge: Cambridge University Press.

Barnett, Michael, and Emanuel Adler. 1998. *Security Communities*. Cambridge: Cambridge University Press.

Barnett, Michael, and Raymond Duvall. 2005. *Power in Global Governance*. Cambridge: Cambridge University Press.

Berger, Peter L., and Thomas Luckmann. 1966. *The Social Construction of Reality: A Treatise in the Sociology of Knowledge*. New York: Anchor Books.

Bernstein, Steven. 2004. "Legitimacy in Global Environmental Governance." *Journal of International Law and International Relations* 1: 139.

Bernstein, Steven, and Benjamin Cashore. 2007. "Can Non-state Global Governance Be Legitimate? An Analytical Framework." *Regulation & Governance* 1 (4): 347–371.

Best, Joel. 1993. "But Seriously, Folks: The Limitations of the Strict Constructionist Interpretation of Social Problems." *In Reconsidering Social Constructionism: Debates in Social Problems Theory*, edited by J. Holstein and G. Miller, 129–147. Rutgers, NJ: Transaction Publishers.

———. 2009. *Images of Issues: Typifying Contemporary Social Problems*. Rutgers, NJ: Transaction Publishers.

Biermann, Frank, and Philipp Pattberg. 2008. "Global Environmental Governance: Taking Stock, Moving Forward." *Annual Review of Environment and Resources* 33 (1): 277–294.

———, eds. 2012. *Global Environmental Governance Reconsidered*. Cambridge: MIT Press.

Blanchard, Olivier, and Jordi Gali. 2010. "Labor Markets and Monetary Policy: A New Keynesian Model with Unemployment." *American Economic Journal: Macroeconomics* 2 (2): 1–30.

Blanchard, Olivier, Florence Jaumotte, and Prakash Loungani. 2013. *Labor Market Policies and IMF Advice in Advanced Economies During the Great Recession*. Washington, DC: International Monetary Fund, Research Department.

Blumer, Herbert. 1971. "Social Problems as Collective Behavior." *Social Problems* 18 (3): 298–306.

Boghossian, Paul. 2006. *Fear of Knowledge: Against Relativism and Constructivism*. Oxford: Clarendon Press.

Büthe, Tim, and Walter Mattli. 2011. *The New Global Rulers: The Privatization of Regulation in the World Economy*. Princeton, NJ: Princeton University Press.

Cashore, Benjamin. 2002. "Legitimacy and the Privatization of Environmental Governance: How Non-State Market-Driven (NSMD) Governance Systems Gain Rule-Making Authority." *Governance* 15 (4): 503–529.

CES/CRC(97)16. *Council Resolution on the Classification and Declassification of Information, Adopted by the Council at the 906th Session on 10 July 1997* (29 August 1997). OECD Archives, Paris Headquarters.

Cook-Gumperz, Jenny. 2006. *The Social Construction of Literacy*. Cambridge: Cambridge University Press.

Cutler, A. Claire, Virginia Haufler, and Tony Porter, eds. 1999. *Private Authority and International Affairs*. Albany: State University of New York Press.

Dahl, Robert Alan. 1957. *The Concept of Power*. Indianapolis, IN: Bobbs-Merrill.

Dubash, Navroz K., and Ann Florini. 2011. "Mapping Global Energy Governance." *Global Policy* 2 (1): 6–18.

Epstein, Charlotte. 2005. *The Power of Words in International Relations: Birth of an Anti-Whaling Discourse*. Cambridge, MA: MIT Press.

Fearon, James D., and David D. Laitin. 2000. "Violence and the Social Construction of Ethnic Identity." *International Organization* 54 (4): 845–877.

Finnemore, Martha, and Kathryn Sikkink. 1998. "International Norm Dynamics and Political Change." *International Organization* 52 (4): 887–917.

Florini, Ann, and Benjamin K. Sovacool. 2009. "Who Governs Energy? The Challenges Facing Global Energy Governance." *Energy Policy* 37 (12): 5239–5248.

Foucault, Michel. 1985. *Discourse and Truth: The Problematization of Parrhesia*. Edited by J. Pearson. Evanston, IL: Northwestern University.

Freudenburg, William. 2000. "Social Constructions and Social Constrictions: Toward Analyzing the Social Construction of 'the Naturalized' as Well as 'the Natural'." In *Environment and Global Modernity*, edited by G. Spaargaren, A. P. J. Mol, and F. H. Buttel, 103–119. London: Sage.

George, Alexander L., and Andrew Bennett. 2005. *Case Studies and Theory Development in the Social Sciences*. Cambridge, MA: MIT Press.

Girling, John. 1997. *Corruption, Capitalism and Democracy*. East Sussex: Psychology Press.

GlobeScan. 2011. "Unemployment Rises as 'Most Talked-About' Problem: Global Poll." Accessed November 10, 2017. http://www.globescan.com/news-and-analysis/press-releases/press-releases-2011/94-press-releases-2011/126-unemployment-rises-as-qmost-talked-aboutq-problem-global-poll.html.

Goode, Erich, and Nachman Ben-Yehuda. 2009. *Moral Panics: The Social Construction of Deviance*. Hoboken, NJ: Wiley.

Goodman, Nelson. 1978. *Ways of Worldmaking*. Indianapolis, IN: Hackett Publishing.

Gopalan, Sandeep. 2008. "A Demandeur-Centric Approach to Regime Design in Transnational Commercial Law." *Georgetown Journal of International Law* 39 (2): 22–51.

Grande, Edgar, and Louis W. Pauly, eds. 2007. *Complex Sovereignty: Reconstituting Political Authority in the Twenty-First Century*. Toronto: University of Toronto Press.

Grint, Keith. 2005. "Problems, Problems, Problems: The Social Construction of 'Leadership'." *Human Relations* 58 (11): 1467–1494.

Hacking, Ian. 1999. *The Social Construction of What?* Cambridge, MA: Harvard University Press.

Hale, Thomas, David Held, and Kevin Young. 2013. *Gridlock: Why Global Cooperation Is Failing When We Need It Most*. Cambridge: Polity Press.

Hall, Rodney Bruce, and Thomas J. Biersteker. 2002. *The Emergence of Private Authority in Global Governance*. Cambridge: Cambridge University Press.

Harman, Sophie, and David Williams, eds. 2013. *Governing the World? Cases in Global Governance*. London and New York: Routledge.

Helleiner, Eric. 2014. *The Status Quo Crisis: Global Financial Governance After the 2008 Meltdown*. Oxford: Oxford University Press.

Hofferberth, Matthias, and Christian Weber. 2015. "Lost in Translation: A Critique of Constructivist Norm Research." *Journal of International Relations and Development* 18 (1): 75–103.

Holstein, James, and Gale Miller. 1993. *Reconsidering Social Constructionism: Debates in Social Problems Theory*. Rutgers, NJ: Transaction Publishers.

Hopf, T., ed. 2002. *Social Construction of International Politics: Identities & Foreign Policies, Moscow, 1955 and 1999*. Ithaca, NY: Cornell University Press.

Hülsse, Rainer. 2007. "Creating Demand for Global Governance: The Making of a Global Money Laundering Problem." *Global Society* 21 (2): 155–178.

Kahler, Miles, and David A. Lake. 2003. *Governance in a Global Economy: Political Authority in Transition*. Princeton, NJ: Princeton University Press.

Kingdon, John W. 2010. *Agendas, Alternatives, and Public Policies*. London: Longman.

Krasner, Stephen D. 1982. "Structural Causes and Regime Consequences: Regimes as Intervening Variables." *International Organization* 36 (2): 185–205.

Latour, Bruno, and Steve Woolgar. 1979. *Laboratory Life: The Construction of Scientific Facts*. Princeton, NJ: Princeton University Press.

Lesage, Dries, Thijs Van de Graaf, and Kirsten Westphal. 2016. *Global Energy Governance in a Multipolar World*. London and New York: Routledge.

Levy, David L., and Peter John Newell. 2005. *The Business of Global Environmental Governance*. Cambridge, MA and London: MIT Press.

Love, Maryann Cusimano. 2010. *Beyond Sovereignty: Issues for a Global Agenda*. Boston, MA: Cengage Learning.

McCoy, Jennifer L., and Heather Heckel. 2001. "The Emergence of a Global Anti-corruption Norm." *International Politics* 38 (1): 65–90.

McGrew, Anthony, and David Held, eds. 2002. *Governing Globalization: Power, Authority and Global Governance*. Cambridge: Polity.

Meyer, John W., and Ronald L. Jepperson. 2000. "The 'Actors' of Modern Society: The Cultural Construction of Social Agency." *Sociological Theory* 18 (1): 100–120.

Mills, C. Wright. 1959. *The Sociological Imagination*. New York: Oxford University Press.

Mooney, Linda A., David Knox, and Caroline Schacht. 2011. *Understanding Social Problems*. Toronto: Nelson College Indigenous.

Najam, Adil. 2005. "Developing Countries and Global Environmental Governance: From Contestation to Participation to Engagement." *International Environmental Agreements: Politics, Law and Economics* 5 (3): 303–321.

Onuf, Nicholas G. 1989. *World of Our Making: Rules and Rule in Social Theory and International Relations*. Columbia: University of South Carolina Press.

Pierre, Jon. 2000. *Debating Governance: Authority, Steering, and Democracy*. Oxford: Oxford University Press.

Posner, Eric, and Jack L. Goldsmith. 2002. "Moral and Legal Rhetoric in International Relations: A Rational Choice Perspective." *Journal of Legal Studies* 31 (1): 115–139.

Ronit, Karsten, and Volker Schneider. 1999. "Global Governance Through Private Organizations." *Governance* 12 (3): 243–266.

Rosenau, James N. 1995. "Governance in the Twenty-First Century." *Global Governance* 1 (1): 13–43.

Rosenau, James N., and Hongying Wang. 2001. "Transparency International and Corruption as an Issue of Global Governance." *Global Governance* 7 (1): 25–49.

Ruggie, John Gerard. 1998. "What Makes the World Hang Together? Neo-Utilitarianism and the Social Constructivist Challenge." *International Organization* 52 (4): 855–885.

Scherer, Andreas Georg, Guido Palazzo, and Dorothée Baumann. 2006. "Global Rules and Private Actors: Toward a New Role of the Transnational Corporation in Global Governance." *Business Ethics Quarterly* 16 (4): 505–532.

Senturia, Joseph. 1931. "Corruption, Political." In *Encyclopedia of the Social Sciences*, Vol. 4, 448–452. New York: Macmillan.

Spector, Malcolm, and John Kitsuse. 1973. "Toward a Sociology of Social Problems." *Social Problems* 20: 407–419.

———. 1975. "Social Problems and Deviance: Some Parallels." *Social Problems*. 22: 584–594.

———. 2009. *Constructing Social Problems*. 4th ed. Rutgers, NJ: Transaction Publishers.

Underhill, Geoffrey R. D., and Xiaoke Zhang. 2008. "Setting the Rules: Private Power, Political Underpinnings, and Legitimacy in Global Monetary and Financial Governance." *International Affairs* 84 (3): 535–554.

Van de Graaf, Thijs, and Jeff Colgan. 2016. "Global Energy Governance: A Review and Research Agenda." *Palgrave Communications* 2. https://doi.org/10.1057/palcomms.2015.47.

Väyrynen, Raimo. 1999. *Globalization and Global Governance*. Lanham, MD: Rowman & Littlefield.

Weiss, Thomas G., and Rorden Wilkinson, eds. 2014. *International Organization and Global Governance*. London and New York: Routledge.

Wendt, Alexander. 1992. "Anarchy Is What States Make of It: The Social Construction of Power Politics." *International Organization* 46 (2): 391–425.

———. 1995. "Constructing International Politics." *International Security* 20 (1): 71–81.

Williams, Michael C. 2004. "Why Ideas Matter in International Relations: Hans Morgenthau, Classical Realism, and the Moral Construction of Power Politics." *International Organization* 58 (4): 633–665.

Woolgar, Steve, and Dorothy Pawluch. 1985. "Ontological Gerrymandering: The Anatomy of Social Problems Explanations." *Social Problems* 32 (3): 214–227.

Young, Oran R., ed. 1997. *Global Governance: Drawing Insights from the Environmental Experience*. Cambridge, MA and London: MIT Press.

CHAPTER 4

Building a New World: Global Claims in the 1970s

The chapter examines the first anti-corruption discussions at global venues and the first instances of global institutional legitimation. Since the 1970s, claims on corruption within international organizations developed in two major directions. The chapter argues that these clashing interpretations of the same condition can be called the Chilean and the American (US) legacies. The major difference between these two approaches was that the Chilean legacy developed at the UN and defined corruption as corporate influence on politics, while the American legacy developed predominantly at the OECD and defined corruption as bribery. The chapter examines the content of global claims at the OECD and the UN in the 1970s and argues that the successful campaign to establish corruption as a global governance problem in the 1990s can only be understood as the legacy of the 1970s. By showing that nation states were pioneers in the process of global social construction, the chapter lays the groundwork for the argument that state power is essential in the creation of global problems and that powerful states can be proactive participants in this process.

The search for the first occurrence of claims-making about corruption being a problem in need of globally organized corrective action shows that the initial legitimation of claims took place in the early to mid-1970s in the UN, the OECD, the World Bank, the IMF and the ICC, but also in the US Congress. It was revelations in the American press, starting with a publication by syndicated journalist, Jack Anderson, that

E. Katzarova, *The Social Construction of Global Corruption*,
Political Corruption and Governance,
https://doi.org/10.1007/978-3-319-98569-5_4

triggered talks at global venues of practices and social conditions that were characterized as 'corrupt.' On March 21, 1972, Anderson published an article in the *Washington Post* that documented the inappropriate involvement of the ITT in the political life of Chile. Based on leaked internal memos, the ITT Corporation had been allegedly trying to prevent Allende's election in 1970 due to fears that his policies would impact negatively ITT's investments in the country. In relation to the revelations, at the third UN Conference on Trade and Development (UNCTAD III) in April 1972, Allende defined the problem of corruption as a question about the role of business in politics and the rising influence of corporate power over the democratic process, referring to corporations' 'powerful corruptive influence on public institutions in rich and poor countries alike' (UNCTAD 1973, 353). These initial claims were ultimately not successful at framing a global corruption problem.

If we are to follow the successful claims, the first formalized appeal that there was a global problem with corruption went under the rubric of 'illicit' or 'corrupt' payments. These claims were made by the US delegations to the UN and the OECD in 1975. The United States submitted a proposal to the OECD for the inclusion of 'illicit payments' in the Guidelines for Multinational Enterprises (IME(75)18).[1] The formal claim was made on September 17, 1975, just before the opening of the regular session of the UN General Assembly in the third week of September where a similar claim was reiterated. In September 1975, informal talks including a number of Finance Ministers from developed nations were carried out by William Simon, US Secretary of the Treasury, in the IMF and the World Bank (US Senate 1975). As the fifth chapter will show, both the Chilean and the US claims were triggered by the ITT affair and the same putative condition–corporate involvement in political affairs. The United States carried out its own internal investigations on the ITT affair, which revealed hundreds of other cases of corporate malpractice, including cases of foreign bribery. The next chapter is dedicated to the US internal investigations and provides more information on the ITT affair and the putative condition that triggered global corruption claims.

[1] Due to the large amount of documents cited from the OECD Archives, in-text citations use the reference code, because this constitutes the most effective method to locate the documents in both the bibliography and the OECD Archives.

The Rising of the Global South

It is only after tracing back the unsuccessful claims of developing nations that the US initiative of 1975 can be seen as *reactive* to the developing nations' claims rather than proactive. The US argument that corruption should be understood predominantly as bribery was made in opposition to a more expansive definition promoted by a number of developing countries in the G77, especially Chile. Chilean President, Salvador Allende, promoted a version of corruption as corporate influence over politics. Unregulated global markets offered opportunities for corporations to influence politics in a way that was detrimental to the public interest. Allende called attention to 'the increasingly obvious conflict between the public interests of the wealthy nations (those which are of real benefit to their peoples) and the private interests of their great international corporations' (UNCTAD 1973, 353).

UNCTAD III has been characterized as a time of 'radicalization' of the Global South (Garavini 2013, 132). Developing nations became increasingly assertive in international affairs and demanded a substantial reform of the international economic system. Chile appeared at the forefront of this radicalization, and the Chilean demands in 1972 to examine the increasing influence of multinationals on politics could be understood within that context.[2] These claims historically led to the UN agenda to create a global framework for corporate conduct and the pursuit of the public interest.

As noted previously, the first UN talks on corruption occurred in relation to a series of corporate misconduct cases, of which the involvement of the ITT Corporation in the political life of Chile became the first and most prominent example (US Congress 1975). The Chilean claim that there was a fundamental clash between the globally unregulated pursuit of corporate profit and democracy emerged out of this context. This claim was first launched at the UNCTAD III (April 13–May 21, 1972), hosted by Chile in Santiago less than a month after Anderson's publications shook the world. Allende later reiterated his claims about the corrupting influence of multinationals during his speech at the UN General Assembly in December of the same year (Allende 1972). The basic argument of Allende's claim about the clash between multinationals and states could have been taken straight out of the highly acclaimed 1971

[2]While the term 'transnational' was preferred to 'multinational' corporations by the UN and the Global South in the 1970s, this book uses the terms interchangeably.

book by Harvard economist Raymond Vernon, 'Sovereignty at Bay.' The attempt to multilaterally regulate multinationals under the auspices of the UN became the chosen path of action for ameliorating potential clashes between multinationals and states.

The impact of Allende's claims occurred through a number of direct and indirect channels. Allende's framing of the ITT affair as a problem of corruptive influence of multinationals on politics and democracy resonated strongly with the UNCTAD III audience. In their highly detailed first-person account of the history of the UN CTC, Hamdani and Ruffing (2015) describe that, influenced by Allende's speech, the Under-Secretary-General for Economic and Social Affairs, Philippe de Seynes, who had already developed a strong interest in the role of multinationals in global affairs, included an appeal to create an international machinery to deal with multinationals in the World Economic Survey he presented to ECOSOC in July 1972. At the same time, Chilean Ambassador Santa Cruz presented a formal complaint about ITT's attempt to influence the political life of Chile to ECOSOC in Geneva. Based on the ITT incident, Santa Cruz submitted a draft resolution, which due to a good working relationship with US Ambassador Zagorin was amended and adopted on July 28, 1972 (Yoder 1993). It was this ECOSOC Resolution 1721 (LIII) that urged the Secretary-General to consult with governments on the creation of the UN Group of Eminent Persons, which recommended international regulation of multinationals in 1974. The UNCTC came to act as a Secretariat for the Commission on Transnational Corporations and the proposed Code of Conduct for governments and transnational corporations, but the binding code came to be vehemently opposed by the Global North and, in particular, the United States.

The first meeting of the Group of Eminent persons took place in September 1973 and coincided with Allende's overthrow. US disagreement with the work of the UN Group was evident from the start. Seven members submitted responses to the Report of the Panel of Eminent Persons. The two US representatives, Jacob Javits and Irwin Miller, as well as Swiss representative Hans Schaffner found a lot of faults with the Report, which they addressed thoroughly.[3] Javits claimed that ITT's involvement in Chile was an isolated case and should not become the basis of the entire endeavor. The American delegate also disagreed with the main premise that there is conflict of interest between the economic power of multinationals and the political power of governments, a

[3]While the other delegates submitted responses of half a page, the Swiss and US responses were of 21 and 35 pages, respectively.

position that was generally accepted by other representatives. Schaffner disagreed on another major point of accord: that developing countries should strengthen their bargaining position *vis a vis* corporations. The Chilean representative, Juan Somavia, to some extent agreed that the entire endeavor should not be based on the Chilean case but should address the general problem of: 'the role multinational corporations play in reacting to and shaping policies and events in home and host countries' (Report of the Group of Eminent Persons 1974, 146). Even after the events of September 1973, the Chilean delegate to the Group of Eminent Persons continued to voice the problem raised by Allende with undue corporate influence on politics in developed and developing countries.

Ironically, the Swiss Delegate became the source of much controversy in the UN regarding corporate influence. A Swiss NGO called 'The Bern Declaration' showed that based on minutes of secret meetings and correspondence, Schaffner was working on a mandate by six multinational corporations, including Nestle and Sandoz. Schaffner, who was a former President of Switzerland, was at the time working for the pharmaceutical company Sandoz. The document from 'The Bern Declaration' commented that: 'while officially classed as a government representative Schaffner was in effect representing the private interests of the six multinationals' (The Bern Declaration 1978, 1). The mandate he was given, according to the report, was to halt the Code of Conduct and employ other stalling techniques. If that failed, Schaffner was to steer negotiations toward an organization that is more favorable to multinationals. The case became highly controversial in Switzerland and the UN, especially because it was presented as an attempt to infiltrate the UN with corporate interests at a time when the UN was facilitating their international regulation.

The direct contribution of the Allende delegation to the UN effort came to an end with the establishment of the military dictatorship in Chile. The US involvement in the overthrow (and ultimate death) of Allende on September 11, 1973, and the establishment of the dictatorship of General Augusto Pinochet is touched upon in the next chapter in relation to US Congress debates on the topic, but it falls outside the scope of this study. Yet, the Pinochet regime as an answer to the economic independence of the *Via Chilena*—Allende's democratic, nonviolent road to socialism—cannot be seen as unrelated. Garavini (2013) finds that the 'deliberate symbolism' with which Pinochet moved his headquarters in the same building that Allende's Popular Unity government had built for the UNCTAD just the year before was meant to send a clear message to other Latin American countries (162). Pinochet's corporate-friendly military dictatorship lasted until 1990 and is considered to be one of the first examples of the neoliberal counterrevolution that was about to sweep the globe. The military junta undid swiftly Allende's reforms by returning nationalized corporate assets and providing compensation to US multinationals, including the ITT. Allende had nationalized the Chilean telephone company, which was operated by ITT, and subsequently refused to pay compensation to ITT in 1973 due to the company's attempt to block his election in 1970 (NYT Archives 1973).

As Qureshi (2009) notes, Nixon's nightmare was expropriation of corporate assets, not communist infiltration. It might be easy nowadays to dismiss the threat Allende posed for American leadership in the early 1970s, but that threat went beyond the symbolic gains and losses of Cold War calculations. Allende's nationalization of selected industries, pertaining to natural resources and public utilities could have set a dangerous precedent for Latin American and other developing countries to follow. As Dinges (2012) argued, all those who study the history of Latin America during this period need to appreciate the fact that 'radical social revolution was a real possibility for millions of people, colouring everyday life with hope or dread depending on the circumstances and political views of each individual' (41). Chile's experiment with democratic socialism could not have been as easily delegitimized as oppressive Soviet-style dictatorships.

The assertive new role that Chile tried to play in international affairs constituted the diplomatic counterpart to Allende's reforms at home. As Harmer (2011) notes, through the use of international organizations Allende 'sought to safeguard his own revolution by changing the world as opposed to sacrificing his cause' (262). Allende's appeals for the Global South to mobilize were well received by other developing countries and championed by his Ambassador to Geneva, Santa Cruz, who was also very active at the G77 (Yoder 1993). As Garavini (2013) points out, the Chilean Ambassador managed to secure Santiago as host for the UNCTAD III, which was central to Allende's international strategy. As noted previously, it was at the UNCTAD III that Allende talked for the first time about corporate abuse of power as corruption. During his meeting on December 4, 1972, with the Secretary-General of the UN, Kurt Waldheim, Allende raised the problem of multinational corporations as his top priority. The issue of regulating the operation of multinationals internationally was also in line with the economic theories of Argentinian economist Raul Prebisch, who was Secretary-General of UNCTAD until 1969. Allende also posed the question about what role was Prebisch about to serve at the UN after the end of his term. As is well known, the Prebisch-Singer hypothesis has served as one of the basic tenets of dependency theory, which was the dominating perspective on global economic relations in Latin America well into the 1970s. Margulis (2017) credits Prebisch for informing a lot of the thinking behind the New International Economic Order (NIEO) and the regulation of multinationals. Following the meeting, Waldheim invited Prebisch to consult the UN Panel of Eminent Persons on multinational corporations.

Prebisch had also contributed to providing developing countries with leverage in international negotiations through his work in UNCTAD. If UNCTAD and the G77 constituted attempts to 'unionize' the Third World (Garavini 2013, 30), the UNCTAD conference hosted by Chile in 1972 constituted a 'radicalization of the Third World' (132). Debates on anti-corruption within the UNCTAD, UNCTC and G77 do not have to be understood as counterproductive, but as an attempt by countries in the Global South to assert their political and economic independence, as well as promote their own theories of how the global economy works. In the early 1970s, the Global South demanded the re-organization of the global economic order and put forward their proposal about how was the increasing economic and political power of multinational corporations be curbed as part of a broadly construed anti-corruption agenda. For a brief time in the 1970s (1972–1981), such an agenda did not seem impossible due to the increased ability of developing nations to influence the global economy. The 1973 oil crisis testified to the newly found power of Organization of the Petroleum Exporting Countries (OPEC) members. While 1973 also saw the end of Allende's attempts to instigate change through international organizations, the Chilean legacy still had an impact on UN organizations, dominated by developing nations up until the early 1990s. Allende's initial framing of the ITT affair as corruptive influence of multinationals on politics and elections had a long-lasting impact on the UNCTC and debates on the regulation of multinationals and the US-sponsored issue of illicit/corrupt payments.

For developing nations, the US-sponsored issue of illicit/corrupt payments that is discussed in the following sections remained closely associated with the Code of Conduct on Transnational Corporations, as Resolution 3514 from 1975 also shows. The Resolution was drafted by a group of 27 developing nations and G77 members (among whom Argentina, Columbia, Pakistan, Somalia, Venezuela and Yemen). The UN Codes of Conduct can also be understood as part of the program for NIEO, launched with an initiative from the G77 in 1974 (Reynolds 1982; Fikentscher 1993). Hence, the US-sponsored issue of illicit payments became caught up in a far larger effort to renegotiate the terms and workings of the global economy. This does not entail, however, that the problem of corrupt payments was hijacked by other priorities—rather in the attempt to define the putative condition, different and controversial opinions appeared. The more limited understanding of corrupt payments as bribery was juxtaposed to a more complex definition that contained a broader variety of practices, which contributed to the transformation of corporations from economic into political actors.

The United States Claims Ownership of Global Corruption

Gusfield (1989) delineated problem ownership as having the authority to define a certain condition as a problem and formulating methods for its amelioration. Two essential aspects of owning social problems are responsibility and exclusion. Responsibility, in this case, does not mean accepting that the problem is one's fault, but that one has the responsibility and authority to define and ameliorate the socially harmful condition. Exclusion means that by successfully owning a social problem, the claimant excludes certain interpretations of what is wrong with a given social condition.

When the US government claimed in 1975 that there was a problem with illicit or corrupt practices, it stressed the global impact of a particular type of (what only later came to be called) corruption, that is, payments by corporations to public officials in foreign countries. The transnational character of this activity made it particularly susceptible to global consideration. While it was illegal for an American corporation to pay bribes within the United States, the corporation was not liable, in the United States, for payments made in foreign jurisdictions. Congressional hearings and investigations after the ITT affair and post-Watergate revealed that a significant number of US corporations have been involved in illicit payments to foreign governments. The Subcommittee on Multinational Corporations uncovered what seemed to be an illegitimate involvement of US corporations in the domestic affairs of a number of foreign countries. Separate hearings on 'The Activities of American Multinational Corporations Abroad' were held with ITT, Gulf Oil, Lockheed and other implicated companies that had also made questionable payments. Gulf Oil had made such payments in Korea; Exxon, Mobile Oil and Lockheed in Italy, the Netherlands and Japan (US House 1975). As Chapter 5 shows, such examples of corporate misconduct were largely discussed as an 'American' problem in the foreign press and this caused much frustration for US legislators, who very well knew that such questionable practices were shared by their competitors. The reason why corporate misconduct was perceived as an American problem was that at the time, according to Cohen and Baumeister (1977), approximately 90% of multinationals had headquarters in the United States and this is why the United States was 'viewed as having a heavy responsibility to control multinationals' global activities' (207).

In the wake of the post-Watergate investigations, the United States government found itself in a threefold legitimacy crisis.[4] First, the investigations deepened an already severe crisis of political legitimacy that the United States had to tackle domestically, and which involved the attempt to dissipate public mistrust toward government and big business. Second, there was the question of the legal legitimacy of American-based multinational corporations. The post-Watergate climate was one of the 'most high-profile periods for attacks on multinational corporations' and 'every Congressman and Senator wanted his or her own investigation committee' (Broehl 1996, 159). Internationally as well, the increasing economic power of the multinational corporation and its ability to evade the grip of national jurisdictions led to discussions about the legal status of these juridical entities—the UN and the OECD Codes of Conduct being two examples

[4]This threefold distinction between political, legal and economic aspects of legitimacy is based on Bakker. Bakker (2000) describes legitimacy in the classic definition of Lipset as 'the capacity of the system to engender and maintain the belief that the existing political institutions are the most appropriate ones for the society' (quoted in Bakker, 22). The three qualifications of legitimacy rather than comprising three different definitions stress three dimensions of the same concept. The central political concept can also be based on legality and adherence to the law as the most important basis for legitimacy and/or economic performance or at least an economic order that is considered just and adequate.

of such international debates. Third, there was an economic legitimacy crisis with developing countries, due to the unsatisfactory progress in growth rates and wealth distribution. A growing disappointment after over two decades of development policies that was quite concisely captured in an OECD report from 1972 as 'development weariness' (DD-300, 5). In addition to the geopolitical impact that this development fatigue could have had in the context of the Cold War, it was threatening the very basis of the relationship between Western investors and Third-World countries.

This domestic legitimacy crisis with foreign policy repercussions, which is given much more detailed attention in the next chapter, constituted the backdrop against which the US legislative and executive branches felt constrained to adopt a tough stance against cases of foreign bribery. The United States brought their own interpretation of global corruption in relation to the same string of corporate abuse scandals to the UN and the OECD in 1975 (IME(75)18). Within the particular climate of post-Watergate investigations and the congressional hearings on multinational corporations (1973–1976), corruption increasingly became the focus of public discontent (Broehl 1996). At the same time, a qualitative shift of meaning as to what constitutes corruption occurred in the United States with corrupt behavior increasingly being understood as *quid pro quo* (or bribery) (Teachout 2014). The understanding of corruption promoted by the United States was ultimately an argument that corruption should be addressed as a 'limited scope' and 'individual actor paradigm' offense (Puckett 2010, 815), and this US position was in direct opposition to the understanding of developing nations that corruption should be regulated at the systemic level.

As stated previously, if we are to follow the successful claims, the first formal US appeal went under the rubric of 'illicit' or 'corrupt' payments. The formal bid for global attention was allegedly made by Secretary of State Henry Kissinger on September 1, 1975, during the Seventh Special Session of the United Nations General Assembly (US Senate 1975). The speech 'Global Consensus and Economic Development,' delivered by D. Moynihan, in the absence of Kissinger, however, did not include any direct reference to the question of illicit/corrupt practices. Kissinger's speech contained rather a response to the 'radicalization' of developing nations evident in: 'their claim for a greater role, for more control over their economic destiny, and for a just share in global prosperity' (Kissinger 1975, 425). In the speech, Kissinger confirmed that the US government is ready to address the concerns of developing nations on the problem of corporations as political actors and that the time was ripe for global standards on corporate and government conduct to be articulated.

The specific claims on illicit/corrupt payments were made by the US delegations to the UN and the OECD in 1975. On September 17, 1975, the United States submitted a proposal to the OECD for the inclusion of 'illicit payments' in the Guidelines for Multinational Enterprises (IME(75)18). A similar proposal was reiterated at the opening of the regular session of the UN General Assembly in the third week of September. The same month, the William Simon, US Secretary of the Treasury, carried out informal talks with a number of Finance Ministers from the Global North in the IMF and the World Bank (US Senate 1975).

The US claims-making activities in the OECD were related to the ongoing negotiations of the Guidelines for Multinational Enterprises, which were successfully completed the following year. The US contribution was placed under the heading, 'Political Involvement.' The Draft Guidelines on Political Involvement of Multinational Enterprises recommended that companies and multinational enterprises evade interfering in the politics of a host country and eschew political contestation (IME(75)19, 4). The UN influence can be readily discerned in this formulation because the problem of corporate political influence remained the major issue. A UK proposal explicitly referred to political influence through monetary payments and recommended that multinational enterprises eschew rendering illegal payments to host governments, as well as political parties and governmental agencies (IME(75)16, 1). The US-modified position simply clarified that: 'Enterprises should neither make nor be solicited to make payments to government officials or (illicit) contributions to political parties and candidates' (IME(75)18, 1). 'Illicit payments' was a formulation reminiscent of the 'irregular payments' by American corporations investigated by SEC at the time, and it remained the dominant formulation of such practices at the OECD. At the UN, reference was made to both illicit and corrupt payments. Simultaneously to the proposal in the OECD, the United States made an official appeal to the UN during the 30th session of the UN General Assembly within the framework of the Commission on Transnational Corporations. In addition to the United States, two other countries submitted draft resolutions to the General Assembly concerning the treatment of international corrupt practices—the Libyan Arab Republic and Iran.

Even early on in the discussions, the work of the OECD Committee on International Investment and Multinational Enterprises (CIME) was explicitly connected to the UN Commission on Transnational Corporations. The OECD Committee discussed an exchange of views with the UN Commission on a permanent basis, but was met with opposition by some delegates, who while principally agreeing to the collaboration stressed that: '…a clear distinction should be made between exchanges of views and attempts to coordinate views' (IME/M(75)2, 8). As the document explains, the debates at ECOSOC and other UN bodies, which concentrate on the formulation of a Code of Conduct, would differ from the same discussions at the OECD because developing nations had specific concerns on multinational companies that were not shared by OECD member states (IME/M(75)2, 8). As we will see shortly, the attempt to keep the two processes separate failed and the development of a legally binding OECD Convention on illicit practices was made conditional on the developments at the UN Commission on the same subject. The connection to the UN talks in itself was problematic, because of the highly contested nature of discussions on corporate conduct at ECOSOC and other UN forums.

Talks at the UN After 1975

At the UN, the US claims on illicit/corrupt payments were incorporated in discussions about the repercussions of the activities of transnational corporations within the framework of the UN Commission on Transnational Corporations, which held its first session on March 17–28, 1975. Three countries submitted draft resolutions concerning the treatment of international corrupt practices to the General Assembly—the United States, Iran and the Libyan Arab Republic. The United States proposal did not differ substantially from that of pre-revolution Iran, except for the emphasis on the role of governments from the developed world in occurrences of corruption. The Iranian proposal:

> called upon Governments to take all necessary measures to prevent corruptive practices; called upon home countries to adopt strict measures against acts of bribery committed by their nationals or corporations abroad; asked the Secretary-General to prepare a study of ways and means to prevent corruptive practices, including the adoption of a code of conduct; asked

> that the Commission on Transnational Corporations include the issue in its programme of work; and called upon relevant governmental and non-governmental organizations to assist in the formulation and implementation of anti-corruptive measures against transnational and other corporations. (487)

The Libyan version of a draft resolution made use of a more forceful language, providing for tougher measures and requesting that states: 'refrain from employing transnational corporations as an instrument for intervening in the internal affairs of host countries for political purposes' (Chapter XIII: UN Yearbook 1975, 487). With this addition, the Libyan claim raised the highly controversial question of government-sponsored illicit payments to foreign governments done through front corporations. While the final version of the UN Resolution is fully available, the draft versions are presented in a summarized version in 'Chapter XIII. Questions Concerning Transnational Corporations' from the UN 1975 Yearbook, with the positions of the three countries which submitted draft resolutions to the 30th Session of the General Assembly presented verbatim. The Libyan version of the draft resolution was withdrawn as the other two, but it most directly addressed the problem of corruption as political influence and the entanglement of interests of foreign public and private actors. These controversial claims, despite not being directly adopted in the position of the G77, presented an extreme case of the position of the developing countries on the question of corrupt practices:

> By the Libyan proposal, the Assembly would have, inter alia: condemned illegal and immoral acts practised by transnational corporations against the safety and security of peoples and States; condemned States which supported, collaborated with or covered up such acts; recognized the right of States to nullify contracts entered into as a result of illegal or immoral practices, and to take action they deemed appropriate in accordance with national laws; called upon all Member States to investigate the illegal and immoral acts of transnational corporations, to exchange information regarding them, and to impose strong sanctions, including boycotts, against the corporations involved. (487)

'Illegal and immoral acts,' the exact content and form of which were to be studied in an ad hoc group, constituted an expansive definition of what was problematic with the interaction of foreign private and domestic public actors. It also revealed a deep-seated distrust in the objectives of foreign investment and skepticism about the status of corporations as independent economic actors, pursuing purely economic i nterests, without being influenced by the country of origin. The most notable twist in the problem's definition is the claim that bribery and other illicit practices and forms of influence are state sponsored and foreign states are part of the corrupt equation. The US proposal also included a reference to state-sponsored corporate bribery by referring to possible 'encouragement' by governments for corrupt practices committed by private agents. The US proposal: 'condemned the offering or solicitation of bribes and other corrupt practices by enterprises, or their encouragement by government officials or individuals' (487).

The US attempt to claim ownership of the problem at the UN was to a large extent unsuccessful because all three draft resolutions were withdrawn in favor of a G77 sponsored Resolution, which included the Libyan Arab Republic, Iran and seven OPEC members.[5] Resolution 3514 (XXX) was adopted on December 15, 1975, with the title, 'Measures against Corrupt Practices of Transnational and Other Corporations, their Intermediaries and others Involved.' The Resolution, which was drafted by a group of 27 developing nations, although devoid of the forceful language of the Libyan draft resolution, left the question open as to the involvement of foreign governments in corporate illicit payments and other illicit practices. The question of (Western) government influence through the employment of private corporate actors as instruments of foreign policy was claimed as relevant to the problem of corruption, as developing nations understood it. Furthermore, Resolution 3514 reinforced the connection between corrupt practices of transnational corporations and the discussions about the Code of Conduct, which aimed at regulating the activities of transnational corporations globally. Resolution 3514 recalled the Declaration NIEO and the Action Plan that provided for the discussion of the Code of Conduct. As noted previously, the NIEO was an initiative of developing nations, who sought to establish what they understood to be more equitable conditions for development, but in doing so were jeopardizing the interests

[5] The draft resolution was forwarded by Algeria, Argentina, Benin, Bolivia, Colombia, Costa Rica, Cuba, Democratic Yemen, Ecuador, Egypt, Gabon, Guyana, Iran, Iraq, the Libyan Arab Republic, Madagascar, Nigeria, Pakistan, Peru, Romania, Somalia, the Syrian Arab Republic, Togo, the United Republic of Tanzania, the Upper Volta, Venezuela and Yugoslavia.

of Western investors with demands for stronger control over foreign investment and the reaffirmation of national sovereignty through more effective control over natural resources and demands for more equitable prices for raw materials (Resolution 3201 S-VI).

The Ad Hoc Intergovernmental Working Group on Corrupt Practices, established on August 5, 1976, by ECOSOC, was also dominated by developing nations. Members included Algeria, Colombia, Iran, Mexico, Nigeria, Pakistan, Sierra Leone, Uganda, the United States, Venezuela and Zaire. The chairman of the group, Rafael Rivas, was from Colombia. The group was meant to 'conduct an examination of the problem of corrupt practices in international commercial transactions by transnational and other corporations, their intermediaries and other parties involved' (Appendix III: UN Yearbook 1976, 1084). This broader mandate did not identify corrupt practices as a payment and allowed for the consideration of other parties, such as foreign governments, as part of the illicit interaction.

Some of the developed countries were opposed to the UN Code of Conduct because they saw it as an offspring of NIEO and because the Code was attempting to regulate Western-based multinationals. Despite their similar mandate, the draft Codes of Conduct at the OECD and the UN were in competition, if not in conflict, with each other, because the former was representing the approach of the industrialized nations of the North, while the latter was to a large extent dominated by the Global South (Sagafi-nejad and Dunning 2008). The US-sponsored problem of corrupt practices in the UN was intertwined with discussions about the influence of Western governments and multinational corporations over the social and economic progress of developing nations. The ultimate paralysis of the negotiations came in 1980, when the G77 finalized its decision that the progress of the drafted International Agreement on Illicit Payments (IAIP) was conditional on the adoption of the Code of Conduct on Transnational Corporations. Although this constituted a decisive blow to the negotiation process, the talks had already stalled in 1976 with the G77 insistence that corporations should terminate their support—legal or illegal—of the apartheid regime in South Africa by stopping illicit payments toward the regime (IME/M(77)1). Although the decision of the G77 looks like a strategic move to hamper the agreement on illicit payments, work on the Code of Conduct started in relation to Chile bringing the case of the ITT Corporation to ECOSOC in 1972 (Horn 1980).

Therefore, making progress on illicit payments conditional on the Code was symptomatic of a different interpretation of what is wrong with the same putative condition; the G77 claimed it was corporate conduct and demanded more restrictions on multinational corporations, while the United States interpreted bribery as the culprit.

The claims made by developing nations included the political impact of FDI, with payments made to the apartheid regime in South Africa as the most controversial example, which ultimately led to the stagnation of the pre-negotiation talks. Developing nations claimed that foreign private enterprises tried to influence the political processes of newly sovereign nations for the benefit of their home governments or for their own purposes. In the case of South Africa, although new FDI flows stagnated in the 1970s due to public pressure against apartheid, it was only in the mid-1980s that foreign corporations started exiting the South African market en masse (Gelb and Black 2004).[6] The involvement of transnational corporations in South Africa was claimed to support the apartheid regime. By pursuing investment interests, in particular in military, police and security affairs, foreign corporations were directly solidifying the regime and were detrimental to international efforts to terminate apartheid. The operations of transnational corporations were also supporting the regime indirectly by confirming to the rules of apartheid, because 80% of the South African workforce was black (Sagafi-nejad and Dunning 2008). The case of the apartheid regime pertained to political corporate power—the power of foreign economic actors to influence even indirectly the political processes of a country in a way that is detrimental to the public interest. This interpretation of what constitutes a corrupt practice was in line with the initial Allende claims of undue corporate influence on foreign political processes.

The claims of the developing nations could not be understood only as a bargaining strategy in which unrelated issues are made conditional on one another. The diverging positions of the developed and developing countries can be more fully understood as ontological claims and counterclaims about the construction of a global problem and as a struggle of definitions over putative conditions and their causal relation to other

[6] Further work at the UNCTC contributed to the withdrawal of transnational corporations from South Africa in the 1980s (Sagafi-nejad and Dunning 2008).

agenda items. Whether it is the support for apartheid, the inability of yet unstable institutional systems to exert effective control over the dealings of transnational corporations on their territory or the use of bribery to secure military contracts, one of the major claims of the developing nations was about corporate influence on politics bought legally or illegally through monetary and non-monetary means.

As Pieth (2007) observed, because of the corporate misconduct revelations in the 1970s, the very legitimacy of the free market system appeared to be under threat. For the developed nations, the operation of the free market, unencumbered by global regulation, as well as the free access of corporations to foreign markets, could have been just and desirable (take away the occurrences of illicit payments). For developing nations, however, the primary source of concern seemed to be the question as to what kind of impact the powerful governmental and corporate moneyed interests had over their, yet inadequate, national political systems.

Talks at the OECD After 1975

Parallel to discussions at the UN, some OECD member states also raised concerns about the increasing flow of FDI from non-OECD members, and in particular, oil-producing countries. The flux of capital from these countries was bound to 'add new aspects to foreign control in key industries' (IME(75)2, 3). This 'reversal' of foreign investment from its usual route from developed to developing countries became a matter of controversy:

> The word "investment" in this particular context could not be interpreted in the sense in which it had normally been interpreted in the past. Normal investments by foreign countries were usually welcome because they permitted the creation of new production capacities and access to foreign technology and mahagerial [sic] skills. But the investments now under discussion were of a different nature, and involved the purchase of the assets of a firm, not for economic reasons but for political reasons, in order to control it and its management. Because of his country's shortage of skilled labour, the Federal Government had always encouraged German businessmen to go abroad and to take with them their knowledge and skills and money. But the motives of the oil-producing countries were not the same, their object was to gain influence on the production structures of other countries. (IME(75)4, 55)

Even though the problem of political influence in a foreign country through FDI reflected the claims of the G77 at the UN, in the OECD the issue, under the general rubric of political influence, was not connected explicitly to illicit payments. The exertion of influence by oil-producing countries in OECD member states was juxtaposed to the benefit of managing current account surpluses globally. Yet, concerns over the political influence of oil-producing nations came center stage and were revealing of a rather uncharted territory in the global economy—the inflow of investment from developing to developed nations. In the 1970s, outward FDI from developing nations was the exception rather than the rule, starting from 1% of total global investment in the 1970s and reaching 6% in the 1990s (Velde and Nair 2006). The unprecedented investment flows from oil producers in the mid-1970s anticipated later debates about sovereign wealth funds and raised concerns in the OECD. As noted previously, this concern mirrored the claims of some G77 members about the influence of foreign investment over the political processes of developing countries, but was not explicitly connected to corruption as it was in the UN. The problem of 'illicit payments' in the OECD remained of a more limited scope, although still under the rubric of political influence.

The question of political influence of multinational enterprises was introduced by the UK delegation to the Drafting Group on September 12, 1975, and aimed to set basic guidelines for private enterprises' political non-involvement in the countries where international investment is carried, 'save to the extent necessary' (IME(75)2, 1). The draft aimed as much to establish standards of political non-involvement, as to safeguard some involvement of multinational enterprises as legitimate. The necessity to stay clear of political controversy is also pointed in the UK Draft, but most importantly the avoidance of 'any payments (other than for manifest public purposes) to a host government, or to its agencies, or to political parties.' The distinct feature of such payments is based on the criterion of lawfulness or legality, as well as on a requirement for full disclosure: 'unless such payments are lawful and deteils [sic] of the amounts and the beneficiaries are published in accordance with a general requirement of the host government' (IME(75)16, 1). The note on the Draft Guideline on Political Involvement, submitted by the United States on September 17, 1975, expanded the criterion of legality by defining the contributions or payments as 'illicit' rather than unlawful or illegal. This shift of definition allowed for arguments that make the issue of political involvement of multinational enterprises and illicit payments, in particular, the prerogative of the 'home government' and therefore promoted a different set of solutions that would be in accordance with the solutions discussed in the US Congress in relation to corrupt payments performed by American corporations. The discussions during the Fourth Meeting of the CIME dismantled such claims as the majority of delegates agreed that while referencing the question of political involvement in the Guidelines might be of some use, the recommendation for behavior could not go beyond 'recommending multinational enterprises to act in conformity with the legislation and practice of the host country' (IME/M(75)4, 3).

The responsibility of the multinational enterprises to act in accordance with the host country's established practices was further strengthened through the revisions of the Draft Guidelines. Multinational corporations were urged to operate:

> within the framework of the laws and regulations of the host country, observe the best standards set by relevant local customs and practices with regard to:
>
> (i) rendering gifts or other benefits to public servants;
> (ii) contributions to political parties and other political organisations;
> (iii) involvement in local political activities. (IME(75)19 (1st Revision) Annex I, 5)

After US insistence, the reference to 'gifts' was changed for 'bribes' and a much stronger overall formulation of the recommendation was achieved. Enterprises were urged to:

> (6) not render – and they should not be solicited or expected to render – any bribe or other improper benefit, direct or indirect, to any public servant or holder of public office; (7) not make contributions to candidates for public office or to political parties or other political organisations except as permitted by law; (8) abstain from any improper involvement in local political activities. (IME(75)2 Annex I, 2)

The shift from 'gift' to 'bribe' is, of course, significant. While 'gifts' rendered in the cultural context of another country, according to the best practices of the host society, seem rather inauspicious as a problem, the rendering of direct or indirect benefits and 'bribes' demands more attention. The former claim provides a supposed excuse for such practices within the sociocultural context of the country in which investment is carried out, while the latter condones such practices as universally unacceptable. Ultimately, the first claim negates that there is a problem with such practices while the second promotes the need to counteract them. While the former claim does not provide a basis for the 'globality' of the problem, because it makes the course of action conditional on the customs and practices of a territorially bound state, the latter universalizes the illegitimate nature of monetary payments or indirect types of influence, independently of the national socio-historical context. The latter text prevailed during the next meeting of CIME on December 18, 1975 (IME/M(76)1), and was included in the final text of the adopted Guidelines.

The controversy of defining the putative condition as 'gift' or 'bribe' between OECD member states was overshadowed by the far bigger controversy about corrupt practices and political influence at the UN. Thus, despite the inclusion of the recommendation in the Guidelines for Multinational Enterprises adopted on June 21, 1976, further work on illicit payments was hampered. The successful adoption of the Guidelines on multinational corporations, and the references to transnational bribery that it made, was of limited success since the code was voluntary. The US goal was to further develop the work on illicit payments in the direction of a treaty. By the end of 1976, such talks were already underway, and the United States argued that certain issues referenced in the code were in need of further work, such as the 'proposed convention to deal with the problem of illicit payments' (IME(76)26/01, 2). For lack of a dedicated ad hoc committee to deal with the subject of illicit payments, CIME was entrusted with the task, but its work became entangled with the negotiations of a binding legal instrument in the Ad Hoc Intergovernmental Working Group on Corrupt Practices at the UN. Despite the initial determination to keep the work of the OECD and the UN separate, because of the differing interests of the developing and the developed nations on the subject of transnational corporations, such separation became unfeasible during the pre-negotiation talks (IME/M(75)2).

Claims and Counterclaims and the Redefinition of Scope

Voluminous exchanges of documentation between the two organizations occurred during 1976 and the discussion of bribery and political involvement at the OECD stagnated in 1977 because of the discussions at the UN (IME/M(77)1). The pre-negotiation talks at the UN were qualified by Jack Blum, a US attorney, who endeavored to draft the anti-corruption Convention at the time, as the 'disaster of 1976.' The reason, according to Blum, was that: 'Ideological differences, commercial rivalries, and national interests overrode what little momentum the anti-corruption initiative had' (Blum 2009, 2). Mark Pieth, a Swiss Professor of Criminal Law, who was Chairman of the OECD Working Group on Bribery in International Business Transactions from 1990 to 2013, had a different insight into the debacle of the 1970s:

> The drafts modeled after the FCPA were, however, caught in the cross-fire between North and South, with developing countries maintaining that the concept of "illicit payments" should be understood in a broad sense, including payments also made to the Apartheid regime in South Africa. (Pieth 1997, 122)

Claims-making about the redefinition of the scope of the problem was at the center of the heated debates, as discussed previously. The position of the developing nations was that the problem of corrupt payments was broader than the limited understanding of bribery, promoted in accordance with the FCPA drafts that were simultaneously being discussed at the US Congress. This redefinition of scope incorporated instances of political influence through means other than commercial bribery and referred to illicit interactions between private and public actors, but also to political influence through FDI. This redefinition of the scope of the problem included, but was not limited to bribery:

> With decolonization, former colonial states, but also newcomers amongst exporting nations, tried to maintain or establish their power-basis with the emerging elites in the southern hemisphere by buying allegiances. Whereas the motivation to bribe will have been primary economic, to a large extent corruption was also used as a political means in the struggle of the Cold War to secure influence across the world. (Pieth 2007, 5)

This shadow of influence has to be understood in the context of suspicion toward multinational enterprises and their likelihood to 'abuse (of) concentrations of economic power and to conflict with national policy objectives' (IME(76)1 Annex, 5). The socioeconomic context of the 1970s is relevant here, not only because of the Cold War, but also because consensus had not yet been reached about the universal desirability of FDI. In light of their colonial heritage, G77 members were apprehensive of the dealings of foreign corporations on their territory. Furthermore, during the Cold War, the G77 had more leverage to claim a different global economic order, a request that was present in the Declaration NIEO. The OECD Guidelines were seen to represent a 'western approach' and at least to some extent to 'render irrelevant' the UN approach (Sagafi-nejad and Dunning 2008, 111). The South–North controversy during the pre-negotiation talks was, however, also a clash of definitions and a clash of different perspectives on the same putative condition and, therefore, on what constitutes the global problem of corrupt practices.

During the 1970s, a redefinition of scope was the primary issue at stake at the OECD and the UN, with *corporate political influence* and *bribes* reflecting different degrees of expansion of the definition. Understanding corrupt practices as payments or as influence entails different approaches for addressing the putative condition that led to the claims in the first place. As noted previously, the empirical condition, which led to both the expansive and the limited scope claims, was a series of corporate misconduct scandals, which started with the involvement of the ITT Corporation in Chile. If the putative condition is broadly and neutrally presented, as the interaction of foreign private (corporate) and domestic public (government) actors, then what is problematic about this interaction is a matter of competing definitions. In addition, while the developing nations questioned to some extent the legitimacy of Western investment, as well as the payment of illicit contributions, the developed nations were interested in establishing the legitimate nature of one form of transaction (investment) and the exclusion of the other (bribery). International corruption, understood either as corporate political influence or as an illicit payment (bribery), demands two different approaches for addressing the issue. While both claims are legitimate definitions of the same putative condition, it is noteworthy that the narrower definition of the problematic situation could be much easier to handle through an internationally negotiated machinery that would tackle the problem of corrupt payments understood as bribery. As noted previously, Spector and Kitsuse (2009) point out that successful claims may limit the scope of problems and make them more manageable. While to address the problem of corporate influence on politics would have been more difficult, it would not have been impossible, and the attempt of the UNCTC and the eponymous commission to create a binding code of corporate conduct can be seen as a step in that direction.

From the vantage point of developing countries in the 1970s, there was a conflict between the pursuit of corporate profit and the pursuit of the public interest. That conflict was not insurmountable, however, and could be addressed if governments regulate corporate conduct in the public interest. When corporations exert disproportionate influence on the direction of politics and public policy, this could hurt the public interest and have a detrimental effect on democracy. This rather simple insight might still be relevant today Especially, in a time of increasing public–private partnerships, the question of what kind of influence is legitimate, and what kind is problematic, becomes difficult to discern. The Lockheed Corporation bribery scandal, which surfaced as a consequence of the Church investigations, provides a relevant example. While Lockheed Martin reformed to tackle the question of bribery, the company's interaction with the Pentagon is still under scrutiny. The last known case of bribery was discovered in 1994 in relation to a 1989 sale of C-130 Hercules transport planes to Egypt, but the influence Lockheed exerts abroad and on American policy-making is still a source for concern. The Lockheed Corporation has remained tightly involved not only in the technological, but also in the policy aspects of national security. As Danielle Brian from the nonprofit Washington-based 'Project on Government Oversight' points out in the New York Times article 'Lockheed and the future of warfare': 'It is impossible to tell where the government ends and Lockheed begins.' Corporate bribery is perhaps superfluous in a world in which big business and government are so comfortably entangled together. As the article argues, Lockheed profits are fueled with government subsidies and revolving door politics ensure a constant flow of officials between the corporation and government agencies. A world, in which 'Lockheed's influence runs so deep,' does not need bribery (Weiner 2004, 1)

An understanding of corruption as corporate political influence, rather than as bribery, would have put under scrutiny the current interaction between Lockheed and the US government. Whether at the UN or at the OECD, the issue of illicit/corrupt payments was always understood within the framework of illicit involvement of corporations in political affairs. The problem of global corruption in the 1970s can therefore be seen to touch on a fundamental topic in the study of international political economy, such as state–business relations in the context of globalization. More specifically, corruption appeared to be intrinsically connected to the question of multinational corporations as political actors. This major element of the debate in the 1970s was completely reversed by the 1990s through the prism of neoliberalism. It was not the corruptive influence of corporations on politics that was the problem; it was the state itself that was the problem and the state as an economic actor. As it will be shown in the following chapters, the idea of the venality and inefficiency of government was intrinsically connected to this argument and to the natural extension of this argument that outsourcing and privatizing more of the former prerogatives of government will lead to less corruption.

This chapter examined the pre-negotiation talks of the 1970s in a number of international forums that formed the backdrop against which the re-launch of global claims was made in 1989. The redefinition of the problem's scope was the primary hindrance at reaching consensus during discussions at the OECD and the UN in the mid- to late 1970s. Claims and counterclaims between developing and developed nations (primarily the United States) made the definition of corruption waver between political influence and bribery. Delegations to the UN from the Global South saw the interaction between public and private actors not only as the influence of foreign business interests over the public interest of their country, but also as the exertion of political influence of foreign countries through business relations. This expansion of the understanding of what was the putative condition implicitly endangered the legitimacy of FDI in former colonial nations and became largely controversial. With talks at the OECD dependent on progress in the UN, both pre-negotiation talks stalled. Faced with the uncertainty of the adoption of a global treaty, the United States enacted the FCPA unilaterally and this decision shaped the content of the talks after the re-launch of global claims in 1989.

In the particular climate of 'post-Watergate morality,' the foreign/illicit payments problem became a serious predicament for the United States.

The approach adopted by the US Congress was criminalization, which entailed a limited scope, individual actor offense. While the global publicity of the revealed corrupt payments compromised trust in American companies and the legitimacy of the global free market system, the FCPA was to a large extent adopted as a domestic anti-corruption measure, as the next chapter will show. The subsequent internationalization of the FCPA can be seen as the global equivalent of turning private (national) troubles into public (global) problems. The problem was 'American,' not because only American corporations were carrying out such questionable payments domestically and abroad, but because due to a constellation of circumstances the United States was the most interested actor in launching a global claims-making campaign on transnational corrupt payments. Other countries involved in the disclosure measures, despite the unfavorable national publicity, did not pursue the issue of corporate payments further, and when they did, it was treated as an essentially domestic (or national) problem. The disclosure of corrupt payments had repercussions in Japan, the Netherlands and a number of countries in the Middle East, but no country investigated the alleged illicit payments by their own corporations or at least did not make the investigations public (Church 1975). The internationalization of the FCPA came forth as an American priority in 1988 with the decision to press the issue at the OECD. The FCPA, therefore, conditioned the second re-launch of global claims in the late 1980s and early 1990s, but it also gave a powerful ally to the US government–American-based multinational companies, who became champions of global anti-corruption efforts.

References

Allende, Salvador. 1972. "Speech Delivered by Dr. Salvador Allende, President of the Republic of Chile, Before the General Assembly of the United Nations." December 4. Washington, DC: Embassy of Chile.

Anderson, Jack. 1972. "Memos Bare ITT Try for Chile Coup." *The Washington Post*, March 21.

Bakker, Heleen, ed. 2000. *Corruption & Legitimacy*. Amsterdam: Siswo Publication.

Blum, Jack. 2009. "Testimony on the Problem of Curbing Grand Scale Global Corruption Before the Committee on Financial Services, U.S. House of Representatives." 111th Cong., 1st sess., May 19.

Broehl, W. G. 1996. "The Persisting Case Against the Multinational Corporation." *Business and Economic History* 25: 159–165.
Church, Frank (Senator from the State of Idaho). 1975. "Testimony on S. Res. 265., A Resolution to Protect the Ability of the United States to Trade Abroad before the Senate Finance Committee, Subcommittee on International Trade." 94th Cong., 1st sess., October 6.
Cohen, Sander, and Richard Baumeister. 1977. "Foreign Bribery by American Multinational Corporations: A Status Report." *Delaware Journal of Corporate Law* 2 (2): 207–232.
DD-300. *The Crisis in Development Strategies.* Development Assistance Directorate (September 13, 1972). OECD Archives, Paris Headquarters.
Dinges, John. 2012. *The Condor Years: How Pinochet and His Allies Brought Terrorism to Three Continents.* New York and London: The New Press.
Fikentscher, Wolfgang. 1993. *Recht und wirtschaftliche Freiheit: Bd. Transnationales Marktrecht.* Tuebingen: Mohr Siebeck.
Garavini, G. 2013. *After Empires. European Integration, Decolonisation and the Challenge from the Global South 1957–1986.* Oxford: Oxford University Press.
Gelb, Stephen, and Anthony Black. 2004. "Foreign Direct Investment in South Africa." In *Investment Strategies in Emerging Markets*, edited by Saul Estrin and Klaus Meyer, 174–208. Northampton, MA: Edward Elgar.
Gusfield, Joseph R. 1989. "Constructing the Ownership of Social Problems: Fun and Profit in the Welfare State." *Social Problems* 36 (5): 431–441.
Hamdani, K., and L. Ruffing. 2015. *United Nations Centre on Transnational Corporations: Corporate Conduct and the Public Interest.* London and New York: Routledge.
Harmer, Tanya. 2011. *Allende's Chile and the Inter-American Cold War.* Chapel Hill: University of North Carolina Press.
Horn, Norbert. 1980. "International Rules for Multinational Enterprises: The ICC, OECD, and the ILO Initiatives." *American University Law Review* 30: 936–939.
IME(75)2. *Attitudes of the Governments of OECD Member Countries Towards Increased Investment by Non-residents.* Note by the Secretariat (February 25, 1975). OECD Archives, Paris Headquarters.
IME(75)4. *Multinational Enterprises—Uniform Standards of Behaviour.* Note by the Secretariat (April 15, 1975). OECD Archives, Paris Headquarters.
IME(75)16. *Draft Guidelines on Political Involvement of Multinational Enterprises.* Note by the United Kingdom Representative to the Drafting Group (September 12, 1975). OECD Archives, Paris Headquarters.
IME(75)18. *Draft Guidelines on Political Involvement of Multinational Enterprises.* Note by the United States Delegation (September 17, 1975). OECD Archives, Paris Headquarters.

IME(75)19. *Guidelines for Multinational Enterprises and Intergovernmental Consultation Procedures on Issues and Policies Pertaining to the Activities of Multinational Enterprises.* Note by the Secretariat (October 9, 1975). OECD Archives, Paris Headquarters.

IME/M(75)2. *Summary Record of the Second Meeting, Held on 28–29 April, 1975* (May 27, 1975). OECD Archives, Paris Headquarters.

IME/M(76)1. *Guidelines for Multinational Enterprises and Intergovernmental Consultation Procedures on the Implementation of the Guidelines* (December 18, 1975). OECD Archives, Paris Headquarters.

IME(76)1 Annex. *Guidelines for Multinational Enterprises and Intergovernmental Consultation Procedures on Issues and Policies Pertaining to the Activities of Multinational Enterprises.* Note by the Secretariat (January 14, 1976). OECD Archives, Paris Headquarters.

IME(76)26/01. *Comments Relating to the Formulation of a United Nations Code of Conduct for Transnational Corporations* (December 30, 1976). OECD Archives, Paris Headquarters.

IME/M(77)1. *Summary Record of the Twelfth Meeting Held on 14–15 February, 1977* (March 9, 1977). OECD Archives, Paris Headquarters.

Kissinger, Henry. 1975. "Global Consensus and Economic Development." Address by Secretary Kissinger Prepared for Delivery at the Seventh Special Session of the UN General Assembly 425. September 22.

Margulis, Matias. 2017. *The Global Political Economy of Raúl Prebisch.* London and New York: Taylor & Francis.

Meeting of the Secretary-General with President Allende of Chile. December 4, 1972. Series 292, Box 18, File 13, UN Archives, New York Headquarters.

NYT Archives. 1973. Allende Scoffs at Funds for I.T.T. Special to the *New York Times*, April 11.

Pieth, Mark. 1997. "International Cooperation to Combat Corruption." In *Corruption and the Global Economy*, edited by Kimberly Ann Elliott, 119–133. Washington, DC: Peterson Institute.

———. 2007. "Introduction." In The OECD Convention on Bribery: A Commentary, edited by Mark Pieth, Lucinda A. Low, and Peter J. Cullen, 3–42. Cambridge: Cambridge University Press.

Puckett, Blake. 2010. "Clans and the Foreign Corrupt Practices Act: Individualized Corruption Prosecution in Situations of Systemic Corruption." *Georgetown Journal of International Law* 41 (4): 815.

Qureshi, Lubna Z. 2009. *Nixon, Kissinger, and Allende: U.S. Involvement in the 1973 Coup in Chile.* Lanham and Plymouth: Lexington Books.

Report of the Group of Eminent Persons to Study the Role of Multinational Corporations on Development and International Relations. June 12, 1974. E/5500/Add1, Series 1003, Box 6, File 22, UN Archives, New York Headquarters.

Reynolds, T. H. 1982. "Clouds of Codes: The New International Economic Order Through Codes of Conduct: A Survey." *Law Library Journal* 75: 315–354.

Sagafi-nejad, Tagi, and John H. Dunning. 2008. *The UN and Transnational Corporations: From Code of Conduct to Global Compact.* Bloomington: Indiana University Press.

Spector, Malcolm, and John Kitsuse. 2009. *Constructing Social Problems.* 4th ed. Rutgers, NJ: Transaction Publishers.

Teachout, Z. 2014. *Corruption in America: from Benjamin Franklin's Snuff Box to Citizens United.* Cambridge and London: Harvard University Press.

The Bern Declaration. "The Infiltration of the UN System by Multinational Corporations." Excerpts of Internal Files. June 6, 1978. Series 0897, Box 7, File 7, UN Archives, New York Headquarters.

UN 1975. "Chapter XIII: Questions Concerning Transnational Corporations." In *Yearbook of the United Nations*, 484–490. Vol. 29. New York: UN.

———. 1976. "Appendix III: Ad Hoc Bodies." In *Yearbook of the United Nations*, 1058–1153. Vol. 30. New York: UN.

UNCTAD. 1973. "Address Delivered by Mr. Salvador Allende Gossens, President of Chile at the Inaugural Ceremony on April 13, 1972." Proceedings of UNCTAD Third Session. Vol. 1 Annex VIII.

UN General Assembly. 2229th Plenary Meeting. "Resolution 3201 (S-VI) [Declaration on the Establishment of a New International Economic Order]" May 1, 1974 (A/RES/S-6/3201). New York: UN.

———. 30th Session. "Resolution 3514: [Measures Against Corrupt Practices of Transnational and Other Corporations, Their Intermediaries and Others Involved]" December 15, 1975, pp. 69–70 in *Resolutions Adopted on the Reports of the Second Committee* (A/RES/3514). New York: UN.

US Congress. House. Committee on International Economic Policy. 1975. *The Activities of American Multinational Corporations Abroad: Hearing Before the Subcommittee on International Economic Policy of the Committee on International Relations.* 94th Cong., 1st sess., June 5.

US Senate. Committee on Finance. 1975. *S. Res. 265., A Resolution to Protect the Ability of the United States to Trade Abroad: Hearing Before the Subcommittee on International Trade of the Committee on Finance.* 94th Cong., 1st sess., October 6.

Velde, Willem, and Swapna Nair. 2006. "Foreign Direct Investment, Services Trade Negotiations and Development: The Case of Tourism in the Caribbean." *Development Policy Review* 24 (4): 437–54.

Weiner, Tim. 2004. "Lockheed and the Future of Warfare." *New York Times*, November 28.

Yoder, Amos. 1993. *The Evolution of the United Nations System*. Washington: Taylor & Francis.

CHAPTER 5

The Corporate Watergate

US claims on illicit corporate payments came to dominate global anti-corruption debates in the 1990s. This chapter traces the steps that led to the re-launch of global claims-making in 1989 and shows how the US concern with illicit/corrupt payments emerged in the first place. The main reason for the United States to re-launch global claims in 1989 was the FCPA, which can be seen as a product of Watergate, as much as a product of the ITT aftermath. While the ITT affair triggered debates in the United States on the foreign policy repercussions of corporate misconduct, Watergate made these debates more domestically oriented. It was the combined work of the Subcommittee on Multinational Corporations, the Watergate Special Prosecution Force and the SEC that shed light on the illicit payments problem and informed much of the thinking behind the FCPA (Koehler 2012). Furthermore, the US Congressional hearings after the ITT affair were the main source of information for other governments to start their own investigations into corporate and government misconduct. As such, these testimonies provide information on the putative condition out of which global claims on corruption emerged. This is why this chapter discusses the content of the US Congress hearings on multinational corporations in relation to corrupt practices. The chapter further establishes the re-emergence of claims after the 1988 Amendment to the FCPA, when the United States chose the OECD as the most appropriate international forum in which to achieve consensus on corrupt practices.

E. Katzarova, *The Social Construction of Global Corruption*,
Political Corruption and Governance,
https://doi.org/10.1007/978-3-319-98569-5_5

The previous chapter demonstrated how consensus on what constituted a 'corrupt practice' proved unattainable, with developing countries insisting on a definition of corruption broader than bribery. These debates over the definition of the scope of the practices that should be deemed 'corrupt' did not remain encapsulated in the UN, but spread, or had an influence, over other organizations such as the OAS and the OECD. In the 1970s, global measures included: OAS Resolution 154 (167/75) from July 10, 1975; UN Resolution 3514 from December 15, 1975; OECD Guidelines for Multinational Enterprises from June 21, 1976; ICC Rules of Conduct to Combat Extortion and Bribery from December 2, 1977. Some of these initiatives were promoted as a wider strategy of the US government to address questionable payments and bribery through international and unilateral solutions (Schmults Memorandum 1976). The ICC Rules of Conduct were published as a self-regulation measure at the same time that the FCPA was signed into law in December 1977. The FCPA, together with the 1978 Ethics in Government Act and the amended Federal Election Campaign Act, became part of a comprehensive regulatory campaign against corruption in American politics (Neild 2002). The FCPA aimed at restoring confidence in American business through a radical measure—a criminalization approach led by Congress that was in direct opposition to the disclosure approach heralded by the US executive in a number of international and global forums. As the US Trade Representative later argued, the US Congress 'reacted quickly and emotionally to daily newspaper headlines and public outcry' in adopting this draconian measure (Brock 1981). The FCPA formed the basis of the second strategic re-launch of global claims-making and to a significant extent shaped the content of the problem of corruption, as it became institutionalized in international organizations starting from the mid-1990s.

Investigations and hearings at the Subcommittee on Multinational Corporations, as well as the US Senate Select Committee to Study Governmental Operations with Respect to Intelligence Activities, revealed inappropriate behavior by US corporations abroad. Senator Church was the central figure in the hearings, first as Chairman of the Subcommittee on Multinational Corporations and then as Chairman of the so-called Church Committee (or the US Senate Select Committee to Study Governmental Operations with Respect to Intelligence Activities). The Chilean case and the ITT affair were the cornerstone in the investigations of both committees. The Subcommittee on

Multinational Corporations held its first hearings (March 20–April 2, 1973) on the role of ITT in Chile. The widely controversial 'Church Committee' also aimed to set the record straight on US involvement in Chile in the decade prior to the overthrow of Allende, but it tackled the role of multinationals only marginally in relation to covert action by the CIA. In publications in The New York Times on September 20 and December 22, 1974, the investigative journalist Seymour Hersh revealed alleged CIA involvement in the Chilean coup and surveillance of US civilians, which prompted the creation of the Church Committee. As William Bader (1975), professional member of the Church Committee, stated: 'our interest in Chile, and in this report, is not only what happened there but what the Chilean experience tells us about covert action as a foreign policy operation of a democratic society' (8).

In a similar way, the ITT case became the basis on which the Subcommittee on Multinational Corporations launched an investigation into the way in which inappropriate corporate behavior clashes with political and foreign policy objectives. While the decision to investigate the ITT case was made in May 1972 (shortly after the Anderson revelations) by the Senate Foreign Relations Committee, the hearings were postponed until after the US presidential election. When the hearings on the ITT case in Chile started in March 1973, the Subcommittee on Multinational Corporations ventured once again to look at what the ITT case meant for the influence of multinational corporations on US politics in general. The first question that the hearings attempted to answer was about corporations and the public interest: 'Do the activities of the multinational corporations advance the interests of the people of the United States taken as a whole?' (US Senate 1973, 1). In the preamble to the hearings, it was further stated that it might be 'critical to the survival and viability of these corporations, that there be agreed upon standards of conduct' (US Senate 1973, 2). The mandate of the Subcommittee on Multinational Corporations to a large extent coincided with UNCTC debates on multinational corporations and the public interest, as well as the negotiation of codes for standards of behavior for multinationals. As the investigations at the Subcommittee on Multinational Corporations progressed, the revelations of inappropriate payments also started to surface. One of the most blatant examples of such questionable payments was the infamous seven-figure offer that the ITT made to the CIA to prevent the election of Allende in 1970. The CIA refused the offer, but the hearings raised the possibility of a legislative response which would criminalize similar corporate contributions (US Senate 1973, 119). The underlying question behind these payments to a significant extent continued to be about 'the appropriate limits for a company in seeking to influence the politics and policies of nations' (US Senate 1973, 111). It was the foreign corporate payments problem, however, which emerged with the SEC disclosure program in 1975 that shifted debates decidedly toward corporate bribery and formed the basis of the FCPA, as well as the US proposal on illicit payments in the UN and the OECD.

Establishing the Global Dimension and Deciding on a Venue

The FCPA was the first, albeit national, law that addressed the question of transnational bribery. The adoption of the law in 1977, however, can be better understood within a domestic anti-corruption program, since the FCPA was a direct consequence of the Watergate investigations (Posadas 2000; Cragg and Woof 2002; Biegalman and Biegelman 2010; Koehler 2014). The connection was immediate because the Watergate Special Prosecution Force, investigating the 1972 campaign of then President Richard Nixon, discovered that the slush funds used at home for illegal party contributions were also used to bribe foreign officials abroad (Sporkin 2003). Judge Stanley Sporkin, who was employed by the SEC at the time (1961–1981) and became Director of the Division of Enforcement (1974–1981) explained in an interview for SEC that the same slush funds, used for illegal contributions in the United States were used abroad for other questionable payments: 'we had developed a horrendous situation where we found out of those slush funds that were being used to give money to political parties, we went into them and we found that those monies were also being used for other various activities, such as bribing officials in foreign countries to get business' (Sporkin 2003, 16). Given the particular post-Watergate environment, the publicity surrounding these investigations created strong support for a unilateral measure that would forbid US companies to perpetuate these illicit practices abroad, leading eventually to the FCPA which is discussed in this chapter.

The first claims that illicit/corrupt practices were a global problem operated in an environment of uncertainty as to the magnitude of the problem and had fluid definitional boundaries. In light of the expected unilateral legislative measure that the US Congress was pushing for, the search for an international solution became a priority for the US executive and for American corporations. One of the primary sources of information on the immediate US position before starting a global claims-making process in 1975 was the Congressional Hearings and Discussions on Senate Resolution 265 'The Resolution to Protect the United States Ability to Trade Abroad' (US Senate 1975). Senator Ribicoff, as a member of the Finance Committee, in the opening of the Congressional hearings pointed to the unfavorable domestic and worldwide publicity for US illicit practices that were not, however, the sole prerogative of American companies:

> The publicity that has accompanied these disclosures has made it seem to many that this kind of corporate misconduct is primary an American practice. It has been argued that if we stop our companies from engaging in these sordid activities we will be ending the problem. But the fact is foreign corporations have been involved too, probably even to a greater extent than our own companies. (Ribicoff 1975, 2)

Despite the unjust focus on American corporations, illicit corporate payments were considered of global relevance because other corporations were also implicated in such practices. Thus, the twin solutions of national legislation and international negotiations on a collective solution become the center of claims as to the proper course of future action. Senator Church (in his capacity as Chairman of the Subcommittee of Multinational Corporations) also made a statement that the investigations led him to conclude that a solution to the problem of political contributions and bribery had to be sought nationally and internationally. Church stated that globally such practices appeared to be a 'way of life' and therefore, not necessarily perceived by the participants as a problem in need of an urgent solution:

> It has been a very sorry, sordid tale that the subcommittee heard - a tale of kickbacks and shakedowns, of bribery and corruption in the very highest military and governmental circles abroad and the condoning of secret slush funds, false bookkeeping, Swiss bank accounts and "fake" subsidiaries by the top of the executives of America's leading firms. Corporate representatives tell us that corruption is an integral part of doing business abroad;

that paying bribes is a common and accepted practice or a way of life, as many of them put it.' (Church 1975, 7)

Church's knowledge and expertise on the subject were central to forming a better understanding of the scope of the problem and its repercussions and subsequently influencing a decision as to why the problem should be tackled and at what level. Senator Church considered the problem of corrupt payments a political and economic, rather than a moral one, and he put emphasis mostly on the repercussion of such payments on American foreign policy. Despite the fact that the hearings in the Subcommittee provided numerous examples of the way in which US foreign policy was hampered by the revelations, Senator Church singled the influence of corporate bribery on a new arms race in the Middle East as the most important foreign policy aspect of corrupt payments:

> Documents and public testimony before the Multinational Subcommittee show that military procurement decisions which were supposed to be made on the basis of fundamental national security considerations, instead, all too often are based on the size of payoffs made to key people in the military and civilian defense establishments (…) The incentive is, therefore, great to buy the most expensive weapons and in greater quantities than are really needed. One country's unnecessarily bloated defense budget then immediately becomes the rationale for its neighbors or potential adversaries to acquire more weapons just to keep up. And so it goes in a vicious and never-ending cycle. (Church 1975, 8)

According to the statement, the payments constitute a problem because legitimate defense requirements should be the basis for making arms purchases rather than private financial interests. In addition, leaving defense budgets to be influenced by private profit incentives may lead to an escalating arms race with grave repercussions for armed conflicts. Bribery could be singled out as the major cause of such distortions, but the issue was more intricate. Senator Church suggested that US authorities could be tolerating the inappropriate use of agent's fees by corporations because higher arms sales contributed to the country's balance of payments, which had been hurt by the OPEC oil crisis. The political commitment to prevent conflict in the Middle East was hampered, however, by aggressive arms sales which provide 'all sides in that conflict with the instruments of another war' (Church 1975, 8). Thus, US commercial interests clashed with other foreign policy objectives.

The effect of corporate bribery on political regimes in other countries, as well as on US foreign policy objectives, was not limited, however, to a spiraling arms race, but involved the use of corrupt payments by American corporations in ideological warfare. The tendency of electorates in other countries to start perceiving their governments as 'handmaidens of foreign and domestic financial interests' was jeopardizing the American foreign policy objective of stabilizing democratic and foreign capital friendly political regimes:

> There is also little doubt that widespread corruption serves to undermine those moderate democratic and pro-free-enterprise governments which the United States has traditionally sought to foster and support. Several oil companies testified before the subcommittee that they had made huge political contributions in Italy and Korea, for example. They claimed to be supporting the democratic forces who are friendly to foreign capital in those countries, but in fact, they were subverting the basic democratic processes of those two countries by making illegal contributions and were, at the same time, providing the radical left with its strongest election issue. (Church 1975, 9)

Foreign policy repercussions of corrupt practices were the main issue for the Subcommittee on Multinational Corporations, but Senator Church argued that these practices committed abroad were also problematic domestically: 'The slush funds and secret bank accounts from which money was drawn to pay foreign politicians also provided the means of disguising corporate contributions to American politicians' (Church 1975, 9). The illicit interaction between private and foreign actors, as well as national public actors, constituted a national as well as an international problem. Illicit payments also constituted a short-sighted understanding of American business interests and, as Senator Church asserted, the business community was already aware of the fact that corruption was not a viable long-term strategy. An analogical international solution had to be sought in addition to a national one since the problem was not only American and the competitiveness of American business should not be compromised with a unilateral solution (Church 1975). Senate Resolution 265 urged the American executive to start talks for a treaty on corrupt practices in the framework of GATT or another trade agreement. A multilateral approach was deemed appropriate in order to preserve the competitive positions of American companies in international trade.

It was more than logical to conclude that the problem with illicit political contributions was not a patented American one, and hearings at the Subcommittee of Multinational Corporations bore testimony by American enterprises that such practices were widely shared in the global business community, but the evidence was scarce. Senator Church admitted that American companies during the hearings: 'spoke in generalities. They said that they believed that these practices which they themselves admitted were commonplace, they believed that foreign firms did engage in them. But they were not able to furnish us specific information' (Church 1975, 10). The Senator himself was positive that this was not solely an American practice, but he referred to the difficulty of discovering definitive proof. The evidence he provided was of anecdotal nature—he referred to two stories he read in the press about Belgian and French bribery cases. In this case, a conventional understanding of problems as objective conditions that are statistically studied and demand an almost automatic response from society and the responsible public authorities, inadequately explains the emergence of social and global problems. Even in cases when the magnitude of the problem appears as the driving force behind building a collective response to a putative condition, it may be the perceived magnitude of a problem (or the publicity it generates) that leads to action and prescriptive, rather than empirical, argumentation for said action. The difficulty of building a statistical database on global corrupt practices is notorious and the fact that at such an early stage of claims-making, the 'data' are anecdotal is more than understandable. The Congressional hearings persuasively show the lack of precise data, but also the struggle to understand the magnitude of the problem quantitatively. This dynamic is evident in the testimony of the Assistant Secretary of Commerce for Domestic and International Business:

> ... I've spent the last 15 years of my life in the field of international trade, and in the last 18 months prior to coming to government, I have participated in the financing of over $300 million of equipment going abroad, and I have never been involved in a transaction of that nature. I do not think that 98 percent of the companies in this country have. I think we are talking about a small percentage. (Reed 1975, 34)
>
> Senator BYRD. You mentioned that 98 percent of the corporations do not engage in such practices as are enumerated in the resolution. That is an encouraging statement, I think. Does that apply to 98 percent of the multinationals as well as 98 percent of the corporations?

> Mr. REED. The Fig. 98 percent is my own estimate. It is not something that is statistically proven.
> Senator BYRD. Yes; but when you applied the 98 percent, do you apply it to all corporations doing business overseas, or do you apply it to the multinationals only? (US Senate 1975, 37)

The geographical scope became another question in relation to the 'globality' of the problem investigated during the hearings. Senator Church concluded that from the information he had gathered during the hearings the rendering of bribes was also from the recipient's side a 'worldwide problem.' American companies admitted to making such payments not only in developing, but also in developed countries (US Senate 1975, 11). On the other hand, the supply part of such corrupt payments that was deemed to be the developed countries was more significant because it required the search for a global solution. Senator Church was not aware of ongoing investigations in other countries with the exception of Germany, but he confirmed that Iran and Saudi Arabia had reacted to the findings of the Subcommittee on Multinational Corporations by passing edicts on the practice of rendering commissions in military equipment purchases (Church 1975, 9). The expected scenario was that after other countries undertake their own investigations, even if only a small number were willing to make the findings public, this small core of states could reach agreement for an international solution. Senator Church supported a mixed solution for these potential partner countries with the enactment of national laws and corollary international agreement. The proposal of the Church Committee for national legislation on corrupt payments was to a large extent driving the need for an international approach:

> Now we have these universal practices all over the world. And American business is being blamed. Talking for myself, personally, I do not intend to sit by and see American business put in a disadvantageous position. And they certainly are in a disadvantaged position because this Congress will, I am sure, follow up the Church committee's proposals and have every type of restriction against American corporations. (Ribicoff 1975, 19)

Senator Ribicoff explained that in including the issue under the Trade Act that both Democrats and Republicans 'expected once and for all that the American negotiators look out for the interests of American business and not be so hypersensitive to what other people do' (Ribicoff 1975, 19).

The framing of corrupt practices as a trade issue, and therefore, an issue suitable for discussion at GATT, was meant to best serve the interests of American business from the viewpoint of the legislature. The function of an international solution was, to some extent, to preempt national legislation banning illicit payments abroad or at least minimize the damage that the ban on such payments would have incurred on the competitiveness of American corporations. This is the main reason why representatives of American trade organizations also endorsed the Senate Resolution with the modifications put forward by representatives of the executive. US companies and representatives of the executive were more eager to export the policy debate on corrupt practices abroad, while in the US Congress there was a strong determination to first ban such practices by US companies with a national law that would go in the line of full disclosure or criminalization. For organized business interests, the search for a global solution was much more preferable to a unilateral domestic measure which would put American business at a competitive disadvantage. Representatives of American trade organizations, therefore, urged that the problem of corrupt payments be addressed at the international level and the plans for unilateral policy measures be abandoned:

> use every resource of the U.S. Government to deal with this problem, and that might include bilateral discussions or any other intergovernmental technique to accomplish the objectives of the resolution. I suggest that the regulatory proposals of the Department of State, which I have entered into the record, are unilateral in character; they are totally unnecessary at the present time; and they would be contrary to the objective of the resolution. (US Senate 1975, 41)

The two main considerations were, firstly, not to rush into a unilateral form of legislation before a global approach has been tested and, secondly, to place a demarcation line between similar practices which would render some legitimate and others not. The second concern was expressed about both domestic and global business transactions and especially in connection to military contracts. Business representatives urged that: 'many relationships carried on by US companies even with the Middle East countries or with Indonesia or with some of the other countries that have received so much attention in the press, are legitimate relationships and are not subject to criticism' (41). Where the line of demarcation between illicit and legitimate types of influence in business transactions lies was subject to claims-making. Representatives of business and trade interests tried to delimit a narrower definition of what are considered 'corrupt payments' and clarify legitimate agent fees, monetary and non-monetary forms of influence and other services that remain outside the 'problem.' The two primary objectives of organized business interests in the mid-1970s were: (1) exporting the discussion of the problem to international forums while preventing the enactment of a unilateral national legislative act; (2) demarcating a narrower definition of what constitutes a corrupt practice. These two objectives shaped much of the strategy of the US executive in addressing corrupt practices internationally. As will become evident with the adoption of the FCPA, different actors had different interests and tried to construct an etiology of the problem that served those interests. The choice of international organization in which to launch the claims was another example of the plurality of positions in which the intent of Congress to direct talks to GATT was challenged by representatives of the US executive and organized business interests.

Senate Resolution 265 directed the American executive (President's Special Representative for Trade Negotiations, representatives of the Department of State, Commerce, Treasury and Justice) to initiate negotiations for a treaty on corrupt payments in the framework of GATT or other trade agreement in accordance with the 1974 Trade Act. The main exchange of claims and counterclaims on the content of the problem and the appropriate international forum in which to address it occurred during the hearings of the President's Special Representative for Trade Negotiations. It was in the contrasting positions between the representatives of the legislative and executive branches of government that the claims-making process became ready for international export.

The Senate Resolution 265 specified GATT as the proper institutional forum for the internationalization of the problem of corrupt payments and insisted on its definition as a trade issue. The Special Representative for Trade Negotiations concurred with the general objective of the Resolution, but not with the definition of the problem as a trade issue and with the chosen institutional setting for launching the claims globally. The President's Special Representative, Dent, insisted that the trade negotiations in Geneva were not the appropriate forum and that a multifaceted issue such as unethical payments should be examined in the OECD and/or the UN. The Special Representative rejected GATT as the proper institution at which to address the claims and reassured Congress that other institutional fora were already approached.

The question of public disclosure of corrupt payments was examined at the IMF and the World Bank with Ministers of Finance from Canada, Japan, Britain, France and Germany. Furthermore, the Secretary-General of the OECD had responded favorably to looking for international corrective action within the organization. Special countermeasures were undertaken in the sphere of defense by the Secretary of Defense who in cooperation with the State Department and the Pentagon was working on a solution for the disclosed cases of fees paid to middlemen in arms sales. Regional approaches were also underway in the framework of the OAS in cooperation with MIT, Stanford Regional Institute and Harvard University. Despite claiming that the problem was predominantly political and governmental in nature, Special Representative Dent stressed that corporate actors were actively working for a solution in the direction of self-regulation. The ICC, as well as the US Chamber, was already starting to develop codes of acceptable conduct for multinational corporations. The Charter on International Investments of the Pacific Economic Council and the Caterpillar Tractor's Code of Worldwide Business Conduct provided other examples of business-sponsored initiatives on solving the problem of illicit payments (Dent 1975).

Special Representative Dent claimed that corruption or unethical payments were not simply a trade issue as 'the problem affects all facets of business and business-government relationships' (Dent 1975, 17). What was problematic with the disclosed payments, Dent claimed, was of moral and political nature. Legislating global morality was hardly the business of the United States, according to his argument. The GATT trade negotiations were already complicated by economic recession, and if these ethical issues were added to an already ambitious round of negotiations, it was doubtful that successful conclusion of both the negotiations and the particular problem laid ahead. The President's Special Representative insisted that corruption was predominantly a moral and political issue, but this did not doom it to failure in other international negotiations since 'no government is likely to concede nonconformity with commonly held principles of morality and decency.' While agreeing in principle that corrupt practices can constitute a trade obstacle, Dent expressed his practical doubts that one could negotiate 'the ethics of trade practices in the MTN' (17).

Within the framework of the social construction of global problems, this preliminary reframing of putative condition justifies the choice of venue for the launch of global claims. Corrupt payments as a trade issue was meant to introduce the issue at GATT where some congressmen believed the United States had clout. Corrupt payments as an ethical problem was meant to steer talks away from GATT. This is why the executive representative referred to 'unethical payments' and insisted that the issue should be brought to a wider web of global and international venues, but most appropriately to the OECD. The insistence of the President's Special Representative that GATT was not the most appropriate forum for working toward a global solution was met with very strong opposition in Congress. The Special Representative suggested amendments to the Resolution that would accommodate the change in preferred venue, and these changes were supported by the business community, but met forceful opposition in Congress. Senator Ribicoff insisted that: 'we felt the time has come to move fast in the international forum where we have clout, and that is GATT, to put the American companies on the same basis as companies from all over the globe' (Ribicoff 1975, 22). The Senator vehemently opposed the change in international organization proposed by the executive arguing that: 'Every nation that is in OECD is in the GATT, but GATT is where the crunch is. GATT is where the power is. Everything else is a debating society' (Ribicoff 1975, 30). The inclusion of transnational corrupt payments under the 1974 Trade Act made the issue suitable for discussion at international trade negotiations. Therefore, it is possible that this particular interpretation of the putative condition was enacted in order to promote the problem at an international forum where the United States 'had clout,' as the Congressional hearings repeatedly put it. The position of the representatives of the executive promoted a different interpretation and another strategy for the internationalization of the issue—these unethical payments would be better managed at the OECD and after a consensus is reached within the group of developed nations, this agreement could be 'transferable' to other international and global institutions (Dent 1975, 23). The strategic value of starting the discussions at the OECD was explained as the following:

> What we are attempting to do is obtain some unanimity of thought within a smaller group, particularly the payers, the people who are making the payments. The OECD, we think, provides a proper vehicle at the moment to attempt to get some unanimity of thought in regard to how this universal code of conduct would be accepted and could then be introduced into GATT or any other appropriate body. (Reed 1975, 35)

While the US Senate Resolution directed the negotiation talks toward GATT, representatives of the executive and business interests managed to establish that a broader approach, involving in particular the OECD and the UN, would be more effective. This strategy of the US executive informed the US anti-corruption initiatives not only in the 1970s but also in the 1990s. To a significant extent, the immediate function of claims-making at this stage was to tackle unfavorable publicity domestically, as well as globally, and to ameliorate the consequences public discontent might have for compromising American leadership. While the US Congress expressed intent to act unilaterally, such projects were suspended, waiting for the results of a multilateral approach.

The FCPA as a Product of 'Post-Watergate Morality'

The failure of talks in the UN and the OECD in the 1970s to generate a viable global solution to the problem of corrupt/illicit payments was due to some extent to varying claims of scope, and in particular, the developing nations' argument that broader range of activities and outcomes were to be included in the category of 'corrupt practices.' The claims of the G77 that foreign corporations become political agents in their countries that strengthen or destabilize the position of ruling governments, as well as channel the national interest of their country of origin, became highly controversial. Viewed from this perspective, the question of corruption was one of corrupt 'influence' rather than 'payment.' The US government had its own reason to pursue a ban on illicit or corrupt payments and this reason can be understood after a careful look at the domestic investigations that the two Church Committees, the Watergate Special Prosecution Office and the SEC, undertook.

Parallel to the UN and OECD pre-negotiation talks, debates were ongoing in the US Congress. The Ford administration insisted on a multilateral solution and favored a disclosure approach (Cragg and Woof 2001). It took a change of administration and Jimmy Carter, who favored a criminalization approach, signed the FCPA into law on December 20, 1977 (Koehler 2012). The new president still envisioned the successful conclusion of the UN negotiations as the international counterpart of the American ban on foreign bribery, but the unilateral adoption of the FCPA further complicated the pre-negotiation talks and isolated the United States in the UN and the OECD (IME/M(77)1).

The chapter discusses the adoption of the FCPA, because its amendment in 1988 leads to the resurgence of discussions at the international level and a strategic re-launch of global claims.

The FCPA was the first national law to address the question of transnational bribery. As it was noted previously, the adoption of the law in 1977 can be placed better within a domestic anti-corruption program and can be understood as an unintended consequence of the post-Watergate investigations (Sporkin 2003). The FCPA is significant in the construction of a global corruption problem for two main reasons. Firstly, the unilateral adoption of a law with extraterritorial implications further complicated the pre-negotiation talks at the OECD and the UN after 1977, and contributed to the failure of a viable multilateral solution. Secondly, the FCPA became the basis for renewed attempts to reopen negotiation talks at the OECD after the Act was amended for the first time in 1988 in Title V of the Omnibus Trade Act. While the attempts to promote the problem of corrupt payments on the international agenda presented transnational corporate bribery as fundamentally a global problem, the adoption of the FCPA pitched corporate corrupt payments as essentially a national problem. The criminalization of corporate questionable payments to foreign government officials was not a 'national' problem because it could not have been better addressed through a global approach, but because the FCPA was predominantly a consequence of the dynamic between the executive and legislative branches of power in the peculiar post-Watergate climate, and the function of the Act was to a large extent to remedy sentiments of suspicion toward the dealings of US business and government.

The general concern of the American legislator had to do with the connections between government and business, whether domestically or internationally, and did not differ so greatly from the UN talks about the role of corporations in politics. Senator Church in a public speech at Harvard University on October 26, 1976, argued that corporations have been transformed into political actors: 'an American multinational corporation can become a political actor abroad whose immediate interests may be antithetical to the foreign policy objectives of the United States.' The problem of political involvement of US corporations abroad and the growing power of corporations to outmaneuver national sovereignty was further complicated by alleged government involvement in the questionable corporate payments:

> I do not ignore that some of these corporations, as in the case of ITT in Chile, acted with the encouragement of government agencies, like the CIA. But more often, as in the cases of Japan, Korea and Italy, the subcommittee has been told by the responsible U.S. government officials that they had no knowledge of the political payments, bribes or questionable commission fees disclosed by the subcommittee. It could be that these are disingenuous denials designed to conceal the background role of our own government in such gross misconduct. But I think it is more likely that the disclaimers reflect the traditional attitude of our diplomats that commercial activities abroad of American-owned corporations are simply none of their business. Such an attitude betrays a failure to understand that multinational corporations often are crucial actors in the international political sphere, whose activities may determine and define U.S. national interests to a degree comparable to the actions of our own government. (Church 1976, 1)

The problem of corrupt payments can therefore be placed at the center of what Senator Church in the same speech referred to as a 'web of entanglement' that cannot be exhausted with the influence of corporate actors over political processes, but rather points to an intricacy between political and business considerations:

> What I have tried to describe to you is the way in which the Lockheed case illustrates a web of entanglement: a major U.S. defense contractor seeks its financial salvation in sales abroad; it penetrates and corrupts the internal politics of major allies of the United States; our own government admits that this fraudulent and corrosive behavior has taken place outside its knowledge and control; and, when a congressional committee proposes to expose the sordid facts and legislate to prevent their repetition, we are told that to do so would endanger the security of the United States. (Church 1976, 2)

Despite attempts from Secretary of State Henry Kissinger to suppress the Lockheed case on the basis of security interests, Senator Church continued the investigations (Biegalman and Biegelman 2010). The main reason why the legislature concentrated on 'payments' (that were called 'irregular,' 'questionable,' 'illegal' or 'corrupt') came from the fact that, as noted previously, while following the money trail of the Watergate investigations, the existence of slush funds was discovered. In 1973, the Watergate Special Prosecution Office was investigating the money trail of domestic political campaign contributions. In a follow-up, SEC discovered:

> falsifications of corporate financial records, designed to disguise or conceal the source and application of corporate funds misused for illegal purposes, as well as the existence of secret "slush funds" disbursed outside the normal financial accountability system. These secret funds were used for a number of purposes, including in some instances, questionable or illegal foreign payments. (SEC Report 1976, 2)

The disclosure program, instituted by the SEC as a consequence, had hundreds of companies participated on a voluntary basis and in 1975 revealed a worldwide bribery web, a global conundrum that Kissinger referred to as 'the Watergate of private industry' (quoted in Biegelman and Biegelman 2010, 17). The Lockheed bribery case was simply the most publicized of the investigations, because it led to resignations of political leaders abroad, and therefore became the emblematic precursor to the FCPA. Legislative response was deemed necessary, firstly because of SEC's obligation to ensure correct disclosure to stockholders and secondly because of the ramifications such payments had for American foreign policy (Cragg and Woof 2002).

The American executive was hesitant to pursue criminalization and the Ford administration focused on disclosure measures, which would have provided a much more lax approach to handling corporate foreign payments. The US Congress was determined to enact tougher measures, however, and an earlier form of the FCPA (Bill S.3133) was introduced by Senator Proxmire (Koehler 2012). The bill was in direct opposition to the proposal backed by the Ford administration, the 'Foreign Payments Disclosure Act,' which did not foresee the explicit prohibition of foreign bribery. The leverage of the US Congress post-Watergate was particularly strong because of the compromised reputation of the executive, severely damaged during the Nixon administration (Fisher 2014). The criminalization approach, promoted by Proxmire, was the most substantial option of legislative action against the questionable corporate payments, and in the particular post-Watergate climate, it overrode strong domestic concerns from the business sector.

The ITT affair and the resulting corporate misconduct revelations by the Subcommittee on Multinational Corporations had a damaging effect on US credibility both domestically and abroad. It was, however, the SEC disclosure program, which came as a follow-up of the Watergate investigations that redirected the debates decisively toward corporate bribery in 1975. The problem with the disclosed corrupt payments had an ideological and a foreign policy dimension, but the reason why the criminalization approach became the preferred mode of addressing the questionable payments had more to do with the climate of 'post-Watergate morality' that had a powerful impact on US politics in the 1970s (Koehler 2012).

Unilateral Criminalization or Disclosure

The FCPA was a complex interplay between a number of actors, most notably the Church Subcommittees, the Ford (and Carter) Administration, the SEC, and the chairman of the Senate Committee on Banking, Housing and Urban Affairs (Koehler 2012). The latter, in the face of Senator William Proxmire, was responsible for drafting what was later to become the FCPA of 1977. In the attempt to criminalize bribery and not simply demand disclosure of information, Proxmire was guided by clear objectives. He wanted the anti-bribery campaign to take the form of a criminal law because that 'would help US multinational companies resist corrupt demands,' but he also argued that corrupt practices carried out abroad would corrode the US political landscape and become the rule domestically as well (quoted in Cragg and Woof 2001, 185). Proxmire's follow-up Senate hearings at the Committee on Banking, Housing and Urban Affairs came as a consequence of the SEC reports and supplemented the Church revelations on Lockheed. The reason why Proxmire could have taken the Lockheed bribery scandal to heart was that he was opposed to the 1971 bailout of the corporation, and the revelations that Lockheed might have used some of the government money to bribe foreign officials must have not fared favorably with him.

The Proxmire-sponsored criminalization of transnational bribery appeared at first as an unlikely course of action, because the proposals of Church, SEC and the Ford administration excluded criminalization in favor of disclosure and measures aiming at self-regulation (SEC Report 2017). The proposal of the Ford administration was based on the investigations of the Task Force on Questionable Payments Abroad, established by the president on March 31, 1976. President Ford considered the 'erosion of confidence' and in particular the public distrust in the free enterprise system as major motives for legislative action (Ford 1976). The proposed Foreign Payments Disclosure Act, however, avoided a criminalization approach because of the inherent element of extraterritoriality, which would have entailed the application of US criminal statues on foreign territories (Ford 1979). The disclosed information about corrupt payments would have been provided to foreign governments on certain occasions, and the relevant foreign authorities were to decide if the information should be made public and/or national jurisdiction on the subject was applicable. The prosecution of transnational bribery was, according to this draft Act, to remain a predominantly national prerogative with limited forms of unilateral or multilateral international cooperation for the exchange of information. The provisions of the Act were minimal in comparison with the approach promoted by Proxmire. Facilitation payments were to be excluded from disclosure, and the Secretary of State or the Attorney General could ban the publication of disclosed payments on the basis of foreign policy considerations (Ford 1979).

The proposal of the Ford administration left a large margin for political discretion. The continuation of 'business as usual' was what the Proxmire proposal for criminalization was trying to counteract. The criminalization approach also entailed a larger responsibility for the bribing corporation. The approach would have, therefore, showed decisive intention to root out American corporate bribery domestically and abroad, and would have also inflicted significant costs on bribing transgressors. During a hearing before the Senate Committee On Banking, Housing and Urban Affairs, Proxmire referred to the impunity and lack of criminal and monetary accountability that corporations involved in the corrupt payments have enjoyed following the disclosures. Promoting a criminalization approach was to some extent a method of instituting more stringent measures against bribing US companies. The approach championed by Proxmire claimed to aim at restoring faith in the US business community and in the ethical standards corporations abide to in their interaction with foreign, as well as US governmental officials:

> The recent revelations of foreign bribes paid by many of our largest corporations threaten to undermine public confidence in our free enterprise system. We cannot condone bribery abroad and expect the public to believe that the same kind of illegal payoffs do not occur at home. Corporate corruption knows no boundaries. If we permit bribery to become a regular policy of U.S. corporations abroad, it will only be a matter of time before these same corrupt practices inflict our domestic economic system.
>
> There are those who condemn foreign bribery but who argue that it should be dealt with only through an international treaty such as the one

> the State Department has announced it is considering. This approach is really a prescription for doing nothing...An international treaty to outlaw bribery is equivalent to a treaty to outlaw war. While high sounding in purpose, it is devoid of any practical effect. (Proxmire 1976, 1)

Proxmire reversed the arguments used earlier to promote corrupt practices as an intrinsically global problem that has to be addressed through a viable multilateral solution. The Senator claimed that, even if desirable, the negotiation of an international treaty would be too lengthy process and would ultimately not provide a practical solution to the problem. Proxmire's arguments had a political underbelly because his criminalization approach was in direct opposition to the proposal by the Ford administration. The proposal also reflected the expressed concern of Congress that the State and Defense Departments, in particular, were not only insufficiently involved in solving the problem of foreign corrupt payments, but were actually actively perpetuating it (Kohler 2012). Congressional hearings suggested that the US government might have been aware of the questionable payments even prior to the disclosure procedures, and this led to suspicions of state-promoted corporate bribery. Senator Helms announced that the US government has not 'leveled with the American people about the government's own involvement with respect to these activities' (quoted in Koehler, 968). As Koehler (2012) observes, Senator Church also characterized the government's inactivity and overall attitude toward the foreign corrupt payments as one of 'indifference or perhaps benign neglect' (969). This suspected indolence of the US government, which was working toward an international solution, but was allegedly circumventing real reform, became the fuel behind the unilateral criminalization approach.

The US Congress and in particular the Senate's suspicion toward the government's approach and possible involvement in the questionable payments were the driving forces behind the FCPA. The initial draft of the bill proposed by Proxmire was the only one providing for the criminalization of transnational corrupt payments performed by US-based companies and their subsidiaries, and the Senator later reworked the bill to accommodate the proposal by the SEC. The SEC initially showed reluctance to support the criminalization approach. In an address by the SEC Chairman Roderick Hills on March 15, 1976, the implications of the disclosures for the US society were presented in the following way:

> Confidence in our business community and its capacity to compete fairly has been badly shaken, perhaps destroyed at least temporarily. We must – for this reason alone – as a government and a society, condemn bribery anywhere. If bribery will get a contract for a manager in a foreign country, and if he is permitted to try it: Who will be convinced that the company that bribes abroad will compete fairly at home.
>
> Disclosure alone cannot restore confidence in our institutions. Indeed, disclosure carried to an irrelevant degree would only obscure its true value, but the discipline of disclosure will be a power catharsis for much of our present cynicism. We are face to face today with the disagreeable fact that too many of our people in government and out do not believe in our free-enterprise, capitalistic system; because they do not believe it's competitive, they do not believe it's free, and the word "capitalist" sounds like another one of those fellows who won't tell the truth. (Hills 1976, 12–13)

The SEC Chairman was expressing a similar sentiment to the one held by Proxmire that the unencumbered proliferation of corrupt payments abroad would compromise the credibility of domestic business-government relations. At the same time, the 'discipline of disclosure' was judged sufficient to purge the American public from the growing distrust toward the dealings of business and government actors. The SEC, however, later came around on the criminalization approach supported by the Senate as the most effective measure against corrupt practices that would restore the confidence of the American electorate in the political system governing the country (SEC 2017).

In his resignation speech, former Vice President Agnew used the term 'post-Watergate morality' to refer to his understanding that 'the things he had done had been … normal and generally tolerated … until Watergate came along' (quoted in Koehler 2012, 943). The decreased tolerance of the American public toward questionable dealings was a central item of this post-Watergate moral sentiment and the members of Congress of this new political era took on the role of guardians of the integrity of the free market system that the United States was championing around the globe. The illicit payments discovered during the post-Watergate investigations became, therefore, part of the ideological battle of supremacy during the Cold War and were seen to compromise the very legitimacy of the free enterprise system (Pieth 2007; Koehler 2014).

Following the enquiries from a number of Senate committees, the SEC and the Task Force on Questionable Payments Abroad, established by President Ford, the US Congress passed the FCPA in December

1977. The US Congress was driven not only by concerns for US foreign policy, being damaged by the bribery scandals of the previous years, but also by much broader ethical considerations, the primary one of which was the integrity of the free market system (US House 1977). This combination of domestic challenges to democratic governance and the foreign policy exigencies in the Cold War era coupled to promote the enactment of the FCPA in 1977 in the particular post-Watergate climate. After being passed by Senate, but not by the House of Representatives in 1976, the bill was re-introduced by Proxmire in January 1977. Prior to his election as President, the Democratic candidate Jimmy Carter had supported the criminalization approach, but as SEC records show, after coming into office showed only hesitant support for Proxmire's bill. SEC believed it had remedied the problem by strengthening corporate governance and addressing the falsification of corporate records. Proxmire's bill, however, retained 'a great deal of superficial appeal' as Commerce Secretary Richardson put it (SEC 2017). The Proxmire-sponsored bill passed the 95th Congress and the report presented in front of the House of Representatives stated that the necessity for the act was primarily driven by the unethical nature of the bribe practices disclosed and the rift with the political values of American public life. The report concluded that such corrupt practices erode 'public confidence in the integrity of the free market system' (quoted in Cragg and Woof 2002, 115).

Adopting unilaterally the FCPA placed American business at a relative disadvantage with respect to foreign competitors. The 'international' or multilateral alternative preferred by the Ford administration remained another option that was pursued at the time by the US executive in the framework of a number of international organizations. From a business point of view, the proposal of the Ford administration to first secure a multilateral framework appeared far more acceptable than the one championed by Senator Proxmire. The multilateral arrangement was more favorable to business interests because it would have resolved the tension between conformity with the national legislation and the competitive pressure of global markets by leveling the playing field. Furthermore, the US proposal at the UN was based on the disclosure approach championed by the Ford administration and the adoption of the FCPA had a negative impact on the international negotiations. The ECOSOC Ad Hoc Intergovernmental Working Group on Corrupt Practices was firmly against home country criminalization of corrupt practices because of the predicaments of enforcement and extraterritorial application that this approach entailed (IME/M(77)1).

Once the FCPA was adopted, the interest of the United States to protect its companies from the adverse effect of the unique domestic anti-bribery act on their global competitiveness appeared as a logical development. In the decade, following the adoption of the FCPA, the US Congress was consistently lobbied by American companies who insisted that they operated at a relative disadvantage in a global marketplace, where bribes remained tax deductible for most of their European competitors. In fact, as Gutterman (2013) observes, corporate lobbying against the FCPA from 1977 to 1988 was so persistent that the question becomes why was it not successful in repealing the act? Despite the Reagan administration's stated intention after 1981 to decriminalize foreign bribery, the FCPA remained intact. According to Gutterman (2013), the reason for the act's perseverance in the face of powerful corporate lobbying and the executive's determination to protect the interest of American business was that repealing the act would have been 'easier done than said' (109). In the enduring tradition of Watergate, public justification for the repeal would have been politically unfeasible, because: 'you simply couldn't get representatives or senators to vote to repeal it … no congressman will want to run for reelection and have his opponent say that he had voted in favor of committing bribery' (Heimann quoted in Gutterman, 112). The debate about revisions spread over three congresses and the first amendment to the FCPA was enacted as part of the Omnibus Trade and Competitiveness Act in 1988. Thus, in 1988 in accordance with the provisions of the amendment, the US Congress pushed the executive branch to initiate negotiations specifically in the framework of the OECD, which culminated in an international convention ten years later.

American corporations lobbied against the adoption of the FCPA prior to its adoption and to repeal it after 1977. Business found itself on the defensive after the revelations of hundreds of illicit high-profile business cases, and the 1970s became a decade of intensive business mobilization (Hacker and Pierson 2010). Despite the strategies of stepping up lobbying and developing personal contacts with politicians, the prevalence of an anti-corruption sentiment post-Watergate made repeal difficult. In the immediate adoption of the FCPA, enforcement efforts were credible, but with the advent of the Reagan administration and the frustrated effort to repeal or amend the act, enforcement patterns changed (Cragg and Woof 2002). The ban on foreign corrupt practices raised specific problems for a range of actors in the United States, starting from the fact that the FCPA placed unique constraints on US business. The re-launch of global claims was intrinsically connected to the criminalization approach established by the FCPA. Previous negotiations were not restricted to criminalization or even to establishing a definitive ban on transnational corrupt practices, but heralded primarily a disclosure approach, which would entail the 'right to know.' The re-launch of global claims at the OECD in 1989, therefore, served a different function than the failed exploratory talks of the 1970s, because it aimed at the specific task of internationalizing the FCPA. The function of the US global claims was, nonetheless, stated as essentially identical to the ones of the previous decades:

> The impetus to move on this issue came from the Congress which called on the executive branch in the Omnibus Trade bill of 1988 to work through the OECD to arrive at a common anti-bribery position. Now, some have asserted that the treaty does not go as far as it was hoped, but nevertheless it sets us on a course to pursue similar actions and efforts and other international arena and to broaden anti-corruption efforts in cooperation with our competitors. (Senator Sarbanes 1998)

The strategy to reach consensus at the OECD and build on it in other international forums was first proposed by representatives of the US executive in 1975 and was adopted again in 1989. The attempt to forge consensus with other economically powerful partners and then export this consensus on corrupt practices as a global problem to other international organizations and global institutions was successful in the 1990s. It determined, to a large extent, the definition of the problem and the mapping of the legitimate range of concerns and responses. In the process, the limited scope and 'individual actor paradigm' (Puckett 2010, 815), promoted by the FCPA, came to tacitly define global attitudes toward corruption as bribery. The tackling of the problem, predominantly understood as one of 'foreign corporate payments,' had to contribute to the global legitimization of the free market system and of multinational enterprises. Furthermore, how to reconcile fighting corruption with the objectives of liberalization, privatization and deregulation became issues of primary concern. The discussions about corrupt practices in the OECD in the 1990s were contextually different from the UN pre-negotiation talks in the 1970s, but were not less problematic. The United States had to persuade their competitors and partners from the Global North that corrupt payments, particularly in the form of bribery, constituted a problem, which had to be addressed multilaterally. The pre-negotiation talks at the OECD, which started in 1989, were central to forging a consensus on what constitutes and how to address the global problem of illicit or corrupt payments.

References

Bader, William (Professional Staff Member of the Senate Select Committee). 1975. "Testimony on S.Res.21. Hearings Before the Select Committee to Study Governmental Operations with Respect to Intelligence Activities." 94th Cong., December 4–5.

Biegelman, Martin T., and Daniel R. Biegelman. 2010. *Foreign Corrupt Practices Act Compliance Guidebook: Protecting Your Organization from Bribery and Corruption*. Hoboken, NJ: Wiley.

Brock, Bill. 1981. "An Official View: Bill Brock on U.S. Trade." *Washington Post*, May 20. Copy in the OECD Archives.

Church, Frank (Senator from the State of Idaho). 1975. "Testimony on S.Res.265. A Resolution to Protect the Ability of the United States to Trade Abroad Before the Senate Finance Committee, Subcommittee on International Trade." 94th Cong., 1st sess., October 6.

———. 1976. "Lockheed: Corporation or Political Actor?" Outline of Speech, Harvard University, Boston, MA, October 26. Accessed September 5, 2014. http://www.thecrimson.com/article/1976/10/26/lockheed-corporation-or-political-actor-pon/.

Cragg, Wesley, and William Woof. 2001. "Legislating Against Corruption in International Markets: The Story of the US Foreign Corrupt Practices Act." In *The Political Economy of Corruption*, edited by Arvind K. Jain, 180–214. London: Routledge.

———. 2002. "The U.S. Foreign Corrupt Practices Act: A Study of Its Effectiveness." *Business and Society Review* 107 (1): 98–144.

Dent, Frederick (Special Representative for Trade Negotiations). 1975. "Testimony on S.Res.265. A Resolution to Protect the Ability of the United States to Trade Abroad Before the Senate Finance Committee, Subcommittee on International Trade." 94th Cong., 1st sess., October 6.

Fisher, Louis. 2014. *The Law of the Executive Branch: Presidential Power*. Oxford: Oxford University Press.

Ford, Gerald. 1976. "Statement on the Task Force on Questionable Corporate Payments Abroad." *The American Presidency Project*, March 31. Accessed 22 September, 2014. http://www.presidency.ucsb.edu/ws/?pid=5773.

———. 1979. *Public Papers of the Presidents of the United States: Gerald R. Ford, Containing the Public Messages, Speeches, and Statements of the President 1976–1977*. Washington, DC: Government Printing Office.

Gutterman, Ellen. 2013. "Easier Done Than Said: Transnational Bribery, Norm Resonance, and the Origins of the US Foreign Corrupt Practices Act." *Foreign Policy Analysis* 11 (8): 109–128.

Hacker, Jacob S., and Paul Pierson. 2010. "Winner-Take-All Politics: Public Policy, Political Organization, and the Precipitous Rise of Top Incomes in the United States." *Politics & Society* 38 (2): 152–204. https://doi.org/10.1177/0032329210365042.

Hersh, Seymour. 1974a. "C.I.A. Is Linked to Strikes in Chile That Beset Allende." *The New York Times*, September 20.

———. 1974b. "Huge C.I.A. Operation Reported in U.S. Against Antiwar Forces, Other Dissidents in Nixon Years." *The New York Times*, December 22.

Hills, Roderick. 1976. "Address by SEC Chairman Roderick M. Hills to the Association of the Bar." Association of the Bar, New York, March 15. Accessed March 12, 2014. https://www.sec.gov/news/speech/1976/031576hills.pdf.

IME/M(77)1, *Summary Record of the Twelfth Meeting Held on 14–15 February, 1977* (March 9, 1977) OECD Archives, Paris Headquarters.

International Chamber of Commerce. *Extortion and Bribery in Business Transactions: Report Adopted by the 131st Session of the Council of the ICC, 29 November 1977*. Paris: International Chamber of Commerce.

Koehler, Mike. 2012. "The Story of the Foreign Corrupt Practices Act." *Ohio State Journal* 73: 930–1013.

———. 2014. *The Foreign Corrupt Practices Act in a New Era*. Northampton, MA: Edward Elgar.

Neild, R. R. 2002. *Public Corruption: The Dark Side of Social Evolution*. London: Anthem Press.

OAS Resolution 154 (167/75), Permanent Council Resolution on the Behaviour of Transnational Enterprises Operating in the Region and the Need for a Code of Conduct to Be Observed by Such Enterprises, OEA/SerG, CP/RES 154 (10 July, 1975). Reprinted in *American Society of International Law* 14 (5) (September 1975): 1326–1328.

Organization for Economic Co-operation and Development. 1976. *The OECD Guidelines for Multinational Enterprises.* Paris: Organization for Economic Co-Operation and Development.

Pieth, Mark. 2007. "Introduction." In *The OECD Convention on Bribery: A Commentary*, edited by Mark Pieth, Lucinda A. Low, and Peter J. Cullen, 3–42. Cambridge: Cambridge University Press.

Posadas, Alejandro. 2000. "Combating Corruption Under International Law." *Duke Journal of Comparative & International Law* 10 (2): 345–414.

Proxmire, William. 1976. "Release from Senator William Proxmire on Legislation Outlawing Bribes to Foreign Government Officials." Wisconsin, March 12. Accessed September 12, 2014. http://www.sechistorical.org/museum/galleries/wwr/wwr04b-three-criminalization.php.
Puckett, Blake. 2010. "Clans and the Foreign Corrupt Practices Act: Individualized Corruption Prosecution in Situations of Systemic Corruption." *Georgetown Journal of International Law* 41 (4): 815.
Reed, Travis (Assistant Secretary of Commerce for Domestic and International Business Administration). 1975. "Testimony on S.Res.265. A Resolution to Protect the Ability of the United States to Trade Abroad before the Senate Finance Committee, Subcommittee on International Trade." 94th Cong., 1st sess., October 6.
Ribicoff, Abraham (Chairman of the Subcommittee on International Trade). 1975. "Hearing on S.Res.265. A Resolution to Protect the Ability of the United States to Trade Abroad Before the Senate Finance Committee, Subcommittee on International Trade." 94th Cong., 1st sess., October 6.
Sarbanes, Paul S. 1998. "Convention on Combating Bribery of Foreign Public Officials in International Business Transactions." Committee on Foreign Relations, 105th Congress 2nd Session, to Accompany Treaty Doc, 105–143, July 16 (Text from: *Federation of American Scientists, Intelligent Resource Program*).
Schmults, Edward to Gerald Ford, Memorandum for the President. 1976. "Questionable Foreign Payments by U.S. Companies," February 24.
SEC Report. 1976. Report of the Securities and Exchange Commission on Questionable and Illegal Corporate Payments and Practices, Submitted to the Senate Banking, Housing and Urban Affairs Committee, May 12. Accessed April 14, 2018. http://3197d6d14b5f19f2f440-5e13d29c4c016cf96cbbf-d197c579b45.r81.cf1.rackcdn.com/collection/papers/1970/1976_0512_SECQuestionable.pdf.
SEC Report. 2017. "Three Approaches, One Law: Foreign Corrupt Practices Act of 1977 and Related Museum Resources." Accessed October 22. http://www.sechistorical.org/museum/galleries/wwr/wwr04b-three-criminalization.php.
Sporkin, Stanley. 2003. "Securities and Exchange Commission Oral Histories with Stanley Sporkin." Interview by Irving Pollack, September 23, edited transcript. Accessed May 22, 2014. http://www.sechistorical.org/museum/galleries/wwr/wwr04a-three-illicit.php.
UN General Assembly, 30th Session. 1975. "Resolution 3514: (Measures Against Corrupt Practices of Transnational and Other Corporations, Their Intermediaries and Others Involved)" December 15, 69–70 in *Resolutions Adopted on the Reports of the Second Committee* (A/RES/3514). New York.

US Congress House. Committee on International Economic Policy. 1975. *The Activities of American Multinational Corporations Abroad: Hearing Before the Subcommittee on International Economic Policy of the Committee on International Relations.* 94th Cong., 1st sess., June 5.

US Congress House. 1977. *Unlawful Corporate Payments Act of 1977: Report to Accompany H.R. 3815 to September 28, 1977.* 95th Cong., 1st sess. H. Doc. 604.

US Senate. 1973. "Hearings before the Subcommittee on Multinational Corporations. The International Telephone and Telegraph Company and Chile 1970–1971." Part I, March 20–April 2. Accessed September 1, 2018. https://babel.hathitrust.org/cgi/pt?id=mdp.39015003294462;view=1up;seq=1.

US Senate. Committee on Finance. 1975. *S.Res.265. A Resolution to Protect the Ability of the United States to Trade Abroad: Hearing Before the Subcommittee on International Trade of the Committee on Finance.* 94th Cong., 1st sess., October 6.

CHAPTER 6

The Road to the New Orthodoxy

In the 1980s, a counterrevolution that re-configured the relationship between state and market took place. The history of neoliberalism as a technical fix would stress the role of stagflation in the 1970s and the emergence of monetarism as a functional correction to the presumed failure of Keynesianism. As Stedman Jones (2014) argues, this might have been the case with monetarist policies, but adopting the doctrine of unfettered markets was a little more perplexing. The idea that the free market provides the best mechanism for allocating resources, of course, delegitimized the role of the state as defender of the public interest against the excesses of global corporate profit maximization. In fact, the neoliberal turn of the 1980s stressed the role of the state in constructing the right framework for business to operate, as the main objective of governance.

The anti-corruption debates in international organizations are perhaps not unrelated to these processes. The 1990s witnessed the transformation of anti-corruption debates from 'bad business' to 'bad government' (Jakobi 2013, 243). The objectives of regulating multinationals internationally and preventing the corruption of the public interest appeared to be relics of the past. If in the 1970s anti-corruption debates were dominated by the problem of corporations as political agents, in the 1990s the role of the state as economic agent came center stage. The Global South lost its strategic importance with the end of the Cold War, but also much changed with the Third-World foreign debt crisis, which became

E. Katzarova, *The Social Construction of Global Corruption*,
Political Corruption and Governance,
https://doi.org/10.1007/978-3-319-98569-5_6

apparent by the early 1980s. The set of structural adjustment programs imposed on debtor countries was starting to work its magic in converting the Global South to neoliberalism. Yet, the UN venues dominated by developing countries, such as the UNCTAD, the G77 and the UNCTC, continued to argue for regulatory activism in the developing world.

The US-sponsored issue of bribery was now re-introduced as a problem of corruption in the developing world. The formal appeal by the US delegation to the OECD to revisit the issue of illicit payments took place in the first months of 1989, before the formal end of the Cold War. Yet, the US drive to convince other major competitors from the Global North to ban transnational bribery could not have but intensified with the prospect of new markets opening up in the East.

Talks at the OECD After 1989: The Positions of Member States

The re-launch of formal claims to address corruption or bribery as a global problem was made by the US delegation at the OECD during a Special Session of the Executive Committee, held on February 28 and March 1, 1989. The US proposed a feasibility study, or an 'inventory of relevant legislation' on illicit payments to be completed through a questionnaire, distributed to member states (C(89)49, 1). The US delegation insisted that further work be carried out by an ad hoc committee, with a small group of legal experts from member states (to be agreed by the OECD Council). The US proposal emphasized the need for an ad hoc group because the issue did not allegedly fit neatly into the standing committees (such as the International Investment and Multinational Enterprises) and also would have interfered with the work and financial resources of other committees since it needed special (mostly legal) expertise.[1] As Spector and Kitsuse (2009) observe, the tactic of establishing an ad hoc group allows for the institutional independence of discussions of the problem and is therefore more conducive to reaching a successful outcome.

[1]The proposal stated that illicit payments constitute a 'broad but discrete subject' and this is why it demanded special attention. The US delegation also suggested that legal expertise is of primary importance in this case: 'We would anticipate that the necessary experts – primary legal experts – would come largely from capitals and would have different sorts of expertise from the officials who attend meetings of the standing committees' (C(89)49, 2).

The US proposal provided a succinct background report on the FCPA and the consequences of the 1988 Omnibus Trade and Competitiveness Act. It also briefly touched on concerns about jurisdictional reach and the contested definition of the problem. The proposal urged swift action and the adoption of a binding treaty that would administer civil and criminal penalties on transgressors from the OECD member states.[2] The document clarified, however, that such practices were not the sole prerogative of OECD nations:

> Bribery is a problem for many countries, not just those of the OECD. But as the U.S. Congress recognized, the OECD has a long history of setting an example for others. In our view, this organization is well suited to examine this problem. OECD members have a common interest in showing they are committed to ethical business practices abroad by their nationals. Moreover, the OECD has the experience and the facilities to serve as a forum for the negotiation of an agreement on illicit payments. (C(89)49, 2)

The US appeal for action was not limited to developed nations and sought to universalize the significance of a future OECD agreement on illicit payments. In fact, US claims concentrated on developing nations as the beneficiaries of such reforms. Economic development in the Third World and economic efficiency for industrialized nations smoothly coalesced in US claims. The universalization of the claims served three primary purposes. First, it was a continuation of the strategy of building consensus among developed nations and exporting it to other organizations with a wider membership base. Second, it helped make the claims less controversial because it presented bribery as a problem of efficiency for both developed and developing nations; for the developed nations, it was imposing undue costs, and for the developing nations, it was causing political instability and was hindering development. Third, the United

[2]The US proposal envisioned a binding international treaty that would harmonize international legal provisions in accordance with the US law: 'The goal of an international agreement would be to ensure that individuals and enterprises in OECD member states are subject to comparable national legal standards governing bribery in conducting international commercial transactions. The central element of such agreement would be a binding obligation by members to enact appropriate civil, administrative and criminal penalties to punish their nationals and corporations who commit bribery in connection with such transactions' (C(89)49, 2).

needed to universalize the claims and to reach a degree of consensus and a global legitimization of the issue because of the transnational nature of corrupt transactions. Without the cooperation of developing nations for information exchange, even a convention targeting only OECD members would not have been implementable.

As we saw in the previous chapter, the United States wanted to take a firm stance against corrupt practices internationally in the 1970s, but failed to convince developing nations in the UN that they had a stake in fighting corrupt payments understood as bribery. Bringing developing nations on board with a broad mandate to address corrupt practices internationally was still needed in the 1990s. Furthermore, presenting the question as a development prerogative was deflecting controversial claims. Playing the development card in an organization with membership from only developed states became a basic strategy in the pre-negotiation talks:

> The issue of illicit payments also is relevant to the OECD's overall concern for the developing world. This organization has long recognized the importance of maintaining a corruption-free environment for international commerce. The use of bribery in international commerce not only poses ethical problems, it also hinders the development of international commerce by adding undue transaction costs and restricting the operation of free and open markets. The United States believes that an international agreement would serve the purpose of eliminating so far as possible bribery and other payments that are both illegal and costly to enterprises and that are disruptive to political stability and sound economic development in developing countries. (C(89)152, 17)

The Council approved the US proposal (already backed by the Secretary-General). A group of experts was formed, which consulted for the first time on a draft questionnaire to be distributed to member states on June 15, 1989, and returned to the Secretariat by October 31, 1989. The preliminary definition of illicit payments was: 'payments or other benefits offered or paid with a view to facilitate commercial transactions.' The question of the political impact of such transactions was dropped altogether, and it was assumed that corporations make such payments with strictly commercial purpose. The questionnaire probed national and transnational bribery legislation as well as issues pertaining to extraterritorial jurisdiction and the tax deductibility of bribes (C(89)49, 22). After the completion of the study in June 1990, the Secretary-General produced a Note about illicit (corrupt) payments in international commercial transactions. This report set the framework for discussion in the following years and also put the problem into comparative and historical perspectives. The study of what were the main factors that caused the failure of the previous talks in the UN and the OECD guaranteed institutional continuity and also pinpointed the most controversial issues that could interfere with the progress in the current talks. The main obstacles were judged to be of a legal and political nature. Referring to previous international attempts at abolishing such practices and in particular the attempt to draft a convention to criminalize corrupt payments, the report stated that in terms of legal obstacles:

> No other general international convention had made criminals of corporations, and this novelty created some of the problems that arose in the course of the negotiations[...] Difficulties of a legal nature were mostly in connection with the issue of territorial jurisdiction. As illicit payments involve activities in several states, effective control would involve concurrent action in these states. As is shown above this was not in accordance with most countries criminal statues against bribery, which generally seek to protect mainly the integrity of their own national officials. Jurisdiction over acts committed abroad is asserted only exceptionally. (C(90)87, 5)

Corporate criminal liability and extraterritorial application of national laws were designated as the two issues of primary concern in the past and would prove to be problematic in future OECD talks on the subject as well. The Secretary's Note examined the principal unresolved legal aspects of addressing corrupt payments at the UN, which were: the issue of extraterritoriality and the publication of payments. However, pending issues of political nature were judged to be: references to 'illegal minority regimes in Southern Africa' and the entanglement of the issue of corrupt payments with the negotiation of a binding Code of Conduct for Multinational Enterprises.

> Political problems also appeared. An article concerning the prohibition of making royalty or tax payments to the 'illegal minority regimes in Southern Africa,' firmly supported by the G77, was opposed by OECD countries. Also, throughout the negotiations, the G77, insisted that corrupt practices involving transnational corporations should only be regulated within the context of the 'Code of Conduct of transnational corporations.' This led to a deadlock. (C(90)87, 33)

As it was already discussed in Chapter 4, both issues were indicative of the different understanding that developing nations had of corrupt practices. Expanding the definition of corrupt practices to include other payments with political impact is reflected in the issue of tax payments to the apartheid regime: 'The article concerning the prohibition from making royalty or tax (p)ayments to the 'illegal minority regimes' in Southern Africa was firmly supported by the G77 and especially by Uganda, Venezuela and Argentina. OECD countries constantly opposed this article' (C(90)87 Annex 2, 41). Even more importantly, developing nations insisted on the issue of bribery, which was introduced by the United States to be regulated within the Code of Conduct because a broader regulatory effort was deemed necessary to counteract what can sometimes be a corruptive influence of multinationals on politics and national development objectives.

Examining the reasons for the deadlock, the report pointed out one striking element of the opposition between developing and developed nations: 'In fact, few developing countries demonstrated interest in the issue, which they perceived as of special concern to some industrialized counties' (C(90)87 Annex 2, 41). The puzzle as to why the developing nations did not show particular concern for the problem narrowly defined as bribery can be approached in a number of ways. Elites of developing nations could have shown lack of interest in addressing the problem of transnational bribery, in which they were in fact implicated, and their disinterest constituted a disingenuous attempt to continue said corrupt practices uninhibited. As the discussions at the UN had previously revealed, however, developing nations did not show particular concern for bribery per se, but lodged claims that there was a more fundamental problem with the influence that Western investment interests and state-sponsored corporate bribery had over their political processes. They demanded that the question of corrupt payments be examined within the broader context of setting different terms of global trade, a strategy that was opposed by developed nations and in particular the United States.

The OECD members were meant to put a common front at the UN, but the significance of the question of transnational bribery did not have unequivocal support within the group. Nevertheless, in 1979 a decision was reached to sign an OECD agreement in case the UN talks faltered:

> Upon the request of the United States, consultations were held among OECD countries in Paris from 31st May to 2nd June 1978 with a view to harmonising these countries positions in the UN Committee. In spite of the efforts made mainly by the US delegation, no consensus was reached on a common declaration setting forth the basic elements of a treaty on illicit payments and proposing to convene a conference of plenipotentiaries in 1979 to conclude that treaty. In the 1980 Venise [*sic*] Summit Communiqué, however, the attending governments committed themselves to the ongoing UN effort and pledged, in the event that initiatives faltered, to conclude an agreement among themselves with the same objective. (C(90)87 Annex 2, 37)

The G7 Summit took place from June 22 to 23, 1980, in Venice, Italy, and considered the question of illicit payments as part of its trade agenda and the final communiqué made the political commitment that the G7 members would pursue the question further:

> As a further step in strengthening the international trading system, we commit our governments to work in the United Nations toward an agreement to prohibit illicit payments to foreign government officials in international business transactions. If that effort falters, we will seek to conclude an agreement among our countries, but open to all, with the same objective. (Venice G7 Summit Communiqué VI: 3)

This political commitment, however, did not prove to be stable. The United States appeared as the only state actor with a strong interest in addressing the question of illicit payments. The choice to tackle the problem unilaterally with the adoption of the FCPA, and without consultation with other negotiating partners, further complicated the matter and alienated the hesitant partners in the developed world. The adoption of the FCPA was viewed unfavorably by other OECD members, despite the fact that it put their multinational corporations at a competitive advantage, because it showed that the US government was unilaterally making decisions about addressing the corrupt payments problem, decisions that it was later intending to impose on other countries. As Pieth (1999) explained, the other partners were suspicious of a hegemonic trade agenda, so despite the impasse at the UN, OECD members did not pursue the issue any further:

> The draft agreement was not finalized because of divergences between participants. In addition to the draft agreement, the Economic and Social Council formulated two draft resolutions on the subject and decided to transmit them to the General Assembly. The General Assembly agreed in 1979 to take no decision on them at that time. No further action has been taken since. (C(90)87 Annex 2, 37)

The talks in the 1990s reopened in the shadow of the impasse from the 1970s, but also as an outstanding issue to be resolved by OECD members. By stressing that the issue of corrupt practices was awaiting settlement for over a decade, in 1990 the Reports of the Secretary-General reopened the debate as an unresolved issue in need of settlement. The Recommendations to the Council suggested a wide mandate and two possible courses of action. The first was in accordance with the US proposal to pursue an international solution through the negotiation of a treaty, and the second was a softer approach of fortifying the already existing national legislation and supplementing it with a set of voluntary guidelines, such as a revised version of the Guidelines on Multinational Enterprises. Furthermore, the US proposal for the creation of an ad hoc group to tackle the issue was countered by the option of CIME taking on the mandate, as it did in 1975. The Secretary-General Note concluded that:

> The problem of prohibited practices, otherwise called corrupt practices, including payments, bribery, extortion and other similar practices, is a universal phenomenon with deep roots and a long history. It poses serious political, economic, social, legal, and moral challenges. With the development of international exchanges, instances of corruption have resurfaced in a dramatic manner, causing serious embarrassment and attracting widespread concern. (C(90)87 Annex 2, 36)

At this preliminary stage of discussion, three primary concerns developed as justification for a course of action at the international level. The first was a concern for developing nations, which had failed to understand their stake in agreeing to accept the so-defined problem of corrupt payments. The second was a preoccupation with economic efficiency and the financial losses that bribery, in particular, was incurring on the global economy. The third was about publicity and the 'embarrassment' factor pertaining not to the actual harm corrupt payments were causing, but to how revelations of their existence were causing international outrage.

During the early stages of discussions, however, OECD member states remained unconvinced of the seriousness the US delegation was attaching to the issue of bribery. As Mark Pieth, who was to become the Chairman of the OECD Working Group on Bribery in International Business Transactions, stated: 'the reactions of other OECD members were at best reserved' (1997, 119). After the Council in March 1989, the US representative forcefully re-established the US interest in the subject during the Council Session on May 21, 1990, referring to his government's plan to 'approach capitals to reiterate its interest in the matter' (C/M(90)13(Prov.)). The US representative claimed that 'increased awareness' or 'consciousness' of the problem of corrupt payments in the developing world is a signal that OECD members should do whatever is in their power to curb bribery in international business transactions:

> The United States believed that OECD governments had a common interest in seeing that business entities based in OECD countries avoided illicit payments, for reasons that were well known: trade problems and persistent problems in foreign relations emerged when such payments came to light. Mr. Lamb thought that there was increasing consciousness of the problem of corruption in economic development in the third world, and that whatever could be done to eliminate illicit payments could help countries address at least part of the problem of corruption of which all were perhaps more aware today and more willing to address openly. (C/M(90)13(Prov.), 6)

The US representative, Denis Lamb, was tactfully presenting the problem of corrupt payments as damaging for developing countries, evading in this way potentially controversial discussions about the involvement of OECD members in such practices. At the same time, the absence of developing nations at an international forum such as the OECD appeared to be a fortunate condition for addressing the issue properly as it could have obliterated many of the hindrances encountered at the UN:

> The United States recognized that dealing with illicit payments on an international basis was not easy, as had been amply demonstrated by the lack of progress in the United Nations. Nevertheless western governments had made progress in recent years in attacking controversial problems such as money laundering, and they would urge the OECD to set a comparable example in addressing illicit payments. (7)

The United States considered the OECD to be the most appropriate forum for tackling this 'generally acknowledged problem' and recognizing the resistance of some delegations, agreed to a broad mandate but insisted on the establishment of an ad hoc group. The Canadian delegation provided vague agreement, without commitment to the outcome, and was specifically against the issue as an extraterritorial offense. Canada also preferred future work to be carried out within CIME rather than an ad hoc group. The representative of Switzerland was skeptical of the feasibility of a legally binding agreement and the UK delegation saw no merit in further work on the subject altogether. The UK argumentation was that national laws were adequate and domestic legislation could remedy the insufficiencies. Insurmountable issues with extraterritorial application of laws and double jeopardy were coupled with the demand for additional resources that could be put toward more urgent matters. According to the UK delegation even if action on the international scale was agreed on, the rules could not be effectively applied domestically. The UK position was backed by Germany with some unspecified reservations.

Spain, the Netherlands and Turkey were in favor of a UN treaty. The Netherlands in particular showed a strong preference for a universal treaty and raised the issue at the UN at the end of 1989.[3] Spain, Australia, Greece, Denmark, New Zealand, Belgium, Italy, Sweden, the Netherlands and Japan also favored CIME as the future forum for work on illicit payments. Only the Austrian and Finnish delegations showed explicit support for an ad hoc group, but Austria had a problem with the extraterritorial application of national laws. Iceland, while generally supportive, demanded further clarification on the definition of 'illicit payments' 'or what exactly – among a multitude of business practices constituted an illicit payment' (C/M(90)13(Prov.), 12). The delegations of Greece, Belgium, Sweden and Norway were more supportive of the US proposal, while Australia, Luxembourg and Ireland demonstrated skepticism over the proposed endeavor. The Greek delegation in particular claimed that illicit payments and illicit receipts were part of the game in international economic relations, but such practices undermined international competition. The Irish position was skeptical but: 'That was not to say that the Irish authorities did not recognize that there was a very serious problem' (11). The problem, however, remained national and the

[3]Attention to this process is given in the following UN section.

extraterritoriality inherent to the US international solution was considered inappropriate:

> The problem of extraterritoriality was one which was not confined to this particular issue: the difficulties which had occurred in a number of other aspects of international law were well known, when countries tried to solve a problem which essentially was one which should first be dealt with at home by reaching out into the legal systems of other countries. The question of illicit payments, Mr. O'Sullivan thought, was a field that would prove to be immensely complex and difficult to tackle. (C/M(90)13(Prov.), 11)

While the governments of the French and Italian delegations had not yet finalized their positions, the Italian delegation was principally opposed to extraterritoriality and requested information about the reaction of the US Congress to the OECD discussions so far, as well as more information on the overall US strategy. The US delegation's response was that members of Congress were very invested in the issue and reasonably satisfied by OECD developments. However, a conclusive decision had not been made about the feasibility of an international agreement or what kind of action the organization and its members intended to take. In light of the expressed opinions, the Chairman of the OECD Council was hesitant about the prospects of success and 'whether something could be done and if so, whether it would be better to envisage a binding or a non-binding instrument' (13).

The United States faced a difficult task of persuading partners at the OECD that illicit payments, defined as bribery in international business transactions, was a matter of global concern. The US government had maneuvered itself into competitive disadvantage and despite the lax implementation of the FCPA, American businesses were facing more uncertainty with the expansion toward new markets after the fall of the iron curtain in 1989, a problem of competitiveness that the Omnibus Act was trying to remedy. The US President had made a commitment to submit a progress report on the work done on illicit payments by August 1991, but the reservations that other OECD members had, as to how important was this issue, made progress incremental (DAFFE/IME/M/(91)1). The political clout of the United remained the most important factor for progress, but also the ability to 'lock' the issue in a working group guaranteed institutional continuity that ensured the problem would not be written off the agenda. Managing controversy became an essential task for the Working Group and aided the US delegation to ultimately forge consensus on corrupt payments.

The OECD Ad Hoc Working Group and Controversy Management

The role of the Working Group, under the auspices of CIME, was essential in foreseeing and managing controversies arising in the OECD Council. The Ad Hoc Group constituted not of independent experts, but of delegates from national capitals and was therefore similar to the constitution of the Council. The delegates were from Ministries of Justice and Finance, Ministries of the Economy, central banks, foreign investment departments, etc. The United States had the most delegates (4)—from the SEC, the Department of Justice, the Department of State and the Permanent delegation to the OECD (DAFFE/IME/PI(91)3). At least initially, the delegates did not strictly represent relative size of the states or financial contribution, but to some extent reflected the level of investment in the issue of illicit payments. The German and the UK delegations, which were both outspokenly opposed to addressing the issue, had just one delegate each from the Ministry of the Economy (Germany) and the Department of Trade and Industry (United Kingdom).

The selection of national, predominantly legal experts, with a broad competence, rather than independent anti-corruption consultants influenced the content and direction of discussions. As Spector and Kitsuse (2009) note, the selection of the members of a working group is not a self-evident choice, but a political one. The selection of sociologists, economists or legal experts already tints the problem in the shade of the expertise that the delegates are expected to provide. The discussions in the Ad Hoc Group on Illicit Payments, therefore, had a decisively legal character and concentrated on the problem of legal feasibility, leaving the decisions, as to the substance of the problem, to member states. This strategy helped the management of controversies arising from the discussion of the ethical, economic and political consequences of corrupt practices. At the same time, the question of legal feasibility became an intrinsic part of the process of definition and the measures taken against the issue. Further work in the framework of the OECD was judged dependent on the attainability of consensus and the practicability of the proposed solutions. This trend had an influence on the scope and definition of the offense with the boundaries of what constituted 'illicit payment' remaining fluid and fuzzy during the discussions. These developments are in line with the argument that practicability and feasibility constitute an intrinsic part of the decision whether there is a 'problem' that demands a collective response (Spector and Kitsuse 2009). At the international level, matters of feasibility are further complicated by competing claims that policy measures are better left to the discretion of individual nation states, and should not become the center of concerted global action. The national principle in the selection of experts for the ad hoc group increases the propensity to consider the problem to be a national prerogative rather than a subject for international measures.

Contact was initiated with consultants for a feasibility study to examine options for international cooperation on illicit payments (DAFFE/IME/PI(91)2, 4). The ad hoc group convened in June 1991 to discuss a Feasibility Study on Available International Means for Dealing with Illicit Payments in International Commercial Transactions (DAFFE/IME/PI(91)1). It had to issue a report by the end of the year, which, after revision, would be sent to the Council as a CIME report (DAFFE/IME/PI(91)4, 5). The ad hoc group divided the options into five categories: (1) multilateral treaty, (2) bilateral agreements, (3) decision of the council, (4) national laws and (5) non-obligatory codes of conduct (DAFFE/IME/PI(91)2).

First, the choice of a multinational convention, especially with an emphasis on criminalization, was pitched as the most effective measure for the prevention of illicit payments. The problem of reaching the 'highest level of consensus' associated with this measure, however, made this option difficult to achieve. The lack of a wide-reaching consensus at the UN in the 1970s was provided as a case in point. Second, the bilateral arrangements had to 'include agreements between OECD Member States and countries where public corruption appeared prevalent; agreements among OECD Member States on taxation issues and mutual judicial assistance; and agreements to implement, enforce, or fill gaps in other international instruments' (DAFFE/IME/PI(91)2). The third option in the form of an OECD Council Decision could have been adopted in combination with other measures and/or with the establishment of an international monitoring body or formal consultation process. The fourth option of revising national laws could have been done with a model law that would encourage reform of national laws or with a recommendation to 'take appropriate measures' and was a highly feasible option because it demanded a 'lower level of consensus' (DAFFE/IME/PI(91)2, 3). Since the OECD and ICC had already issued guidelines on corrupt payments, reinforcing and endorsing those voluntary guidelines remained the last option.

Despite the fact that the definitional boundaries of the offense remained ambiguous and unspecified throughout the talks, the Ad Hoc Group claimed that consensus existed on the principle that bribery should not be taking place between enterprises and members of foreign governments. Singling the United States as the only state that had enacted legislation against such transactions, the Group reaffirmed that the choice of the term 'illicit payments' also came from US legislative debates. However, consensus as to whether illicit payments were to be addressed internationally remained a challenge. Discussing the failure at the UN and the insufficient impact of the ICC Guidelines, the Report affirmed that:

> The lack of success in finding an effective international solution to the illicit payments problem appears to reflect a lack of consensus on a fundamental point: is it appropriate and feasible to proscribe corrupt arrangements between private enterprises and the public officials of other sovereign states? The United States has long urged that the answer to this question should be affirmative, so long as a recognized basis exists for exercising prescriptive jurisdiction. Other nations, however, have repeatedly urged that efforts to police another state's governmental processes would constitute an impermissible assertion of "extraterritorial" jurisdiction or, at least, officious and self-righteous intermeddling. (DAFFE/IME/PI(91)2, 4)

This lack of consensus reflected a fundamental disagreement on whether the issue could and should be tackled through the transnational measures proposed by the United States. The question of feasibility became intertwined with the question of 'globality' because other OECD member states disagreed with the claim that illicit payments, defined as bribes, should be tackled outside the borders of nation states and saw the problem as a national one. How the anti-corruption initiative would be received beyond the OECD area was another area of contestation. While previous efforts to tackle bribery were met with the opposition of non-OECD members, the ad hoc group claimed that the tide had turned for developing nations, which had come to appreciate the deleterious effect that corruption had on their social and economical systems and were less likely to oppose an OECD initiative, like they did in the 1970s: 'they (developing nations) may, as a group feel less aggrieved by a joint effort of the OECD Member States to prevent illicit payments in international commercial transactions' (5). This position was already taking into consideration the recent UN Economic and Social Council Official Records

Decision 111/104 which recommended 'that all nations take appropriate means in combating corruption of public officials,' as well as the proceedings of the International Seminar on Corruption in Government, which took place in The Hague (11–15 December 1989, 3–19).

The Ad Hoc Group's Report is indicative of the importance of feasibility in the construction of social problems. This feasibility works on two levels. The first level is administrative, and it pertains to the effectiveness that the proposed measure would have in terms of compliance and presumed efficacy in ameliorating the condition.[4] The second is political feasibility, and it pertains to the likelihood of reaching a final agreement. The interplay between what is feasible in terms of political consensus and what is effective in terms of addressing a putative condition becomes part of the makeup of the problem and the proposed solutions:

> In considering the options presented in this Discussion Paper, it is important to evaluate not only their intrinsic merits but also the extent of consensus likely to support them. In the past, there has been no consensus favoring strong international action to prevent illicit payments. An overriding issue is the extent to which such a consensus has now – or can be – developed. (DAFFE/IME/PI(91)2/REV1, 5–6)

The feasibility of reaching an agreement on the need for international action became an intrinsic part of the development of the putative condition into a global problem. Consensus on the severity of the condition, what it was, and what was the proper mode to handle it, was at the center of such debates. Different states or group of states had a diverging understanding of 'what is wrong' and what the best mode of handling the alleged problem was. The understanding of problems as natural conditions has created a success bias, which naturalizes the final definition of a putative condition, forsaking the divergent interpretations of the problem prior to institutionalization. The lack of consensus on illicit payments in the UN reflected a divergence in understanding what was problematic with the putative condition (which could

[4]As noted, the content and definition of the actual problem remained unspecified with the US definition of bribery being continuously challenged from other member states at the UN, the OECD and OAS. The preliminary documents made reference to broadly defined 'illicit payments'.

most broadly be defined as illicit interaction between public and private actors). This lack of consensus worked at different levels:

> Three draft UN Conventions failed to reach fruition because of a lack of consensus (1) between the developed and developing countries and (2) among the developed countries themselves. The lack of consensus between developed and developing countries is unlikely to reoccur (at least in the same form) in negotiating a multilateral convention among OECD Member States. The lack of consensus that emerged among the developed countries, however, is potentially more significant. Indeed, based on a review of the ECOSOC deliberations, one commentator has concluded that 'the bulk of the important struggle over the proposed convention has been between the United States on the one hand and the other OECD nations on the other. (DAFFE/IME/PI(91)2/REV1, 9)[5]

Because of the institutional continuity, the impact of the failed talks was weighing heavily on the new ones. The OECD work program also showed that in addition to taking into consideration previous efforts, international organizations may go to great lengths not to duplicate efforts by other international organizations on the same topic. The OECD talks in the 1970s were put on hold because the main forum for discussion had become the UN, and any further work at the OECD was made conditional on forging consensus at the UN. This development suggests that, as the US strategy stated, consensus is indeed 'transferable,' but also that the main institutional setting for the talks matters. The rationale behind the choice of venue in transnational litigation, also known as forum shopping (Bell 2003), was very much part of the choice of the OECD by the United States. The OECD provided favorable conditions because an agreement between its members to put a stop to transnational corrupt payments perpetuated by their corporations would have been easier than establishing consensus at the UN. As the Report of the Ad Hoc Group argued, the lack of consensus between the Global South and North would not be repeated in the same form. This was apparent for negotiations at the OECD where developing nations were not present; it also implied that the UN would not become the primary

[5]The reference was to a study published by Seymour in 1980 (Seymour, Bruce Illicit Payments in International Business: National Legislation). It is noteworthy that the studies made by Seymour (consisting mostly of the history of the pre-negotiation process in the UN) were the only broadly cited academic scholarship in the Group's Report.

forum for discussion. However, even if the OECD was to remain the central forum for work on illicit payments, the lack of consensus between the developed nations could be a serious hindrance.

In the 1990s, the United States was still isolated in its concern for bribery or illicit payments. This isolation raises the question as to why other developed nations appeared so blasé about said practices. Was the United States the beacon of moral fiber in international business? A more functional explanation would be that while in 1975, the United States had a problem with illicit payments, after 1977 it had a problem with the FCPA. The issue of bribery of foreign officials became a problem for the United States in its national legislative order, and in this sense, the problem of corrupt practices was a 'private trouble,' which the US executive was trying to turn into a global concern. This was applicable to an even greater extent after the re-launch of global claims in 1989, when the explicit mandate of the US executive was to internationalize the FCPA, particularly among developed nations. For other OECD states said practices did not become problematic, and therefore, it was the task of the United States to break this relative isolation and convince the other OECD member states to take the issue seriously.

The failed UN model of US action post-1977 provided one alternative for future work at the OECD:

> The draft UN illicit payments agreement provides one model for a multilateral convention among OECD Member States addressing the illicit payments problem. The U.N. approach was to draft a comprehensive criminalization convention designed to incorporate all mechanisms available to deter illicit payments in international transactions and to punish anyone engaging in corrupt practices. Effectively, it would have incorporated the U.S. Foreign Corrupt Practices Act, together with a number of additional enforcement mechanisms into international law. (DAFFE/IME/PI(91)2, 11)

As noted earlier, after the adoption of the FCPA in 1977, it was even more difficult for the United States, to convince its partners not only of the definition of illicit payments as bribery, but also of the adoption of a criminalization approach, which due to the extraterritorial character of the measure would allow the United States to police its application. On the one hand, this was because other OECD nations had an incentive to be free riders and not adopt the legislation that was imposing restrictions on US business. On the other hand, however, the adoption of the FCPA in the midst of talks at the UN and the OECD in the late 1970s showed that the US government was going ahead unilaterally with a widely contested issue and trying to impose the same definitions and solutions on other states. In fact, the problem that the United States had in the 1990s had more to do with the FCPA itself, rather than the corrupt practices per se. Nothing short of a multilateral convention criminalizing transnational bribery would have been a satisfactory outcome for the United States. Adopting a criminalization approach for other OECD members was the major objective. From the US perspective, the work of the Ad Hoc Group was important in steering the discussion toward the direction of a multilateral option or in case this was unfeasible, to direct attention to preliminary steps that would secure a basic level of consensus that would later be used as a basis for a multilateral legally binding agreement.

The discussion of the 'sub-options' of a criminalization convention involved a choice of remedies, and the advantages and disadvantages of the multilateral option were evaluated in terms of benefits and costs, a common model for US documents on the subject of illicit payments. The benefits of a multilateral convention would have been to prevent illicit payments more effectively, to level the playing field and cut unnecessary costs for business. In addition, the pros of a multilateral convention were deemed to be the binding nature of the agreement, uniform application and efficient enforcement mechanisms. The cons of the multilateral approach were that it was not flexible, it demanded a high level of consensus and it was difficult to change once adopted (DAFFE/IME/PI(91)2/REV1). The major costs of a multilateral convention would have been its inherent inflexibility and the prospect of future amendments:

> If the definition of "illicit payment" or a particular enforcement mechanism created unforeseen problems for one or more parties, they would have to persuade the other parties to agree to a change. As the recent amendment of the U.S. Foreign Corrupt Practices Act demonstrates, the definition and control of illicit payments can well require change in light of experience. (DAFFE/IME/PI(91)2/REV1, 14)

Even more relevant were the 'extrinsic problems' and the trade-off between effectiveness and feasibility. An agreement achieved at the expense of reservations would have been one likely outcome of a binding treaty that in any case would have been a multiannual project. The high degree of consensus that the adoption of a multilateral treaty required could have led to failure to pursue the issue further in any form as it had happened in the UN:

> As the experience of the draft UN convention shows, there may well be no consensus even among the OECD Member States on important elements of a criminalization convention. At worst, lack of consensus could result in failure to agree on any text to recommend for signature. Alternatively, lack of consensus might lead to agreement among only a subset of Member States which, for competitive reasons, might ultimately refuse to proceed on their own. (DAFFE/IME/PI(91)2, 5)

Characteristically, the feasibility of reaching consensus on addressing the problem became part of the discussion whether it was desirable to tackle the issue multilaterally: 'the most important consideration in determining whether to pursue a multilateral convention on illicit payments is the likelihood of success. For agreement to be reached, a broad political consensus must exist among Member States' (DAFFE/IME/PI(91)2/REV1, 15). The consensus was to go 'beyond agreement that illicit payments are reprehensible' and extend to the questions of extraterritorial jurisdiction and the proper measure to address illicit payments (15). Later, the development of a matrix presenting the controversies that may arise in pursuing an international agenda became the centerpiece of preliminary discussions. The reports reveal the extent to which the proposed solutions became part of the discussions about whether to address the condition. Feasibility, rather than an inquiry into the severity of the condition or its negative global impact, became the center of discussions in the Working Group. The following matrix was developed and revised multiple times in order to foresee any sources of controversy within the OECD member group (Table 6.1).

Controversies pertaining to the definition of corrupt practices beyond bribery were one source of difficulty. The US delegation insisted on a definition of corrupt payments as bribery, while the majority of OECD Members challenged this limitation. The question of corporate criminal liability was also deemed central. Other potentially controversial topics were questions about private agents as recipients, and the use of intermediaries, as well as government involvement in cases when official approval was needed for commercial transactions. The question of monitoring corporations was also deemed highly controversial, as it raised fears of

Table 6.1 Issue controversy

Issue	*Controversy*	*Comments*
Definition of offense as bribery	No	Has to be illegal under national jurisdiction
Definition including other illicit payments	Yes	Problems in adopting a definition beyond traditional bribery
Type of transaction—sale to governments	No	
Type of transaction—sales in need of government approval	Yes	
Purpose of payment	Yes	'Market conditioning' and other payments would become controversial
Public agents as recipients	No	
Private agents as recipients	Yes/No	Payments to private agents would be controversial, but will probably not be discussed as an option
Corporate payers	Yes	Criminal liability for corporations would be very controversial
Intermediaries	Yes	Payments through intermediaries would lead to controversy
Secondary offenses	Yes	It would be in conflict with the legislation of a number of MS to include conspiracy and other secondary offenses (in the case of criminalization)
Actions at the national level		
Criminalization of illicit payments	Yes	
Tax deductibility	Yes/No	The degree to which the issue of tax deductibility would be controversial depends on the definition of the offense
Disclosure and keeping records	Yes	A disclosure approach could become as controversial as criminalization depending on offense definition
Conditioning public actions	Yes	Similar considerations to disclosure
Civil measures	Yes	Caused problems at the UN
Territorial Jurisdiction	Yes	Very controversial in UN draft. A solution might be to define the offense so that it demands adequate territorial nexus
International measures		
Information exchange	No/Yes	

(continued)

Table 6.1 (continued)

Issue	*Controversy*	*Comments*
Mutual (administrative, civil, criminal) assistance	No	
Extradition	Yes/No	Extradition instruments already exist and the principle is not controversial
Monitoring MS	No	
Monitoring corporations	Yes	Entails delegation of sovereignty
Dispute resolution	Yes	Controversial at UN and ICC

Adapted from: DAFFE/IME/PI(92)3/ANN, DAFFE/IME/PI(91)2/REV1, DAFFE/IME/PI(91)7/ANN1

too much government involvement in the economy. A dispute resolution tribunal and securing compliance with the multilateral convention would have posed significant challenges. An opening through which to address the illicit payments indirectly came from the subject of tax deductibility of bribes, on which consensus appeared possible.

The draft matrix prepared by the Ad Hoc Group is revealing of the element of feasibility that is intrinsic to the construction of social problems, according to Spector and Kitsuse (2009). The matrix was regularly updated and became central to evaluating the trade-off between the administrative and political aspects of feasibility. Based on the matrix, the choice of convention appeared unfeasible according to the working group. The assumed unfeasibility of reaching a degree of consensus necessary for the adoption of a binding multilateral instrument was judged more important than the fact that a multilateral treaty would have been arguably the most effective measure against corrupt practices. Other measures that demanded a lesser degree of international consensus were therefore deemed necessary. Bilateral agreements came as a 'second best' alternative to a multinational treaty:

> Unlike multilateral conventions, which seek to create a multinational web of identical legal rules, bilateral agreements generally focus on matters of reciprocal interest between the two contracting states.[6] To assist its investigation of allegations that Lockheed Aircraft Corporation had made

[6]Prolific examples existed in the field of investment and double taxation, but it was unusual for such instruments to be used for criminalization of some forms of transnational behavior.

> illicit payments, the United States negotiated a series of ad hoc bilateral assistance arrangements in the 1970s. A series of much broader bilateral treaties followed, providing the assistance in locating witnesses, obtaining witness testimony, production and authentication of business records, and service of judicial and administrative documents in criminal matters. (DAFFE/IME/PI(91)7/ANN1, 4)

Four secondary options to bilateral agreements with host countries (defined as countries where corruption was 'prevalent') were developed. These bilateral agreements would have resolved the question of extra-territoriality, but were deemed politically unfeasible because the host country would have to implicitly admit the existence of endemic corruption on its territory. Therefore, it was judged that excluding developing nations and enacting a 'network of such bilateral undertakings among OECD Members (or a multilateral convention to that effect) might provide useful political cover for non-OECD countries to enter into such agreements' (DAFFE/IME/PI(91)7/ANN1, 17). This formulation implied that such agreements between OECD members would otherwise be completely superfluous, despite the fact that after the Lockheed affair the bilateral agreements enacted were precisely between OECD member states. This redirection of focus from the developed to the developing world once again was strategically keeping controversy under control by presenting the problem as one peculiar to developing countries.

At the same time, the question of tax deductibility of bribes was one of central importance to US interests because it was creating an even more acute disadvantage for American business. Option 2 was dedicated to this aspect of bribery and concerned Bilateral Tax Agreements dedicated to the treatment of the deductibility of illicit payments that could use the model OECD treaty on double taxation. Option 3 was Mutual Assistance Agreements (MOU) for the facilitation of current laws, but would have been helpful as a deterrent only in the United States. Finally, Option 4 constituted a combination of bilateral agreements with other measures such as a multilateral treaty or a voluntary code. The benefit of bilateral arrangements was that they were legally binding, yet could be easily adapted to specific needs (a MOU was even easier to negotiate and adopt, but was non-binding). The cons of bilateral agreements in 'non-host countries,' however, were significant because: 'Absent a parallel series of agreements making the same or similar rules applicable to all principal international competitors, non-host countries would be unlikely to agree bilaterally to prohibit their own nationals from competing for international business' (DAFFE/IME/PI(91)7/ANN1, 18). The disadvantages of expanding the web of bilaterals, created with the initiative of the United States after the Lockheed case, were deemed significant enough for this option to be deemed feasible but impractical. The third substantive option concerned an OECD Council Decision. This would have fallen under Art. 5(a) and 6 of the OECD Convention which entitles the Council to issue decisions by consensus that are binding, but do not demand ratification and allow for reservations. An OECD Decision could come in the form of a recommendation, but it had not been used to criminalize private actions. The advantages of a Council Decision and relevant sub-options would have been that they are phrased generally and are coupled easily with other options, which can lead to incremental progress in the given area (DAFFE/IME/PI(91)7/ANN1, 2).

The prospect of incremental action was advantageous because it would have allowed for a low degree of consensus in order to adopt a Recommendation with general language, leaving significant discretionary power for member states. The disadvantage was that Decisions had not been used previously for such substantial changes, such as the criminalization of private conduct. This option was, therefore, considered in combination with strengthening national laws (fourth substantial option). The advantage of taking this combination was that a Council Decision would make it easier to reach international consensus. This route allowed for flexibility and possibly increased effectiveness, because a multilateral treaty might lead to the lowest common denominator. The disadvantage was that legislation would remain 'spotty' (DAFFE/IME/PI(91)7/ANN1, 23).

The last and fifth substantial option concerned Codes of Conduct and voluntary Guidelines. This option was already explored with the 1976 OECD Guidelines, which included a reference to illicit payments. The ICC Guidelines, issued following the Shawcross Commission Report, 'Rules of Conduct to Combat Extortion and Bribery,' also established a panel to monitor the application of said rules; but any study of infringement had to secure the agreement of the accused enterprise, and the procedures were to remain undisclosed. The UN Guidelines also constituted a precedent. The OECD Guidelines and the Shawcross Report both took less than 2 years to be concluded, but the UN Code of Conduct on Transnational Corporations took more than 15 years of talks and remained inconclusive. This raised questions about the trade-off between the velocity of adoption and the effectiveness of the measures. The advantages of the non-binding measures were that they were faster to negotiate and could provide good ground for further work. Experience showed low efficacy of such measures, however, except for the practice of courts to make use of the guidelines and treat them as international norms. Precedents existed with non-binding instruments on money-laundering. To the extent that such guidelines were already enacted and seemed to be of little consequence, this option was also considered feasible, but unlikely to be effective.

The talks on corrupt payments at the OECD in the period 1989–1994 were to a large extent dominated by the impasse of the 1970s. Managing controversy and deciding on the trade-off between effectiveness and feasibility became the dominant goals of the pre-negotiation talks in the early 1990s and the options for future work were each examined against these criteria. Unlike the 1970s, however, the OECD remained the primary venue for discussions on policy solutions to corrupt practices with the UN retaining a subsidiary position.

Talks at the UN After 1980: Economic Crime and Good Management

After the US delegation raised the question of illicit payments at the OECD during the Special Session of the Executive Committee on February 28, 1989, another OECD member state found a less formal channel to re-launch the debates at the UN. The government of the Netherlands, which during the OECD Council meetings expressed a strong preference for a universal treaty, hosted an Interregional Seminar on Corruption in Government as a preparatory meeting for the 8th UN Congress on the Prevention of Crime and the Treatment of Offenders. The Interregional Seminar took place on December 11–15, 1989, in The Hague, and was attended by officials from 18 developing countries and 8 developed countries as observers, as well as representatives from academia, NGOs and other independent anti-corruption organizations. The Seminar participants drafted an anti-corruption manual that was presented at the 8th Congress on crime prevention.

The UN Congresses on Prevention of Crime, which took place every five years, had continuously discussed the topic of corruption since the 1970s. The perspective on corruption was different, however, with what was seen as sophisticated new forms of economic crime being at the center of graft and corruption as problems of international concern. In the period from 1980 to 1989 when talks about what the United States had introduced as illicit/corrupt payments had virtually stopped at other UN bodies, the Congress on Prevention of Crime continued talks on corruption, but its take on the issue was in the tradition of ECOSOC and differed significantly from the OECD discussions. During the 6th Congress in Caracas (August 25–September 5, 1980) questions of corporate crime and the abuse of power of high-level officials were at the forefront of discussions about corrupt practices. The abuse of economic power by transnational corporations and the impunity with which they and high government officials perpetuated corrupt practices was pointing to the problematic relationship between global business and political elites worldwide, and was not concerned with bribery in particular. The inability of developing states to handle effectively transnational corporations and the 'various aspects of offenses relating to the abuse of power and the perpetuators of such offenses at the global and regional levels' with a stress on economic crime revealed a much broader understanding of corruption (Travaux Preparatoires UNCAC 2010, xv).

During the 7th Congress (Milan, August 26–September 6, 1985), the controversial subjects of NIEO and corporate criminal liability also resurfaced. Corruption was discussed as leading to distrust in government and cynicism because of a socially presumed 'inevitability of a corrupt society and the inability to achieve a state of communal well-being and economic stability and prosperity' (xv). At the same time, the solutions to corruption as a form of 'economic crime' were seen to be in building the institutional capacity of developing nations, so they could prosecute complex economic crime. The question of corruption appeared as part of the area of economic crime in which corporate and organized crime appeared intricate:

> "crime as business" referred to heterogeneous groups of crimes characterized by specific features, such as the underlying objective of economic gain and the involvement of some form of commerce, industry or trade; the use or misuse of legitimate techniques of business and industry; and the high social status and/or political power of the persons involved in the commission of the crimes concerned. Crimes of corporations, on the one hand, and so-called "organized" or syndicated crime, on the other, were found to have many similarities and interrelations and, typically, both might involve the corruption of law enforcement and political authority. (Travaux Preparatoires UNCAC, xiii)

Economic crimes exhibited ever-evolving sophistication and were often committed with impunity. The goal was to develop equivalent treatment of economic and conventional crimes, and this required a dynamic penalization approach for corporate offenders. It was in the line of this 'developing nations perspective' that the interregional seminar discussed forms of corrupt practices and the possibility for an international convention to address transnational corruption. During the 8th Congress, corruption was discussed under agenda item 3 and a paper prepared by the Secretariat claimed that 'corruption had become more transnational, plaguing all societies, and that its consequences were much more deleterious in developing countries' (xiii). Political commitment was needed in the form of strengthening of national laws and international cooperation for their effective application. The stress was, however, on the responsibility of the host country to prosecute such crimes, which involved a higher degree of government authority over transnational corporations. The position that corruption and bribery were just tools in the toolbox of a number of more sophisticated economic crimes constituted a major difference with discussions at the OECD where bribery was pitched as the central problem. Attempts by developing countries to strengthen their grip over foreign investors operating on their territory and a high level of discretion in the prosecution and definition of economic crimes and corruption could have been undesirable for the developed countries.

During the 8th Congress, a resolution demanded that the Crime Prevention Branch forward a draft code of conduct for public officials to the next Congress and a report on the position of NGOs and governments on the distributed anti-corruption manual. The Committee on Crime Prevention and Control had to: 'keep the issue of corruption under constant review' and to submit an update to the 9th Congress (xviii). Resolution 45/107 reiterated the mandate of the Crime Prevention and Criminal Justice Branch on corruption and requested the production of materials on special training of national prosecutors and judges. In parallel, corruption was included in the agenda of the Commission on Human Rights with a stress on high-level government officials:

> Following the Eighth Congress, the Commission on Human Rights adopted resolution 1992/50, entitled "Fraudulent enrichment of top State officials prejudicial to the public interest, the factors responsible for it, and the agents involved in all countries in such fraudulent enrichment", in which it stressed the necessity for determined action to combat the

> fraudulent or illicit enrichment of top State officials and the transfer abroad of the assets thus diverted, as well as to prevent those practices which undermined the democratic system in countries throughout the world and constituted an obstacle to their development. (xviii)

Before the 9th Congress in 1995, which took place in Egypt, the UN International Drug Control Program launched a preparatory Ministerial Forum Against Corruption in November 1994. The previous Congress in Havana discussed measures against corruption and stressed the importance of international cooperation in addressing the issue globally, as well as the role the UN should play in the process. The Congress, however, was taking place every 5 years and did not provide a consistent framework for discussion of the issue of corruption per se. It provided, however, for the re-introduction of the issue of foreign illicit payments on the agenda of the UN, and in particular, in the UNCTC. The Commission on Transnational Corporations requested the Secretary-General to issue a report on corrupt practices in international business transactions in 1991. The Report recalled previous efforts on the subject and noted that national approaches to tackling corruption could benefit from international cooperation on the subject. The following year, the Code of Conduct, which was connected to the question of illicit payments in the 1970s, failed and therefore opened the door to a new take on the subject. It was only after the Recommendation of the OECD in 1994, however, that the UN intensified talks on the subject of illicit payments (Posadas 2000). With the exception of the above initiatives, the US-sponsored question of illicit/corrupt payments remained of limited importance in the UN until some degree of consensus was reached at the OECD. In this sense, the discussions of the 1990s mirrored those of the 1970s, but the issue of corrupt payments remained contained as the prerogative of the OECD. This had significant influence over the process of reaching consensus and the definition of the offense. The exchange of venues between the OECD and the UN, as the central forum for discussion in the 1970s and 1990s, raises the relevant question of how to contain the discussions of a potential global policy issue within a certain organization. The Netherlands did not manage to re-introduce corruption in the UN in the same forceful and persuasive way that the United States did with the illicit payments issue in the OECD. In the 1970s, it was the inability to manage controversy at the UN, which raised the stakes of the issue of corrupt payments, and made further OECD talks conditional on finding a successful resolution to the controversy at the UN.

The enduring differences between the OECD and the UN takes on the question of corruption are reflected in an exchange of views that took place on April 25, 1991 (C/M(91)9/PROV/ANN). The United States was still isolated in its interest to address transnational bribery at that point, and the bulk of the discussion took place between the US Permanent Representative to the OECD, Alan Larson, and the Secretary-General of UNCTAD, Kenneth Dadzie. During his presentation of the 8th Session of the UNCTAD, Dadzie made a reference to 'good management,' which the US representative took as a window of opportunity to raise the issue of corrupt activities:

> With regard to Mr. Dadzie's interesting comments on the question of good governance and in particular on the specific point he had made concerning the efforts of developing countries were making to structure their economies in a way as to minimize the opportunities and incentives for corrupt activities, Mr. Larson asked whether it would be seen as desirable to have greater discipline on the activities of representatives of industrial countries through some sort of international agreement or national activities which would discipline illicit payments by their citizens. (C/M(91)9/PROV/ANN, 22)

The US Permanent representative continued to refer to 'good governance,' a concept that had recently gained an, albeit limited, currency after the 1989 World Bank Report on Sub-Saharan Africa called the situation in the region a 'governance' crisis (World Bank 1989, 60). The UN representative consistently referred to 'good management,' and this difference was symptomatic of diverging explanations for the culprit of unsatisfactory development, as well as what was the role of corruption in the process. The UN representative affirmed that the concept of 'good management' was already included in the agenda of UNCTAD VIII, but remained highly contested. 'Good management' was at the interface of market forces and public policy at which government intervention was supposed to compensate for market inefficiencies. To this extent, good management was not seen as the withdrawal of the government from the economy, but as a vantage point for more intervention—a position that would have been inconsistent with the neoliberal turn. The rules of global trade and investment were equally culpable for insufficient development. The position of the UNCTAD representative was that corruption constituted part of a web of problems—a development *problematique*, rather than a problem of its own right (C/M(91)9/PROV/ANN, 4).

At the current stage of discussion at the UN, the issue of good management was primarily understood as market transparency for foreign investors. The four primary objectives of a good management agenda were: to establish a predictable framework for foreign and domestic investors, to manage conflict, to manage market deficiencies and to manage government intervention in the economy. The 'good management' agenda justified government intervention in the economy. The free market was deemed insufficient to solve the problems of development: 'market solutions to problems of poverty and inequitable distribution income often result in conditions incompatible with societal values' (C/M(91)9/PROV/ANN, 14). Altogether, market mechanisms were deemed to not provide for public goods and not deal effectively with externalities. Government intervention (and a lot of it) was still deemed necessary to set the conditions for a free market system. Sustainable development was also provided as another example of the insufficiencies of unregulated markets (C/M(91)9/PROV/ANN).

Without making an explicit reference to New Institutional Economics (NIE), the UN representative concurred in this exchange of views with the basic NIE insight that domestic institutions, defined as the 'rules of the game,' matter in managing economic uncertainty (North 1990). At the same time, Dadzic pointed to the rules of the global economy as the main detriment to successful economic development. The performance of some East Asian economies, as well as India and China, appeared to support the argument that it was domestic rather than global policies which mattered in development strategy, but the UN representative challenged this perspective and claimed that the global economic environment was hostile to development and some of the aspects of the problem were: 'the collapse in financial flows, the burden of the debt overhang, historically high interest rates, depressed real commodity prices, and formidable barriers in developed countries markets' (C/M(91)9/PROV/ANN, 7).

In the early 1990s, under the influence of NIE, the theoretical groundwork was laid for the culprit for unsatisfactory economic growth to be found in domestic politics. The call to reform the global rules of the game did not negate the importance of domestic policies, but revealed a more varied and complex picture. The developing governance literature stressed the role of institutions (defined after North as 'the rules of the game') and the role of political authority *within* the nation state (Kaufmann 2010). The underlying argument was that the culprit of slow development was to be found in domestic politics and that was challenged by developing nations in the preliminary discussions of the parameters of what they called 'good management.' The question of corrupt payments was thrown in the vortex of discussions about good governance but, understood initially from the perspective of developing nations, the concept of good governance/management was meant as a policy tool, which could create a predictable framework for foreign investment, and was therefore a matter of primary interest for Western investors. The difference in positions on what constituted 'good governance' became a matter of debate during the OECD session. The representative of the Netherlands remarked that he was astounded by the degree of convergence between UNCTAD and the OECD on economic policies, but that there was one notable exception:

> There has been however one exception: Mr. Dadzie had mentioned that the question of good management and good governance had aroused considerable controversy whereas Mr. Labohm was under the impression that a consensus was emerging worldwide on the desirability of good management and good governance. (C/M(91)9/PROV/ANN, 21)

The United States joined on that note stating that the delegation: 'had been struck by the emerging consensus on development policy, particularly with respect to the role of private enterprises, human resources and democratic institutions' (21). The views on good management/governance, however, were not synchronized, and as noted earlier, the US representative introduced the future OECD program to tackle the supply side of bribery in the discussion of good governance. The UK representative also welcomed the 'emphasis on good governance' and commented that the 'UNCTAD was not, after all, missing out on the change of atmosphere—with emphasis on partnership and flexibility rather than confrontation and regulation—which had taken place over the last few years' (22).

The softening of the position of the developing countries was also due to the changing global environment in which they had collectively lost bargaining power. The strategic importance of the Third World had diminished with the end of the Cold War. The UN Representative stated that while: 'welcoming the ending of the Cold War many developing countries have also been concerned that their vital interests would lose their salience on the international agenda' (6). The alliances of developing nations were changing, but UNCTAD remained the most essential forum 'to deal ...with trade and development from the particular point of view of developing countries' (7). Together with the G77 (which now has 131 members), UNCTAD was still seen to have a distinctive developing nations' perspective on global issues.

The position of the developing nations was that the global rules of the game and, in particular, the rules governing Western enterprises remained the most pressing element in the development agenda, but the developed nations did not seem disposed to revisit the question of international regulation of multinationals. The rules of the global economic game appeared to be made in organizations to which the developing nations either did not have access or had limited influence:

> These phenomena have accentuated the vulnerability of those economies, particularly in the developing world, that are open enough to come under considerable influence from abroad but are not sufficiently large for their own policies to make a significant impact on others. Thus, the volume and terms of trade of developing countries has come to depend significantly on the overall stance of macro-economic policies in major OECD countries... (C/M(91)9/PROV/ANN, 8)

The Secretary-General of UNCTAD responded to the question regarding good management, which had been raised by the representative of the Netherlands, explaining why the question of good governance had recently become controversial at the UNCTAD:

> The controversy to which Mr. Dadzie had referred was a controversy within the UNCTAD rather than any controversy external to UNCTAD. Within UNCTAD, the way an issue was presented was seen as being just as important as the issue itself. As it had happened, the issue had been advanced in the first place as a problem of corruption in developing countries, and this approach had generated negative vibrations and cast a cloud over subsequent discussions: every time a suggestion was made, it was seen by one side or the other as an accusation. Finally, following some months of acrimonious discussion, agreement had been reached on the concept of good management. There were still some suspicions that the Secretariat might treat good management as simply an issue of corruption (by and involving only developing countries) but Mr. Dadzie thought he had demonstrated in his presentation that the view was somewhat more balanced than that. (C/M(91)9/PROV/ANN, 33)

The question of 'good management' emphasized the economic side of 'good governance' that the US and UK representatives referred to in accordance with the recently developed World Bank terminology. The World Bank also came to define governance with broader, more neutral language, namely as 'the manner in which power is exercised in the management of a country's economic and social resources for development' (World Bank Group 1992, 1). Stressing the economic and political aspects of public authority, the definition of good governance as 'sound development management' was developed for the purpose of feasibility (Santiso 2001, 5). The UNCTAD's stress on good management, as the economic aspect of public authority, showed that there is still space for government that does not simply serve economic objectives. The concept of governance, to a large extent, blended the political and economic capacities of governments for the sole purpose of economic development. At the same time, corruption did not become the centerpiece of the Bank's good governance agenda. A case in point is that the WGI, published since 2002 and covering the period after 1996, use Control of Corruption as one of six governance indicators (World Bank 2014). As the Secretary-General stated, during these preliminary talks at the UNCTAD, at the time corruption in developing countries was put forward as the centerpiece of a good management/governance agenda, which led to rancorous disputes. It is this understanding of governance as national-level management in order to establish a predictable framework for investment that the UN representative was referring to in response to Alan Larson's question about corruption:

> relevant rules and regulations should be effectively removed from an ad hoc or arbitrary intervention by the politically powerful and must not be subject to excessive discretionary power which offered temptations to economic agents and their interlocutors in administrative structures to engage in corrupt practices. Whether there was need for an international agreement was another matter. There was no doubt that all countries must achieve a more uniform understanding of practices which are allowable and which are not. (C/M(91)9/PROV/ANN, 3)

Without appearing fundamentally opposed to an international agreement on corrupt payments, the UN representative outlined broadly the general aspect of the problem and the spectrum of possible measures: 'Different instruments might be required in the field of crime – possibly some sort of international agreement. In other areas, codes of behavior, either binding or non-binding, might be appropriate' (24). The decoupling of the political and economic authority of national governments constituted a compromise that could have led to some level of consensus on the desirability of 'good management.' It was a compromise that stripped anti-corruption policies from their ubiquitous political facet but also reconciled an anti-corruption agenda with the objective to remove market regulation. The degree of disagreement on questions of state intervention in the economy and the global terms of trade was, however, unlikely to lead to an agreement on the definition of corruption or the methods to tackle it at the UNCTAD at that time. The essential step at reaching global consensus on the content of corrupt activities, and the design of the program that would address them, proved to be reaching agreement at the OECD as pre-negotiation talks advanced.

In the 1990s, as in the 1970s, one international organization became the locus of discussion of the problem of corrupt payments. The repercussions of the choice of venue, the UN or the OECD, were significant because of the difference in the membership base of the two organizations. The potential global governance problem was discussed in a different light at the two venues, which had an impact on international consensus. It is not possible to neatly group the position of developed and developing nations as there was significant variety of opinions within each group, yet there appeared to be some level of convergence between a 'developing' and a 'developed' nations' perspective on questions of good governance and corruption.

In the aftermath of the failed UN process, feasibility became the most essential element for future work at the OECD. The study of feasibility meant that in addition to what the problem consisted of, the question whether the problem could be tackled internationally became just as important (Spector and Kitsuse 2009). The protracted work on corrupt payments at the OECD and the UN reveals international organizations as incubators in which global issues can remain encapsulated for a number of years or even decades while state actors remain central to any progress. On the one hand, the study of the social construction of the problem of corruption shows how through the rather mundane internal dealings of working groups and Council meetings, meaning and definitions are shuffled and transformed. On the other hand, the essential impetus for the successful completion of the work of expert committees is political and comes from influential state actors.

The pre-negotiation talks at the OECD were no less difficult for the United States than the UN talks, and the US delegation found itself isolated in its concern for corrupt payments at the OECD. The United States had a problem specifically with bribery because of the FCPA and leveling the playing field with its major competitors from the developed world became the main task. This did not entail that the United States was the only country that was implicated in corrupt dealings, but that under particular domestic and international contingencies in the 1970s, this implication became a problem for the United States in a way that it did not for any other state. The corrupt payments problem was jeopardizing domestic stability post-Watergate and complicating the US position in ideological warfare during the Cold War. Tackling the problem with illicit payments set in course a mechanism of internationalization that was successfully completed in the 1990s. The success of the United States to forge consensus on corrupt payments is examined in the next chapter and shows how the ability to turn your national (private) troubles into global (public) concerns is an essential aspect of state power.

References

Bell, Andrew S. 2003. *Forum Shopping and Venue in Transnational Litigation*. Oxford: Oxford University Press.

C(89)49. *United States Proposal on the Issue of Illicit Payments*, Note to the Secretary General (March 22, 1989). OECD Archives, Paris Headquarters.

———. Annex. *United States Proposal for an International Agreement on Illicit Payments* (March 14, 1989) OECD Archives, Paris Headquarters.

C(89)152. *Illicit Payments in International Commercial Transactions Request to Delegations for Information*, Note to the Secretary General (August 2, 1989). OECD Archives, Paris Headquarters.

C(90)12. *Medium-Term Priorities*, Note to the Secretary General (January 30, 1990). OECD Archives, Paris Headquarters.

C(90)87. *Illicit Payments in International Commercial Transactions*, Note to the Secretary General (June 12, 1990). OECD Archives, Paris Headquarters.

———. Annex 1. *Illicit Payments in International Commercial Transactions, Description of the OECD Countries Legislation and Practices Concerning Illicit Payments* (June 12, 1990). OECD Archives, Paris Headquarters.

———. Annex 2. *Description of the Work Done on the Issue of Illicit payments in International Transactions at an International Level* (June 12, 1990). OECD Archives, Paris Headquarters.

C(90)90. *Council Communiqué* (June 12, 1990). OECD Archives, Paris Headquarters.

C/M(90)10(Prov.). *Minutes of the 733rd Session*, Council (July 18, 1990). OECD Archives, Paris Headquarters.
C/M(90)13(Prov.). *Minutes of the 736th Session*, Council (July 6, 1990). OECD Archives, Paris Headquarters.
C/M(90)16(Prov.). *Minutes of the 739th Session*, Council (September 27, 1990). OECD Archives, Paris Headquarters.
C/MIN(90)11. *Council Meeting* (October 24, 1990). OECD Archives, Paris Headquarters.
C/MIN(90)11. *The 1990 Review of the 1976 Declaration on International Investment and Multinational Enterprises*, Council at Ministerial Level (May 27, 1990). OECD Archives, Paris Headquarters.
C/M(91)2/PROV/PART2. *Minutes of the 749th Session*, Council (February 13, 1991). OECD Archives, Paris Headquarters.
C/M(91)4/PROV. *Minutes of the 751st Session*, Council (March 7, 1991). OECD Archives, Paris Headquarters.
C/M(91)9/PROV/ANN. *Minutes of the 756th Session* (June 11, 1991). OECD Archives, Paris Headquarters.
C/M(91)11/PROV. *Minutes of the 758th Session*, Council (October 22, 1991). OECD Archives, Paris Headquarters.
C/M(91)12/PROV. *Minutes of the 759th Session*, Council (October 16, 1991). OECD Archives, Paris Headquarters.
C/M(91)20/PROV/ANN. *Minutes of the 767th Session* (July 22, 1991). OECD Archives, Paris Headquarters.
C/M(91)22/PROV. *Minutes of the 769th Session*, Council (December 6, 1991). OECD Archives, Paris Headquarters.
C/M(91)25/PROV. *Minutes of the 772nd Session*, Council (February 17, 1992). OECD Archives, Paris Headquarters.
DAFFE/IME(90)4. *Symposium on the OECD Guidelines for Multinational Enterprises*, Note by the Secretariat (June 15, 1990). OECD Archives, Paris Headquarters.
DAFFE/IME(91)2. *Committee on International Investment and Multinational Enterprises, Summary Record, Held on the 10th–12th April 1991* (April 26, 1991). OECD Archives, Paris Headquarters.
———. (91)10. *The 1991 Review of the OECD Declaration and Decisions on International Investment and Multinational Enterprises*, Note by the Secretariat (April 16, 1991). OECD Archives, Paris Headquarters.
———. (91)10/ADD1. *The 1991 Review of the OECD Declaration and Decisions on International Investment and Multinational Enterprises*, Note by the Secretariat (May 22, 1991). OECD Archives, Paris Headquarters.
———. (91)15. *Illicit Payments*, Note by the Secretariat (April 9, 1991). OECD Archives, Paris Headquarters.

———. (91)26. *Illicit Payments in International Commercial Transactions*, Note by the Secretariat (November 26, 1991). OECD Archives, Paris Headquarters.

———. (92)14. *Illicit Payments*, Note by the Secretariat (April 21, 1992). OECD Archives, Paris Headquarters.

DAFFE/IME/A(91)4. *Agenda*, CIME (November 19, 1991). OECD Archives, Paris Headquarters.

DAFFE/IME/BR/A(96)6/REV1. *Agenda*, Working Group on Bribery in International Business Transactions (November 6, 1996). OECD Archives, Paris Headquarters.

DAFFE/IME/M/(90)4. *Summary Record of the Committee on International Investment and Multinational Enterprises Held on 27th–29th November 1990* (December 21, 1990). OECD Archives, Paris Headquarters.

———. (91)1. *Summary Record of the Meeting of the Committee on International Investment and Multinational Enterprises Held on the 6th–8th February 1991* (March 26, 1991). OECD Archives, Paris Headquarters.

———. (92)1. *Summary Record of the Meeting of the Committee on International Investment and Multinational Enterprises Held on 4th–6th December 1991* (February 4, 1992). OECD Archives, Paris Headquarters.

———. (92)2. *Summary Record of the Meeting of the Committee on International Investment and Multinational Enterprises Held on 5th–6th May 1992* (June 23, 1992). OECD Archives, Paris Headquarters.

DAFFE/IME/PI(91)1. *Agenda*, Ad Hoc Group on Illicit Payments (June 13, 1991). OECD Archives, Paris Headquarters.

———. (91)2. *Feasibility Study on Available International Means for Dealing with Illicit Payments in International Commercial Transactions*, Ad Hoc Group on Illicit Payments, Note by the Secretariat (June 13, 1991). OECD Archives, Paris Headquarters.

———. (91)2/REV1. *Feasibility Study on Available International Means for Dealing with Illicit Payments in International Commercial Transactions*, Ad Hoc Group on Illicit Payments, Note by the Secretariat (September 30, 1991). OECD Archives, Paris Headquarters.

———. (91)3. *Summary Record of the Meeting Held 13–14 June 1991*, Ad Hoc Group on Illicit Payments (September 23, 1991). OECD Archives, Paris Headquarters.

———. (91)4. *Agenda*, Ad Hoc Group on Illicit Payments (September 23, 1991). OECD Archives, Paris Headquarters.

———. (91)5. *Illicit Payments in International Commercial Transactions: Question of Future Work in OECD*, Ad Hoc Group on Illicit Payments, Note by the Secretariat (October 2, 1991). OECD Archives, Paris Headquarters.

———. (91)5/ANN2. *Annex 2*, Ad Hoc Group on Illicit Payments (October 2, 1991) OECD Archives, Paris Headquarters.

———. (91)7. *Illicit Payments in International Commercial Transactions*, Report by the Ad Hoc Group on Illicit Payments (November 21, 1991). OECD Archives, Paris Headquarters.

———. (91)7/ANN1. *Annex 1: Feasibility Study on Available International Means for Dealing with Illicit Payments in International Commercial Transactions* (November 21, 1991). OECD Archives, Paris Headquarters.

———. (91)7/ANN2. *Annex 2: Observations by the Italian Delegation* (November 21, 1991). OECD Archives, Paris Headquarters.

———. (92)2. *Agenda*, Ad Hoc Group on Illicit Payments (June 16, 1992). OECD Archives, Paris Headquarters.

———. (92)3. *Illicit Payments in International Commercial Transactions*, Ad Hoc Group on Illicit Payments, Note by the Secretariat (18 June, 1992). OECD Archives, Paris Headquarters.

———. (92)3/ANN. *Annex: Substantive Elements to Be Considered Together with Procedural Options* (June 18, 1992). OECD Archives, Paris Headquarters.

DAFFE/IME/PI(92)3/REV1. *Illicit Payments in International Commercial Transactions*, Ad Hoc Group on Illicit Payments (October 9, 1992). OECD Archives, Paris Headquarters.

———. (92)3/REV2. *Feasibility Study on Illicit Payments in International Commercial Transactions*, Ad Hoc Group on Illicit Payments (December 4, 1992). OECD Archives, Paris Headquarters.

———. (92)3/REV3. *Feasibility Study on Illicit Payments in International Commercial Transactions*, Ad Hoc Group on Illicit Payments (December 17, 1992). OECD Archives, Paris Headquarters.

Foreign Corrupt Practices Act (Amendments), Pub. L. No. 100–418, 102 Stat. 1415 (1988).

Foreign Corrupt Practices Act of 1977, Pub. L. No. 95–23–, 91 Stat. 1494 (codified as amended at 15 U.S.C. 78m, 78dd-1 to 78dd-2, 78ff (1994) [Hereinafter FCPA] as Amended by International Anti-bribery and Fair Competition Act of 1998, 15 U.S.C.A. 78dd-1 to 78dd-3, 78ff (1999) [IAFCA].

International Chamber of Commerce. 1977. *Extortion and Bribery in Business Transactions: Report Adopted by the 131st Session of the Council of the ICC, 29 November 1977*. Paris: International Chamber of Commerce.

Jakobi, Anja P. 2013. "The Changing Global Norm of Anti-Corruption: From Bad Business to Bad Government." *Zeitschrift Für Vergleichende Politikwissenschaft* 7 (1): 243–264.

Kaufmann, Daniel. 2010. "Daniel Kaufmann on State Capture." *World Policy Journal* 27 (1): 3–4.

Omnibus Trade and Competitiveness Act of 1988, Pub. L. No. 100–418, 3001–3604, 103 Stat. 1372 (1988) (Codified as amended in scattered sections of U.S.C. (1988)).

Pieth, Mark. 1997. "International Cooperation to Combat Corruption." In *Corruption and the Global Economy*, edited by Kimberly Ann Elliott, 119–133. Washington, DC: Peterson Institute.

———. 1999. "International Efforts to Combat Corruption." Paper Presented at the 9th International Anti-Corruption Conference (IACC), Durban, South Africa, October 10–15.

Posadas, Alejandro. 2000. "Combating Corruption Under International Law." *Duke Journal of Comparative & International Law* 10 (2): 345–414.

Santiso, C. 2001. "Good Governance and Aid Effectiveness: The World Bank and Conditionality." Accessed October 23, 2017. http://agris.fao.org/agris-search/search.do?recordID=GB2013203594.

Spector, Malcolm and John Kitsuse. 2009. *Constructing Social Problems*. 4th ed. Rutgers, New Jersey: Transaction Publishers.

Stedman Jones, Daniel. 2014. *Masters of the Universe: Hayek, Friedman, and the Birth of Neoliberal Politics—Updated Edition*. Reprint edition. Princeton and Oxford: Princeton University.

Travaux Préparatoires of the Negotiations for the Elaboration of the United Nations Convention against Corruption. New York, NY: United Nations, 2010.

UN. 1990. Corruption in Government: Report of an Interregional Seminar 11–15 December, The Hague. New York: UN.

Venice G7 Summit. "Communiqué." (June 22–23, 1980). Accessed October 22, 2017. http://www.g8.utoronto.ca/summit/1980venice/communique/trade.html.

World Bank. 1989. *Sub-Saharan Africa: From Crisis to Sustainable Growth*. Washington, DC: IBRD/ World Bank.

———. 1992. *Legal Framework for the Treatment of Foreign Investment*. Washington, DC, U.S.A. (1818 H St. N.W., Washington 20433).

World Bank Group. 1992. "Report to the Development Committee and Guidelines on the Treatment of Foreign Direct Investment." In *Legal Framework for the Treatment of Foreign Investment*, vol. II. Washington, DC, U.S.A.

———. 2014. "WBI Governance and Anti-Corruption." Accessed October 23, 2017. http://web.worldbank.org/WBSITE/EXTERNAL/WBI/EXTWBIGOVANTCOR/0,,contentMDK:20678012~pagePK:64168445~piPK:64168309~theSitePK:1740530~isCURL:Y,00.html.

CHAPTER 7

The OECD Convention and Beyond: State-Powered Coalition Building in a Broken World

In the period 1994–1997, the foundation of the global anti-corruption governance was laid out. As this chapter shows, the success of the anti-corruption endeavor was to a large extent determined by a systematic approach of state-sponsored coalition building. The advancement of talks at the OECD and the adoption of the RBIBT led OECD member states to introduce the topic of corrupt practices in the OAS, the CoE, the EU, the UN and the G7/8. Non-state actors contributed to the process of coalition building, but much of what they achieved was shaped by previous efforts of state actors, in particular the United States, and the ongoing intergovernmental dynamics. The instrumental use of publicity and the change of venues contributed to the success of the OECD initiative to outlaw transnational corrupt payments and led to the spread of talks in a number of regional organizations. The formal agreements reached at organizations such as the OAS, the CoE, the EU, the OECD and the World Bank then provided the legal and discursive underpinnings for the re-introduction of the subject at the UN. Building on Chapter 6, the first part of this chapter zooms closer in on the way in which the decision for the RBIBT was reached and discursively shaped. The second part then goes on to zoom out and show the bigger picture of how, in relation to progress at the OECD, the subject of corruption was introduced in regional organizations. In this way, this chapter works toward striking a balance between showing how the social construction of problems is negotiated within organizations and how the interconnection and overlaps

E. Katzarova, *The Social Construction of Global Corruption*,
Political Corruption and Governance,
https://doi.org/10.1007/978-3-319-98569-5_7

between organizations also shape the processes of collective definition and the formulation of an official plan of action.

Pre-negotiation talks constitute the most essential step in the social construction of global problems, but researchers have largely ignored them. In a constructivist research agenda, the decision to open negotiations reveals a high degree of consensus on the recognition of a condition as a global problem. While bargaining during the negotiation stage is the biggest showcase for power imbalances, power also matters before opening negotiations because not every actor can raise an issue at an international organization and actually see it through.

The work of ad hoc groups and other committees provides essential continuity for pre-negotiation debates, but is not in itself sufficient for reaching a successful outcome. As Spector and Kitsuse (2009) note, the vast majority of social concerns drown in the swirl of ad hoc groups and committees. Through the rather mundane and detailed internal dealings of working groups and Council meetings, meaning and definitions are shuffled and transformed, and feasibility becomes the central element of the process. Rather than defining the problem and the measures to address it in some ideal vacuum of technical expertise, the definition of the offense, its relation to the most effective instruments and to the putative condition itself remain contested and dynamic. The study of feasibility, therefore, has an impact on what is defined as the problem, and in judging if anything can be done about the fuzzily defined condition and with what tools. The expertise of national delegates convening at the OECD Ad Hoc Group was instrumental in delimitating the most feasible option for future action but at no time did their technical competences supplant the agency of member states. The supremacy of nation states over this process of internationalization of the problem of corruption was institutionally enshrined in the role of the OECD Council in the organization's decision-making processes, but also became part of the very discussions of feasibility within the Ad Hoc Group and CIME. Previous chapters traced the undercurrent of intergovernmental talks on corrupt practices since the 1970s, and this chapter shows how starting in the 1990s other actors became incorporated into these ongoing talks.

Talks at the OECD Advance: Toward a Fragile Consensus 1991–1994

This section shows how the study of political and administrative feasibility led to the narrowing down of options and establishing a plan for future work, which proved to be fundamental for incremental progress, and led to the adoption of the RBIBT in 1994. After establishing the list of four primary options, the Ad Hoc Group had to receive CIME's approval for choosing a combination of an OECD Decision and Recommendation (options 3 and 4). The choice of these options did not per se exclude option 1 (International Convention) when consensus was forged on the issue, but pursuing the Convention route was deemed unfeasible at the moment (DAFFE/IME/PI(91)2).[1] The Ad Hoc Group had to 'provide the Council with the elements necessary to allow it to assess the feasibility of the different options without prejudicing the outcome of its deliberations on this issue' and at the same time help the Council decide as to whether pursuing future work on the question of illicit payments was necessary and/or desirable (DAFFE/IME/PI(91)4, 2–3).[2] Member states, therefore, retained a firm grip on the decision-making process and even the preliminary recommendations of the Ad Hoc Group were not issued independently, but in collaboration with the delegations. A list of 'elements and issues' (provided by the Secretariat in a Room Document) formed the basis for revisions that incorporated the opinion of the delegations. The refined inventory of elements on which agreement was reached was later to provide the contents of the RBIBT, the Recommendation on tax deductibility and to some extent the Convention itself. Corrupt practices were presented as a problem of competitiveness, which made them contrary to OECD objectives in global economic exchange (DAFFE/IME(91)26). The criterion of 'controversy' was the centerpiece of the study of feasibility: 'Are there any elements, which are considered so controversial that

[1] During a meeting on the June 13–14, 1991, the Ad Hoc Group members re-elected Mark Pieth as Chairman. Pieth had been instrumental for the successful outcome of the discussions on money-laundering (DAFFE/IME/PI(91)3).

[2] The list of the members of the Ad Hoc Group revealed an increased interest in the issue of corrupt practices with a more extensive national representation from Ministries of Finance and the Economy, Departments of States, National Banks from almost all OECD member states (DAFFE/IME/PI(91)3).

their inclusion in any type of instrument would meet little, or no international consensus? If so, which ones and why? ... What is the nature of the controversy?' (DAFFE/IME/PI(91)5, 1). Based on the matrix of potential controversies, the Ad Hoc Group had to suggest the exclusion of controversial elements out of the program.[3] Once again the trade-off between effectiveness and feasibility was taken as the primary consideration: 'which uncontroversial elements must be included in order to have an effective instrument and why?' (DAFFE/IME/PI(91)2/REV1, 10). Using the matrix revealed that the potential and most controversial elements are the definition of the offense and the identification of the actors (DAFFE/IME/PI(91)2/REV1). The continuous management of the controversial elements showcases that expert recommendations were not made in a political lacuna in which technical solutions were matched to clearly defined natural problems, but that these expert recommendations were imbued in the context of what appeared to be politically feasible.

The interplay between optimal solutions and what was to be realistically expected led to estimates as to what kind of definitions of offenses were to be paired with what type of instruments in order to achieve the ultimate match between effectiveness and feasibility: 'If these were the only elements on which agreement could be reached, does the Group feel that they are sufficient for developing an effective instrument? If not, what element would be lacking? Does their inclusion depend on being able to reduce potential controversy?' (DAFFE/IME/PI(91)5, 3).[4] In this study of feasibility vs. effectiveness, the Group had to concentrate on, '(a) the degree of consensus that is likely to be achieved on the different options as presented in the consultant's feasibility study; and (b) the legal/political effectiveness of those options for dealing with illicit payments' (3). Based on this trade-off, the Group had to exclude certain

[3]Basing the recommendations on the provided matrix, the Report stated that a number of such highly controversial elements had been individuated: 'such elements may include a definition of illicit payments which would cover payments other than traditional bribes, including sales requiring government approval, the reaching of payments through intermediaries, and the issue of jurisdiction absent a sufficient territorial nexus' (DAFFE/IME/PI(91)5).

[4]This search for optimal solutions in the context of what is deemed to be in the realm of the politically feasible was concerned with questions such as: 'Is there an inverse [relationship] proportionality between the controversial elements and the type of instrument? For example, does the controversy diminish as one gets further away from the more legally constraining type of instrument?' (DAFFE/IME/PI(91)5, 3).

future routes and promote others, all the while not prejudicing the decision of the Council. This interplay between technical expertise and political authority was at the core of discussions on the subject and showcased the manner in which political feasibility is intrinsically connected to technical fixes from the very beginning of the evolution of the global issue. Furthermore, the methodology of the matrix became contested and the meaning of 'feasibility' became a question in itself: 'What should be the criteria for determining feasibility? Would it be the amount of international consensus a particular option is likely to enjoy, or would it be the extent to which Member states would be legally bound to their commitments, or how much political credibility the instrument can achieve? Are there other criteria?' (DAFFE/IME/PI(91)2/REV1, 4).

The ingredients of a technical evaluation, therefore, already included a significant amount of reflection on issues of practical feasibility, such as estimations of political will and chances of successful consensus building. Since the most important aspect of the Group's consultation was deemed to be legal expertise (in accordance with the US claim), it was legal feasibility, rather than ethical and economic considerations, that took central stage in deciding on a plan for action.[5] In managing controversy, from a legal standpoint, the consideration of what was politically feasible was more readily included in the 'technical analysis.' The diagnostics of the problem did not take place in a vacuum of technical (legal) expertise in which optimal solutions were later matched to the realities of political constrictions, and the distinction between technical and political processes was not clear-cut. Nonetheless, the report retained a claim of separation between technical expertise and political decision-making:

> Having examined the feasibility study on the available international means for preventing illicit payments, the Group should be in a position to make a technical evaluation of which of the available instruments seems the most worthwhile pursuing. This technical evaluation, which will be taken into consideration by the CIME in developing its report to the Council, will help the Council to make the <u>political</u> decision whether or not to pursue work concerning illicit payments. (DAFFE/IME/PI(91)5, 5)

[5] Economists or sociologists, for example, would have provided different type of expertise, but might have also given rise to more controversy, because more claims might have centered around the relationship of the putative condition to the definition of the problem, as they did in the UN.

Following these preliminary interactions between the Ad Hoc Group and the Council, as well as the expressed remarks of the delegations, further work on the feasibility study remained slow and incapsulated within the Ad Hoc Group for almost a year. On June 9, 1992, the Secretariat submitted a note for consideration to the Group in which the option of multilateral negotiations was deemed unfeasible and a combination of a Recommendation and Decision was judged to best reflect the attitude of the Council (DAFFE/IME/PI(92)3). These options could be considered as 'vehicles for political agreement' which would incrementally lead to the more substantive treaty option (DAFFE/IME/PI(92)3/REV1, 3).

Political disagreement and controversies are usually seen as obstacles to solving otherwise practical problems, but this more nuanced picture of pre-negotiation talks reveals that political considerations become an integral part of the way in which problems are studied and constructed. The Ad Hoc Group's technical expertise included an attempt to foresee controversial areas and take them off the negotiation table, so that emerging discord would not lead to a deadlock. Through this process, the members of the Ad Hoc Group, who were also representatives of member states from state departments and ministries, remained attentive to the preferences of the Council and reflected the expected attitudes of member states. Member states remained unconvinced of the US FCPA approach. The majority in the Council was pushing corrupt payments as the prerogative of national legislation and challenging the extent to which the issue should be seen as global (DAFFE/IME/PI(92)3/REV3, 3). The central elements of this national approach to tackling corruption had to be broad enough to allow countries the discretionary power to use them according to their specific needs: 'The language of these elements would be general and non-technical, to provide guidance easily adaptable to different legislative approaches' (4). The only possible intrusion could have been a model law, based on the FCPA, but that would have still left a lot of space for political and legislative maneuvering for individual OECD members. The prospects for international or transnational cooperation remained rather limited, and challenging the extent to which the issue should be treated beyond the borders of the nation state became a primary concern, but questions of definitional scope remained just as relevant.

The Recommendation would have had provisions for intergovernmental cooperation, such as exchange of information, but a network of agreements expanding the network of bilaterals between the

United States and other OECD members, which had been in place since the 1970s, was all that delegations were disposed to concede to. This mutual assistance perspective was firmly routing the responsibility for treating corrupt practices as a predominantly national prerogative. This was claimed to be the case, because difficulties with 'global coverage and jurisdiction' made civil and administrative rather than criminal measures more suitable for addressing the differences between member states (DAFFE/IME/PI(92)3/REV3, 5).

Three other points of fundamental disagreement were the definition of the offense, the actors and the reach of the jurisdiction (DAFFE/IME/PI(92)3/REV3, 11). First, throughout the discussions the precise definition of the problem remained contested and ambiguous:

> The term "illicit payment" has been used as a generic term for all payments that are made with the intention to influence a decision improperly – payments for the purchase of public decisions – broad interpretation that covers financial and non-financial payments, may include the payment of a direct monetary bribe, or payment in the form of political contributions, payments in violation of exchange control regulations, gifts and favours, etc. (DAFFE/IME/PI(92)3/REV1, 5)

Even the understanding of the problem as a 'payment' was not definitive. In later revisions, it was specifically added that the term 'payments' is somehow misleading because the definition is: 'interpreted broadly enough to cover financial and non-financial payments, may include the payment of a direct monetary bribe, or others' (DAFFE/IME/PI(92)3/REV2, 4). The advantage of this definition was to cover benefits which did not possess any intrinsic value in themselves: 'social or other advantage of no necessary significant value to someone other than the recipient' or 'anything of value granted to the recipient, to which the latter would not be otherwise entitled (an 'undue' advantage)' (DAFFE/IME/PI(92)3/REV1, 6). While this interpretation of the offense would have been much closer to an understanding of corruption as influence rather than monetary exchange, the definition was later to be stirred in the direction of bribery. Defining the offense as 'bribery' had little to do with the 'problem itself' and its relation to the putative condition, and more to do with feasibility: 'While there is a certain consensus on the definition of "bribery" (...) the concept of other "illicit payments" is not easily definable and that there may not be a consensus to reach beyond classical "bribery", at least for criminal law purposes' (DAFFE/

IME/PI(92)3/REV2, 12). The US delegation was firmly behind the definition of illicit payments as 'bribery' and this position was intrinsically connected to the FCPA statute and the quest for criminalization of the offense.

Second, after the definition of corrupt payments, the identity of the proponent of the bribe became a source of significant controversy because it entailed corporate criminal liability (CCL).[6] Most countries did not have any provisions for CCL at the time or had only administrative and civil measures and some limited CCL (acting through natural persons, such as board members and employees). Since the questions of private recipients and intermediaries also became controversial, establishing feasibility and managing controversy on the topic of actors involved in the corrupt transaction constituted a central part of the talks.

Third, the question of jurisdictional reach or 'extraterritoriality' became another example of how controversy was managed. The feasibility study had a legal and political component. In terms of legality, legal action was to be taken for a payment made in a foreign territory. The ramification of addressing the supply side of corrupt payments was the exercise of extraterritorial jurisdiction, which was highly contested and this is why it demanded a high degree of consensus. The future CIME report had to address the concerns of delegations, and in later revisions, 'extraterritoriality' was substituted by 'concurrent jurisdiction.' In concurrent jurisdiction, states share the responsibility of prosecution, but some delegations saw this, yet again, as an 'inappropriate interference in the sovereignty or interests of another state' (DAFFE/IME/PI(92)3/REV3, 12). The question of extraterritoriality was nominally absent from the last draft, despite the fact that the substance of extraterritorial jurisdiction was still inherent to the proposed solutions. This rephrasing

[6]The definition of the offender covered natural and legal persons and the recipient could be a public/governmental official or a private party. The definition of public official was broad enough to include all persons with public decision-making or implementing roles. Relevant was also the inclusion of a private person with the ability to influence public policy whether this person works in a firm or NGO. The definition of who makes an offer included 'any corporation, partnership, association, joint stock company, business, trust, unincorporated organization or sole proprietorship which has its principal place of business (or center of activity related to the commercial transaction in question) in the member country' (DAFFE/IME/PI(92)3/REV3, 5). It is noteworthy that there did not occur at any point a discussion of the offeror being a public or governmental agent in their official capacity, while a private recipient remained an albeit contested option.

made no significant difference to the position of the member states, who were opposing the extraterritorial element of the transnational anti-corruption measures. Reaching international consensus was judged to be more likely than it was at the UN more than 10 years ago, but political feasibility still faced considerable hindrances because:

> Some Delegations believe that it is inappropriate for Member countries to assume responsibility for sanctioning conduct which should be primarily the concern and responsibility of the government of the official. Moreover, despite the official anti-corruption policies of all countries, an OECD initiative could be resented by non-OECD countries. (DAFFE/IME/PI(92)3/REV2, 12)

This is why non-member attitudes toward countermeasures to corrupt payments became relevant to the OECD initiative. The participation and inclusion of non-members were judged important and entailed 'a commitment to promote anti-corruption policies within and beyond the OECD area, including through a policy dialogue with non-OECD countries' (11). This expansion beyond the OECD served the dual purpose of providing legitimacy and broader support for an OECD instrument, thus turning the OECD initiative into a catalyst for global anti-corruption action. Furthermore, as early as 1992–1993 policy dialogue with the World Bank was considered and the Guidelines on the Legal Framework for the Treatment of Foreign Investment were referenced, in which a bid to states to control 'corrupt business practices' was made (DAFFE/IME/PI(92)3/REV1). The World Bank Group Guidelines were in the line of work of the UNCTC and the eponymous UN Commission, but the World Bank had, of course, a different take on business—state relations. Instead of looking at the behavior of corporations and calling for international regulation of corporate behavior, the World Bank addressed governments and their ability to promote FDI (World Bank Group 1992). While curbing the economic and political influence of transnational corporations, to the extent to which they may go against the public interest, constituted issues of concern for the UNCTC and the agenda on corrupt practices, such apprehensions were dissipated in the post-Cold War era. The World Bank avoided addressing the behavior of corporations, presumably in order not to duplicate the work of the UNCTC and the Commission on Transnational Corporations, but the UNCTC was abolished in 1992. The program was moved to UNCTAD and the focus shifted toward FDI promotion (UNCTAD 2002).

After the OECD Council gave CIME a mandate on February 25, 1993, to draft the text of a Recommendation, the initiative to promote anti-corruption policies more broadly was claimed as an intrinsic part of the process (DAFFE/IME(93)21). This was the beginning of the expansion of the OECD work on illicit payments into a broader network of other intergovernmental organizations, non-state actors and IFIs, which is discussed in the second part of this chapter.

The Impact of the United States on the OECD Anti-Bribery Recommendation

The work program for 1994 included the preparation of an OECD Recommendation on 'illicit payments in international trade and investment,' which would provide for modes of getting non-members on board. A report had to be filed with the Council by February 1994 and the OECD Council agreed on the Recommendation option in the same month (DAFFE/IME(93)17). The catalyst for progress within the OECD was the change of leadership in Washington in 1993. President Clinton gave new impetus to the American initiative by making the anti-bribery agenda a foreign policy priority (Larson 1997; Glynn et al. 1997). Furthermore, Warren Christopher, who became Secretary of State under Clinton, had been personally involved in drafting and discussing the FCPA in 1977 under Carter (Pieth 2013). Together with the Assistant Secretary of State for Economic and Business Affairs, Daniel Tarullo, who was also a lawyer with good knowledge of the FCPA, Warren Christopher turned the OECD anti-bribery agenda into a major US priority (Abbott and Snidal 2002; Glynn et al. 1997).

With increased political dedication and resources, the United States was very influential in the drafting of the Recommendation. Other member states, such as the Netherlands, Italy and Germany also submitted drafts and commentaries, which, however, were not reflected in the final Recommendation. The Netherlands made suggestions for the draft recommendation in line with prior UN efforts, but was more supportive of the OECD initiative than in 1989. The Dutch delegation still showed a strong preference for a universal approach to bribery that it claimed was not limited to developing countries: 'Far from being restricted to developing countries, bribery is a worldwide phenomenon occurring also in business transactions between OECD member countries.

An OECD initiative, which could act as a catalyst for global action, is therefore appropriate' (DAFFE/IME/PI(93)1, 2). While the Dutch delegation conceded on the definition of the offense as bribery, the Italian delegation made a proposal that concentrated precisely on the definition of corrupt payments, and in particular, the distinction between bribery and other illicit transactions (DAFFE/IME/PI(93)2). The US delegation continued to use the formulation of 'illicit payments' while substituting it with bribery in later drafts (DAFFE/IME/PI(93)3). The German delegation submitted a proposal on assimilation as an alternative to extraterritoriality. According to the Germans, assimilation—a criminal act with foreign elements is assimilated and treated as a domestic act—was suitable, because it would have allowed for a comprehensive international agreement without changes to national legislation on the subject (DAFFE/IME/PI(93)2).

While some of the comments and draft proposals by the delegations concerned the modes of addressing the problem, uncertainty over what was the exact content of the offensive behavior persisted. Delegations were discussing methods to tackle the question of illicit payments without having managed to settle the parameters of what was included in the definition of such activities. Referring to the controversies over the definition of illicit payments, the Report to the Council agreed on the elements of the behavior, the advantage, the transaction and the identity of who offered the bribe, recipient and intermediary, but not on the actual content of these aspects of the definition. In later drafts, the concept of 'illicit payments,' however, was altogether replaced by 'payment of bribes' and 'bribery,' discursively displacing in this way the contestation that illicit payments contained a broader spectrum of activities than traditional bribery (DAFFE/IME/PI(93)9). The position of the United States that illicit payments were more or less exhausted by bribery, which was challenged by OECD members, and previously at the UN, prevailed.

The reasons why the United States insisted on the definition of the offense as bribery were both practical and historical: practical, because a more limited definition of any problem, especially a criminal act, would be more feasible for negotiation and implementation. The United States wanted to criminalize transnational bribery because this was the approach chosen in the FCPA. An expansion of the scope of what constitutes an illicit payment might have also proven more difficult to negotiate. In fact, the United States referred to bribery as 'illicit payments' in order to manage controversy in the international organizations where talks were held.

Hiding the concept of bribery under the more ubiquitous heading of 'illicit payments' constituted a strategy to avoid controversy up to the moment when some level of consensus on the necessity to act had been reached. The underlying reason for this definition was that historically, it was bribery of foreign public officials that crystallized as a problem for the United States after the Congressional hearings, the SEC disclosure program and the subsequent adoption of the FCPA. Therefore, the term 'illicit payments' as a cover for bribery was not meant to raise the questions of scope and definition that it did at the OECD and the UN. While these controversies about what constituted an 'illicit payment' could be seen as a bargaining game in which other state actors try to dilute the US demands and make the problem unfeasible, in the social construction of problems these controversies also reveal competing definitions of the same condition, in this case broadly defined as an illicit interaction between public and private actors.

Empirical studies of the illicit payments in question were understandably difficult because of the political sensitivity of the issue. The work on tax treatment of illicit payments was the only data source that provided some limited glimpse into the empirical dimension of the problem and some, albeit insufficient, quantitative understanding of the extent of transnational bribery in particular. The tax treatment of illicit payments was to be featured as an element of the Recommendation (DAFFE/IME/PI(93)6). The results of the questionnaire to which 16 members responded showed a varied treatment of bribery across the OECD area.[7] Most respondents had at least some provision for the deductibility of payments that could be considered illicit.[8] In addition to the United States, six other members had some provisions of non-tax deductibility of certain general payments.[9] Except for the United States, however, these provisions were not aimed at illicit payments abroad, although Austria and Canada had some extended jurisdiction in tax matters and non-deductibility of illicit payments. Under specific conditions, deductibility was possible for all respondents,

[7] The questionnaire was filled by Austria, Belgium, Canada, Finland, France. Germany, Italy, Japan, the Netherlands, New Zealand, Portugal, Spain, Switzerland, Turkey, the United Kingdom, the United States and included information about Denmark, Greece and Luxemburg from a previous study (C(90)87).

[8] The 'non-deductibility' of illicit payments meant that they were not considered as legitimate business expense, and their deductibility meant that governments were implicitly subsidizing illicit payments by making them tax free as business expenditure.

[9] Namely, in Austria, Belgium, Canada, France, Luxemburg, New Zealand, Norway and the United Kingdom such prohibition was underway (DAFFE/IME/PI(93)6).

including the United States, where facilitation payments for a 'routine government action' enjoyed tax deductibility at the time (6). In some cases (United States and France), prior government approval was necessary for the deductibility of such payments. In France under a confidential procedure, the Minister of Finance deemed payments with an undisclosed recipient abroad deductible, but this procedure had just been abolished. After 1993, such approval was no longer granted, but companies could still enjoy tax deductibility of certain payments as long as they met the legal requirements.

Only four members provided specific information about the number of illicit payments detected or reported in their tax system. In Belgium, 109 such payments were revealed between 1988 and 1992. In France, 200 annual requests were made. While New Zealand had only one reported case, Norway reported 5 such cases and a number of other domestic payments currently under investigation. In conclusion, since most countries imposed certain restrictions on the tax deductibility of illicit payments, harmonization was deemed feasible, albeit difficult (DAFFE/IME/PI (93)6). The work on the prohibition of tax deductibility of illicit payments provided an opening through which to push the anti-bribery agenda further as it led to a second Recommendation that was adopted by the Council on April 17, 1996 (C(96)27/FINAL). This incremental approach of building agreement on different facets of the issue was indicative of the excellent role of the OECD as a facilitator.

The facilitating role of the OECD was also instrumental in providing a forum for a broader range of actors. The anti-corruption work of the organization was presented not as an end in itself but as a first step in a broader anti-corruption agenda. OECD members had to consider undertaking: 'a commitment to promote anti-corruption policies within and beyond the OECD area, including a policy dialogue with non-OECD countries, which would permit the identification of the most suitable modalities for enhancing international efforts' (DAFFE/IME/PI(93)5, 4). The policy dialogue with non-members aimed to:

> [i]ncrease the awareness in non-Member countries of the importance of concerted actions to combat corrupt practices and illicit payments. Member countries could associate themselves with recent efforts by independent organizations such as Transparency International, as well as work already underway in the Development Assistance Committee, in order to jointly encourage and influence policy discussions of these issues in non-Member countries. (4–5)

TI was officially founded in May 1993, only three months prior to the report, and was already seen as a valuable partner in the talks (DAFFE/IME/PI(93)5. In 1993, President Clinton sent US officials to ask for TI's support and managed to secure it (Pope 2011). As Jeremy Pope, co-founder of TI, stated: 'We agreed – not on the basis of providing corporate America with a level playing field for export competition, but in the interest of the victims of corrupt practices, most notably the poor in the developing world' (158). With the initiative of the US executive, TI became a valuable ally in the pre-negotiation talks at a number of organizations, of which more will be said in this chapter.

At the same time that the subsequent drafts of the OECD Recommendation limited the problem of illicit payments to bribery, they universalized the relevance of the OECD initiative and to some extent discursively framed future debates on the subject: 'an OECD initiative to combat bribery could act as a catalyst for global action and could help companies to refuse to engage in such practices in host countries by setting standards of behavior to which they can refer' (DAFFE/IME/PI(93)9, 2). Furthermore, the Recommendation required the acceptance by non-members of the legitimacy of an anti-corruption agenda, because the cooperation of so-called host countries was necessary for successful implementation. Therefore, the Recommendation was seen as an element that would boost future cooperation with non-members as well:

> An important question in considering the effective application of the OECD Recommendation was how to associate non-OECD Member countries in the efforts to combat bribery. The Recommendation appeals to non-Member countries to join with OECD Members in their endeavours to combat the payment of bribes. It further asks Member countries to actively promote anti-corruption policies within and beyond the OECD area and to encourage non-Member countries to join in the OECD effort. (DAFFE/IME/PI(93)9, 5)

The policy dialogue promoted by the Recommendation had its first formal event in the form of an international symposium with non-OECD members in 1994 (later moved to 1995) (DAFFE/IME/PI(93)11). The symposium was tailored to 'increase awareness' of corruption with a broader audience of state and non-state actors and formulate a proposal for future course of action (3). The Ad Hoc Group on Illicit

Payments was further encouraged to make 'the results of their efforts to combat bribery more easily accessible to wider audiences' through the publication of their annual reviews and information exchange with non-members (6). The symposium and the efforts of the OECD to engage a wider audience in the anti-corruption effort, as early as 1993, are indicative of the coalition of governmental and non-governmental actors that was built with US leadership, and are discussed in the second part of this chapter.

The draft recommendation located the impetus for action in that: 'bribery is a widespread phenomenon in international business transactions, including trade and investment, raising serious moral and political concerns and distorting international competitive conditions' (DAFFE/IME/PI(93)11, 7).[10] The impact of the US delegation was not limited to the establishment of bribery as the offense, but was also influential on the hierarchy of proposed measures. The earlier drafts of the Recommendation did not promote criminal action as the top priority in addressing bribery and left considerable space for national maneuvering within the boundaries of the recommended behavior. In fact, criminalization of bribery did not initially make it as one of the recommended measures, with possible civil and administrative measures left to the discretion of member states. International cooperation was limited to actions in the line of bilateral agreements to provide information upon request. This hierarchy of priorities was not consistent with the US intention to use the Recommendation as a stepping-stone for the criminalization of corrupt transactions, possibly in an anti-bribery Convention. On December 6, 1993, the United States submitted an alternative draft recommendation which was adopted almost verbatim as the final text of the recommendation (DAFFE/IME/PI(93)10). The US draft added a definition of the offense and completely reshuffled the proposed measures for domestic action by placing criminalization as the top priority (DAFFE/IME/PI(93)10, 3). The US draft also appealed to the global relevance of the OECD initiative, highlighting the importance of relations with non-members and strengthening the links between the

[10] In the Draft Report to CIME, 'illicit payments' were already substituted with 'bribery' and a more forceful language was employed. The Report highlighted, however, that consensus has not been reached in a number of areas despite the fact that the feasibility of cooperation among OECD members has been developed since July 1990 (DAFFE/IME/PI (93)11).

OECD initiative and the other organizations. The United States urged the Secretariat to: 'consult with other international organizations and IFIs on effective means to combat bribery as an aid to promote the policy of good governance'. Member states were also invited to: 'promote anti-corruption policies within and beyond the OECD area and, in their dealings with non-Member countries' (DAFFE/IME/PI(93)10, 4).

The new draft recommendation reflected very closely the American text and did not incorporate the substance of the commentaries of other delegations, such as the Netherlands, Italy and Germany. The influence of the US delegation on the formulation of the actual text of the Recommendation was very significant, yet the notion of 'bribery' employed in this draft was far broader than a payment, reflecting the position of members who insisted on a definition of corrupt payments beyond traditional bribery.[11] Similar controversies emerged over the hierarchical list of measures promoted by the US delegation with criminal laws being the top choice of civil, administrative and other measures that were reflected in the new draft.[12]

In compromising about including criminal measures in the inventory, some delegations insisted that the list of recommended actions was not meant to be exhausted and that individual member states had discretionary space to decide which measures were applicable:

> While all Member countries agree to review all the areas listed under "domestic action", there are different opinions as to whether action will be necessary in every case. – It is agreed that domestic tax laws and regulations are to be reviewed by all Members, but there are different views on whether tax deductibility of bribes should be mentioned explicitly in the Recommendation, and on whether action to change tax laws and

[11]The definition of bribery was set in the draft as: '[such bribery can involve an intentional offer, promise, or giving of any undue pecuniary or other advantages to or for the benefit of a foreign public official (including members of a law-making body, candidates for a law-making body or public office and officials of political parties) whether or not solicited by the official, in violation of the official's legal duties, whether directly or indirectly through an intermediary, in order to obtain or retain business]' (DAFFE/IME/PI(93)10, 4). The bracketed text indicated that consensus had not yet been reached on the particular definition.

[12]The controversies over the definition were settled temporary with a 'working definition of bribery for practical purposes,' but the controversy over the list of measures was not so easily dissuaded (DAFFE/IME/PI(93)11, 7).

> regulations should be expected in every case. While Member countries agree that action in the area of criminal laws would be the most effective ways [sic] to deal with the problem of bribery in international business transactions, they also agree that it raises complex issues for implementation. Aside from outright criminalization, other possible means of action include criminalization if the act is criminal offence also in the target country, assimilation of the offence in the domestic legislation on request of the target country and extradition. (DAFFE/IME/PI(93)11/REV1, 3–4)

These battles between the US delegation and other OECD members are significant because they show differing claims on the question not only of bribery, but also of the proper actions to handle it. While the first text specified the prohibition of transnational bribery in the style of the FCPA, the second version concentrated on domestic prohibition of bribery and could have been interpreted far more liberally by individual member states. OECD members tried to oblige US demands but at the same time retain the ability to maneuver independently and retain discretion in their application of the new rules. The US delegation was not only determined to limit the offense to traditional bribery, but was also insisting on promoting criminalization along the lines of the FCPA and the latter formed the basis for future discord. Following the amendments of the FCPA in 1998, after the criminalization approach to transnational bribery was enshrined in a binding OECD Convention, the US law became applicable to foreign corporations. Companies such as Telia (Sweden), Siemens (Germany) and BAE (United Kingdom) were imposed record fines (FCPA Enforcement 2018). Enforcement records as of 2018 reveal that 8 out of the top 10 companies fined under the FCPA were foreign. Acceptance of the criminalization approach from the OECD partners allowed foreign companies to be prosecuted under the FCPA, and it also showed consensus on the highest possible level of condemnation of bribery. The United States also specifically connected the question of bribery to the good governance agenda, which was gaining momentum at the World Bank, and intended to get other organizations and financial institutions on board with the anti-bribery agenda (DAFFE/IME/PI(93)10).

The OECD Recommendation (RBIBT) adopted by the Council on May 27, 1994, demonstrated the political will of member states to tackle corrupt practices in international business transactions. It was an important signal for other international organizations and non-state actors that some level of intergovernmental consensus had been reached on the existence of a serious issue in need of a global remedy. While such general political commitments were also evident with the Resolutions of the 1970s, the choice of instrument this time entailed that OECD member states would have to take concrete measures in their respective national jurisdictions. The effectiveness of the instrument is the first way in which to understand the RBIBT as a breakthrough. Not all 'soft law' is made equal, and the peer review and monitoring system of the OECD Recommendations is a case in point. The FATF (FATF) Recommendations successfully developed and implemented global standards on money-laundering through 'soft law' (Pieth 1999). The second political aspect of the importance of the RBIBT is that it became a stepping-stone for further work at the OECD, but also the centerpiece of a systematic approach of state-sponsored coalition building in and between organizations.

The Making of the Global Anti-Corruption Eruption

In the 1994–1997 period, the foundations of the global anti-corruption architecture were laid out. The RBIBT constituted a landmark in this process because its adoption led to the introduction or re-introduction of the problem of corrupt practices (now predominantly understood as bribery) in the CoE, the EU, OAS, G7 and the UN. This section traces how this was carried out by OECD member states and how the agreements in different venues developed and started influencing each other. While non-state actors played a role in this process, their efforts were shaped and reinforced by previous endeavors of state actors, in particular the United States, and the ongoing intergovernmental dynamics. The change of venues coupled with the instrumental use of publicity contributed to the success of the OECD initiative to outlaw corrupt payments and led to the adoption of anti-corruption instruments in other regional and global forums. The formal agreements reached in other venues then provided the legal and discursive underpinnings for the re-introduction of the subject at the UN.

An understanding of global problems as natural would treat the anti-corruption eruption of the 1990s as an automatic response to a worsened condition. International organizations started adopting formal anti-corruption rules because levels of corruption increased and different organizations more or less automatically started trying to mitigate this increase. This approach brackets the role of member states as agenda setters in international organizations, as well as the overlapping membership base of many organizations. The former means that except for the notable case of the European Commission, much of the agenda of international organizations is dominated by the interests of their members. The latter means that because of their overlapping membership, especially with EU member states, an agreement reached at one organization might require talks to be held at another. The latter also means that states can hop from one international venue to another in search of a suitable environment for their grievances. Venue shopping (Baumgartner and Jones 2009) would be one prism through which to see the dynamics of the 1990s, but there is another element to this diffusion of venues. In the 1990s, the OECD became the major forum for the anti-corruption talks, and as this section shows, agreements in other venues were to some degree used instrumentally for reaching an agreement at the OECD.

The optimal solution of internationalizing the FCPA through a binding treaty was deemed not to be feasible at the OECD in the early 1990s. One of the major stated obstacles was getting developing nations on board. Having made some progress with European partners at the OECD with the RBIBT, the US government approached the member states of OAS. The US Office of Government Ethics and the US Information Agency launched the First International Conference on Ethics in Government in Washington DC in November 1994 (Feinberg 1997). The following month, the Summit of the Americas in Miami made addressing corruption a priority for the organization. Feinberg (1997), who was personally involved in the negotiations, traces how the US government engaged other state actors prior to the topic being raised for the first time in OAS. An Interagency Working Group (IWG) was created in 1993 to deal with corruption in the framework of Inter-American relations and was later renamed as the Democracy IWG. Michael Skol, who became Head of the IWG, had excellent knowledge of Venezuelan domestic politics through his work as US Ambassador to Caracas and expected that the US bid would be received well by the new Venezuelan government because the corruption-related scandals the country recently experienced had led to the impeachment of the president. Feinberg singles out winning Venezuela as an ally and receiving its support for the internationalization of the FCPA (in exchange for the inclusion of measures on extradition) as one of the major factors for the successful anti-corruption campaign in OAS. As part of the US consensus building strategy, a series of meetings were organized in

Washington through the embassies of a small core of member states (Venezuela, Chile, Honduras and Ecuador) that carried out a considerable amount of work prior to the official announcement of corrupt practices as an agenda item in the Miami Summit (Feinberg 1997). The OAS Working Group on Probity and Ethics worked in close cooperation with the Washington Working Group. The drafts produced by the two groups 'paralleled' each other and the US government managed to imprint its influence on the final draft of the Convention (119).

Even though the anti-bribery agenda constituted a top priority for the United States at the Summit, President Clinton was evasive of naming the practices 'corrupt' (Elliott 1997). As much as the word 'corruption' had a negative connotation, the trouble was that calling the practices 'corrupt' was also a direct reference to the 'corrupt' practices act that the US executive was trying to internationalize. It was the Vice President of Ecuador Alberto Dahik who was chairman of the Advisory body of TI who promoted the explicit use of 'corruption' as an agenda item.[13] The anti-corruption project was introduced into the general theme of probity and civic ethics raised by Chile in the post-Pinochet era (Manfroni and Werksman 2003). As mentioned previously, the US government was interested in introducing the subject of transnational bribery and Venezuela was interested in establishing extradition and mutual assistance procedures in order to mitigate the consequences of the 1994 banking crisis (Feinberg 1997). The Chilean Ambassador to OAS, Edmundo Carreño presided over the Working Group on Probity and Ethics (Manfroni and Werksman 2003). The Working Group, comprised of national experts mandated by almost all member governments, met at the Washington headquarters of OAS a number of times in order to amend and prepare the draft text of the Convention (Carreño 2000). During the Summit of the Americas in Miami, the United States persuaded its partners to establish cooperation with the OECD Working Group on Bribery, which superseded the Ad Hoc Group on Illicit Payments in 1994 (Elliott 1997). As a consequence of this liaison, the OAS Group adopted a definition of the offense that almost verbatim reproduced the OECD preliminary definition (DAFFE/IME/PI(93)1). The Convention was successfully adopted on March 29, 1996, and Article VIII in practice internationalized the FCPA for the first time (Elliott 1997; Feinberg 1997).

[13]Dahik himself had to leave Ecuador in 1995 on corruption charges, an incident that according to Galtung and Pope (1999) made TI realize that politicians should not be included in TI's higher management.

The leadership of the US executive through a technique of issue-specific coalition building was instrumental for the successful adoption of the Convention (Feinberg 1997). Feinberg credits the careful US preparatory work for diffusing the North–South tension on the global anti-bribery initiative. Furthermore, the liaison between OAS and the OECD Working Group proposed by the United States showed that the inter-American consensus would have positive repercussions for furthering the work of the OECD. The OAS Convention was indicative of an agreement between developing and developed nations on a common anti-bribery approach. The primarily US interest remained in the OECD, as internationalizing the FCPA among the members of OAS would not have been as consequential as convincing the major European investors to impose restrictions on their companies. The OAS progress, therefore, provided a bargaining chip for the United States at the OECD. Developing countries were finally on board with the US-sponsored anti-bribery campaign.

The OAS agreement also testified that the US issue-specific coalition building was effective. An essential aspect of the coalition building was that intergovernmental cooperation was enriched by meetings between the Democracy IWG and a number of INGOs such as the US section of the ICC and TI. Feinberg who was a special assistant to President Clinton and senior director of Inter-American Affairs at the National Security Council sought out TI's support in early 1994 (Vogl 2012). Vogl, co-founder of TI, agreed to utilize TI's connections in Latin America in order to convince another government to officially raise the question of corruption on the OAS agenda because: 'the United States could not diplomatically raise the issue itself as this would be resented' (185).[14] The US success in building this broader coalition with non-governmental actors even before the topic was raised in OAS was fundamental for the quick negotiation and successful adoption of the OAS Convention.

Involving INGOs and business actors has become a successful US strategy for issue-specific coalition building (Feinberg 1997). Proposals to include TI in the work of the OECD on corrupt payments were made immediately after the INGO was founded in 1993 (DAFFE/IME/PI(93)5). As noted previously, President Clinton managed to secure TI's support for the OECD initiative (Elliott 1997; Pope 2011). TI was

[14] This is how the support of the President of Costa Rica, Oscar Arias, and the Vice President of Ecuador, Alberto Dahik, was secured (Vogl 2012).

also very invested in facilitating a global solution to corrupt practices in international business transactions in particular. The US Chapter of the INGO carried out most of the correspondence with the OECD and it is emblematic that its slogan at the time was, 'The coalition to curb corruption in international business transactions' (TI-USA 1998). The main interlocutor with the OECD who submitted and presented reports at the Meeting of the OECD Working Group on Bribery in International Business Transactions was the Chairman of TI-USA Fritz Heimann. He was advocating a synergetic anti-corruption approach between governments and companies and was urging governments to adopt the Recommendation on the tax deductibility of bribes, which was the next stepping-stone in the signing of a binding treaty in 1997 (Heimann 1996a). The TI-USA Chairman also contributed in his dual capacity as a representative of the ICC and as a Counselor to the General Counsel of the General Electric Company (Heimann 1996b). The triple capacity of the main interlocutor with the OECD is revealing of the way in which the experience with the FCPA shaped the interests of American corporations and organized business in becoming anti-corruption activists. In the mid-1990s, a series of high-profile prosecutions by the Department of Justice, such as General Electric in 1994 and Lockheed in 1995, reminded US business to get on board with the government agenda of internationalizing the FCPA (Pieth 2013). The Chairman of the OECD WG on Bribery pointed to the 'effective lobbying of the US business sector' as a major contributing factor for the success of the OECD anti-corruption agenda (17).

While American companies were firmly behind their government's agenda to promote an international anti-bribery pact, their major competitors from other OECD member states were opposed to the endeavor and TI got involved in turning the opinion of members of the business community in the United Kingdom, France and Germany with some success (Vogl 2012). A series of meetings was carried out by TI with the German business representatives at the Aspen Institute in Berlin during the decisive years prior to the adoption of the OECD Convention (Eigen 2013). TI managed to influence the position of the German business community on countering transnational bribery and this had an impact on the German government signing the OECD Convention.

TI is celebrated for its coalition building, but TI was also part of an intergovernmental coalition-building strategy with US leadership. Furthermore, a broad network of interlocutors of civil society and business actors, as well as intergovernmental organizations and global financial institutions, was established from within the OECD. In March 1995, as a follow-up of the Symposium on Corruption and Good Governance, an anti-corruption network was created between the OECD as organizer and the OAS, CoE, the IMF, the World Bank, the UN, as well as other organizations (Symposium 1996). The Symposium gained considerable media attention in the Financial Times (FT), the International Herald Tribune and the BBC among many (Coburn 1995; Glynn et al. 1997). The reference of the former Costa Rican President, Oscar Sanchez, to the 'cancer of corruption' was particularly well received in global media outlets and the FT in particular (Adonis and Jack 1995). Reminiscent of the words of Senator Church in 1975 that: 'A cancer is eating away at the vitals of Western society and that cancer is corruption' (quoted in Vogl 2012, 164), the 'cancer is corruption' slogan would later come to symbolize the policy change in the World Bank. By the time President Wolfensohn made his emblematic 'cancer of corruption' speech in October 1996, the anti-corruption agenda already had the intergovernmental seal of approval with the OAS Convention and the work underway in the OECD, CoE and the EU.

The role of the OECD as a facilitator was particularly important in creating broad coalitions among a range of actors. Special meetings with the private sector and INGOs (including TI and ICC) in the OECD were organized and they included representatives of the World Bank. Such formal meetings were carried out in 1996, for example, to inform the private sector about the Recommendation on tax deductibility of bribes and to receive feedback from business representatives on the proposed route to criminalization (DAFFEE/IME/BR/A(96)6/REV1). In 1996, the ICC revised its Rules of Conduct adopting much of the language of the RBIBT and specifically urging governments to implement the measures proposed in the OECD Recommendation. In addition to a reference to the RBIBT, the revised text urged the World Bank and the European Bank for Reconstruction and Development (EBRD) to contribute to the anti-corruption agenda (ICC Rules of Conduct 1996).

While the United States was keeping busy at the OAS, to which the Europeans had no access, European governments were shuffling the anti-bribery agenda item through organizations that the United States was excluded from. The RBIBT which led to the resurgence of the negotiations at the OECD was immediately followed by the 19th Conference of European Ministers of Justice in Valletta in June 1994, which issued recommendations that prepared the ground for the Programme of Action against Corruption adopted by the Committee of Ministers of the CoE in November 1996 (Civil Law Convention on Corruption 1999b). The 19th Conference was carried out under the theme of 'Administrative, civil and penal aspects, including the role of the judiciary, of the fight against corruption' and it examined the consequences of the RBIBT and the future work on predominantly civil and administrative (but also possibly criminal) measures against transnational corruption and bribery (CM(94)117). The Secretary-General of the CoE stressed the 'European dimension of the problem facing old and new democracies alike' and argued that the 'response to the problem must be European as well' and it entailed collective measures of European states (3). The Ministers of Justice discussed the issues raised at the OECD and the choice of remedies set out in the RBIBT. Resolution 1 was indicative of the overlap with the agenda of the OECD Working Group and also established a Group on Corruption within the CoE which would map future action for European states (including the drafting of a Convention) that would be enacted in coordination with the OECD and the UN (19–21). The preference for administrative and civil measures was clearly discernible in these early CoE talks, and it was indicative of the vigor with which European countries opposed the US criminalization approach at the OECD.

The considerable overlap between the membership base of the OECD and the CoE made the latter a useful forum for the coordination of anti-corruption policies of European states. In 1994, nineteen members of the OECD were also members of the CoE, and after the accession of the Czech Republic (1995), Hungary (1996) and Poland (1996) to the OECD, the overlap increased to 22 common member states. Furthermore, the fact that most CoE members were also EU member states caused not only the spread of discussions from one organization to another, but also later the explicit coordination of the negotiations leading to the Common Position of October 6, 1997, and the Second Joint Position of November 13, 1997, concerning the coordination of work on corrupt practices underway in the three organizations, so as to avoid conflict or duplication (Szarek-Manson 2010).[15] The need to coordinate positions and policies in order to achieve a common legal basis on issues

[15]When work advanced at the UN, coordination was necessary in 4 organizations and this was reflected in the Coordinated Position for the UN, adopted by the Council of the EU on February 28, 2001 (Szarek-Mason 2010).

between EU members led to the inclusion of anti-corruption measures in the Convention on the Protection of the European Communities' Financial Interests, adopted on July 26, 1995. Later, the EU Convention against Corruption Involving Public Officials was adopted on May 26, 1997, and its main goal was to ensure that members adopted criminal provisions which would cover cases of bribery not only of their national public officials, but also of holders of public office in other EU member states. In this way, the EU created an albeit limited system of criminalization of corruption of foreign public officials within its own membership base before the adoption of the OECD Convention on Combating Bribery of Foreign Public Officials in International Business Transactions in December of the same year. The key here was that the EU agreement was not valid for third parties, but only between the members of the organization. This seemingly innocuous detail was a powerful bargaining tool for the OECD talks. If the approach adopted here was to be applied in the OECD Convention that would have meant that bribery of foreign officials would have been criminalized only among the members of the OECD and not in developing countries, for example.

The EU and CoE initiatives are best understood in conjunction with the progression of the OECD talks after the adoption of the RBIBT. As it was evident in the negotiation of he RBIBT itself, at first the European states were interested in discarding the criminalization approach that the United States was promoting in relation to internationalizing the FCPA. Later on, in preparation for increasingly likely negotiations of a binding treaty in 1997, if criminalization was to be chosen, it was preferable that the EU model of an *inter partes* treaty be applied to the OECD instrument as well. These ingenious tactics of the European countries and the United States led to the diffusion of the talks into a number of venues and are given further attention in this chapter.

The Instrumental Use of Venues and Publicity: The OECD Convention and Beyond

If we are to look at the anti-corruption eruption of the mid-1990s with the fresh eyes of somebody, who was unaware of the confidential intergovernmental talks that had been going on for decades, a clear picture would emerge. An explosion of corruption scandals in the mid-1990s was clearly driving the anti-corruption campaign. That was particularly valid for the European member states in the OECD. An imposing number of European partners were facing domestic crises concerning what Harris (2003) calls the small 'c'—that is, corruption scandals that are symptomatic of the broader phenomenon of corruption, but do not exhaust it. Italy, France, Germany, Spain and the United Kingdom all experienced a series of corruption-related political scandals and instability (Della Porta and Mény 1997). It looked like a number of state actors within and outside of Europe faced similar crises of political legitimacy as the United States did in the 1970s. All of these cases of alleged corruption within nation states led the FT to categorize 1995 as the 'Year of Corruption' while a joint survey of FT, The Economist and New York Times showed that there had been a fourfold increase in reporting on corruption between 1984 and 1995 (Tanzi 1998). At the same time, as Vogl (2012) also observes, the corruption-related political scandals of the 1970s were no less turbulent. They were severe in the United States, but also implicated other Western democracies. Yet, the corruption scandals of the 1970s did not generate enough support for the US international ban on bribery. What was different in the 1990s? While the next chapter tries to articulate a more systematic response to this question, this chapter argues that the instrumental use of venues and publicity was the determining factor for the success of the US bid on transnational bribery in the 1990s. It was the US strategy to connect these national, highly reported, occurrences of the small 'c' to the issue of transnational bribery through the 'calculated use of public diplomacy' that made the difference in the 1990s (Glynn et al. 1997, 20).

The corruption accusations in OECD member states, such as France (Fay 1995), the United Kingdom and Spain, influenced the climate of the OECD negotiation process in the mid-1990s (Della Porta and Mény 1997), but were in no way sufficient in and of themselves to steer an international approach to corruption, and in particular to transnational bribery. The 'sensitization' of the European public to the subject of corruption was successfully employed by US officials, who 'observed the high level of European public interest in all aspects of corruption, including the OECD discussions' (Abbott and Snidal 2002, 164). As Abbott and Snidal observe, political scandals culminating in the mid-1990s made the European public highly attentive to issues of corruption and State Department officials managed to link the preoccupation with domestic corruption to the question of transnational bribery. It is a valid assumption to make that these cases of national corruption scandals must have made some of the US partners more susceptible to support an OECD-sponsored anti-corruption instrument. This is why the success of the 'vague' RBIBT has been attributed to the US attempt to bring 'domestic political pressure, motivated by value considerations' to the negotiation table (Abbott and Snidal 2002, 164). At the same time, there was no indication that these national troubles with corruption would become a global issue with a formidable global governance architecture. The scandals in European countries from the mid-1990s might have caused national reforms and even international declarations of concern, but in no way were they in and of themselves related to the US bid to criminalize transnational bribery, and as we already saw, it was that bid, which was driving the talks at the OECD, the OAS, and to a significant extent the EU and the CoE.

In addition to US leadership, other factors inherent to the internal workings of the OECD, such as controversy management and the progressive study of feasibility, as well as the expert Chairmanship of Mark Pieth, contributed to the success of the OECD talks. The Council Recommendation of 1994 differed from the general political statements against corrupt practices of the 1970s because of the specific provisions for review and follow-up procedures that were included under title VIII (C(94)75/FINAL). The monitoring provisions prompted a peer review process, which turned 'into one of the most dynamic instruments of international law' (Pieth 2013, 17). Title IX specifically provided for a review within 3 years, which led to the revision of the Recommendation on May 23, 1997, this time specifically in the line of criminalization (C(97)123/FINAL). Furthermore, on April 11, 1996, another issue which had come out of the feasibility study of the Ad Hoc Group, the tax deductibility of bribes, was adopted in the Recommendation on tax deductibility (C(96)27/FINAL). In fact, the two Council Recommendations remained the major testimonies of the political commitment of states to tackle bribery even after the adoption of the binding treaty (Pieth 2013). The RBIBT, in particular, set in motion a process of peer review and monitoring that secured steady progress.

After the RBIBT, the battle was not to agree on the existence of a problem, which the United States managed to narrow down to bribery, but to push for criminal measures. European partners, in particular Germany and France (at first joined by the United Kingdom), were resisting the US attempt to promote criminalization by internationalizing the FCPA (DAFFE/IME/

BR/RD(95)1).[16] The US State Department wanted a binding treaty, but as this appeared infeasible was content with the recommendation on tax deductibility and the revision of the RBIBT in the direction of criminalization (Abbott and Snidal 2002). Germany and France, however, proposed a binding treaty, with the former choosing the UN as the venue for negotiation and the latter preferring the WTO (Pieth 2013). This seemingly counterintuitive joint move by the German and French delegations was done in order to deflect talks for a binding instrument to organizations that were chosen because of the likelihood of stalemate. The pre-negotiation talks at the UN were still referred to as the 'disaster of 1976' (Blum 2009, 2) and the US executive had historically avoided raising the issue of illicit payments at GATT and the WTO.[17,18]

Pieth (2018) credits the Deputy-Director of Directorate for Financial, Fiscal and Enterprise Affairs (DAFFE) at the time, Rainer Geiger, for calling the European bluff and proposing a Convention at the OECD. While prior to the RBIBT in 1994, the US delegation was pushing for a Treaty, Pieth managed to convince them to explore the Recommendation option, based on the positive experience with FATF. The return to the Convention route at the OECD, therefore, came as an unexpected turn of events at this stage. The threat by the reluctant European partners to move the talks to the UN or the WTO provides another example of the instrumental use of venues during the pre-negotiation talks.

The OECD partners were also bringing agreements reached in other organizations to the negotiation table. Work underway in regional organizations, such as OAS, the EU and the CoE, became part of the persuasion strategies of both camps. The United States was using the OAS Convention to invalidate the argument that criminalizing the supply side of bribes constituted interference in the domestic affairs of another state (or the sovereignty of the so-called host countries). In

[16]The 're-discovery' of the 1906 Prevention of Corruption Act and the repercussions of the 'cash for questions' controversy had a definitive impact on the UK position and the new government (formed in May 1997) wanted to take a strong stance against corruption (Alldridge 2012; Bean 2012).

[17]As discussed in Chapter 4, Senate Resolution 265 of 1975 specified GATT as the institutional forum for negotiations, but representatives of the US executive did not concur with this strategy, as they judged it would have been highly unlikely to reach consensus at GATT.

[18]The United States did raise the issue of transparency in procurement at the WTO, but after the adoption of the OECD Convention (International Trade Commission 1997).

fact, after the adoption of the OAS Convention, Tarullo argued that the member states of OAS 'suggest that governments of developed countries... by failing to act against foreign bribery by their own multinationals, [are] complicit in the bribery' (quoted in Ashe 2005, 2912). While the US delegation used the agreement at OAS as a bargaining tool, the European partners used the agreements reached at the CoE and the EU to set the tone of the OECD agreement. France and Germany presented a draft Convention based on the texts negotiated at the EU and the CoE (Pieth 2013). The EU Convention against Corruption Involving Public Officials (May 26, 1997) was adopted prior to the negotiations for a binding Treaty at the OECD, which commenced in October, and it criminalized bribery of holders of public office in other EU member states, but not in third counties (European Union 1998). If this approach was to be applied to the OECD Convention, as Germany and France wanted, it would have entailed criminalization only among members of the OECD (or the countries that sign the Convention); in other words, Germany, for example, would have made it illegal for a German company to bribe an official in Canada, but not in Bangladesh or Venezuela. This, albeit significant, concession would not have been satisfactory for the United States, because it would not have provided global coverage and would have internationalized the FCPA only incompletely. The United States rebuffed the European *inter partes* approach by arguing that only a global coverage would be legitimate (Abbott and Snidal 2002). The goal of the US delegation was to reach an agreement for the criminalization of bribery in countries outside the OECD area.

Targeting the OECD as the primary forum to address the corrupt payments issue in 1989 was a strategic move to internationalize the FCPA among the main US investment competitors at the time. The US preference can also be explained with the historic and financial influence that it has at the OECD—historic because the organization was created in 1948 to implement the Marshall Plan for postwar Europe, and financial because the United States was still the biggest contributor, providing 22% of the organization's budget. As Carolyn Ervin, counselor at Directorate for Financial and Enterprise Affairs (DAF) at the OECD, put it in a fax to Pieth referring to a visit of the organization's Secretary-General to the United States: 'He [Donald Johnston] intends that bribery be one of his major points for persuading Washington of how useful is the OECD.' The US delegation to the OECD had the political clout to retain the issue of corrupt payments on the agenda of the organization for the period 1989–1994 when little concern for the transnational aspect of such practices existed among other member states.

While what was happening in the OECD was important, external strategies were just as important, and they did not concern solely the OAS, the EU and the CoE. The most important external element that contributed to the success of the OECD talks was the instrumental use of publicity or the use of public diplomacy (Glynn et al. 1997; Abbott and Snidal 2002). As discussed previously, just because all the major European OECD members (Germany, France, United Kingdom, Italy and Spain) underwent a series of corruption-related political scandals did not mean that an international approach would be automatically sought after. In fact, connecting these broader domestic corruption issues to transnational bribery through the instrumental use of publicity was a way of turning national troubles into global problems, to paraphrase the famous formulation by Mills (1959). US officials managed to interlock public concerns over democratic accountability and national corruption with transnational bribery through the European press, which was attentive to suggestions that national politicians appeared supportive of bribery in an international context (Abbott and Snidal 2002). As Glynn et al. (1997) also confirm: 'American officials took their case to the international media, which proved remarkably receptive' (21).

The OECD press reviews from the period 1994–1997 show an overwhelming interest in the OECD talks with thousands of publications referring to the organization's anti-corruption effort and relating it to national corruption scandals. At the same time, media interest peaked around the adoption of the revised recommendation in May 1997 and the months covering the negotiation of the treaty (October–December 1997). The Journal of Commerce, the Washington Post, the International Herald Tribune, The New York Times, The France Press Agency, Le Monde, The Yomiuri Shimbun all published series of articles reflecting on the position of France and Germany as obstructive and quoting US officials who criticized the strategies of the two European countries to block the US proposal to outlaw bribery (Blustein 1997). While the tax deductibility of bribes was discussed at CIME with the Fiscal Affair Committee, the US Trade Representative, Michael Kantor, threatened that the United States would impose trade sanctions on the reluctant European partners and that (most likely unsubstantiated) threat received broad media coverage (Glynn et al. 1997).

This mounting pressure through the media in which the positions of countries were publicly exposed was the culmination of the strategy of public diplomacy that ultimately provided part of the external impetus to adopt the Revised Recommendation in May 1997 and the OECD Convention in December of the same year. From within the OECD and CIME, in particular, work on controversy management continued and a list of 'Agreed Common Elements' was provided on which consensus for the Revised Recommendation and/or the proposed binding instrument would later be built (Pieth 2013). While these elements provided the backbone for agreement, the key to the successful resolution of the OECD talks was lying in another change of institutional setting: the G7. As a TI Press Release (1998) put it later: 'G7 Summit holds the key to Global Anti-Bribery Treaty.' While OECD member states were the target audience for US efforts to internationalize the FCPA, the US strategy from the start was to concentrate on the G7 (Pieth 2018). A series of meetings were organized prior to the 23rd G7 Summit in Denver. The meeting of the G7 Ministers and Central Bank Governors on April 27, 1997, in Washington produced a statement of support for the anti-corruption work of the (IFIs) and the OECD (Washington G7 Meeting). Following the Communiqué of G7 Finance Ministers was a series of preparatory meetings between Washington, DC and Airlie Center, VA on May 22–24, 1997, that proved to be decisive for reaching a compromise between OECD member states (The White House 2014).

The US executive was prepared to move forward without France and Germany and requested the support of the United Kingdom, but Tarullo, who was Clinton's personal representative to the Summit, attempted to secure the Franco-German agreement, as the following telegram from the OECD Archives reveals:

> He [US Representative to OECD, Alan Larson] thought that the Germans might be prepared to move towards accepting the US conditions. Since the ECSS, the US had lobbied them at high level (letters from Attorney General Reno and Commerce Secretary Daley to their counterparts). In circulating the revised draft G7 statement, they had made clear US readiness to take this to the Summit. Tarullo would be pressing hard at Airlie House. Kohl would not wish to be embarrassed at Denver. (Washington Embassy Telegram 1997)

As Pieth (2018) notes, 'between spring and autumn 1997 intensive lobbying took place' through US embassies in key capitals (83). Reaching, what Pieth (2013) calls the 'compromise of May 1997,' ensured that in case the negotiations of a binding instrument failed by April 1, 1998, members would nonetheless enact criminalization measures in accordance with the Revised Recommendation (19). The fate of the OECD Convention was also decided when the G7 members agreed to proceed with ratification (Pieth 2013). The exact way in which the compromise of May 1997, which essentially secured the criminalization of bribery, was reached remains unspecified, but the change of venues, the instrumental use of publicity and the 'embarrassment factor' remained an effective part of the persuasion arsenal of the US President's personal representative. Abbott and Snidal (2002) note that: 'Tarullo carried with him (or told people he did) a list of the 10 largest bribe-paying companies in the world' and he would threaten to make the list public with a tap on his pocket (164). Through public diplomacy and the threat of publicity, the US executive would essentially recreate the consequences of the public revulsion that took over Europe and the United States in the 1970s, but as Abbott and Snidal point out, the public distaste for corrupt practices in Europe was not mobilized in the 1970s, the way it was in the 1990s.

The key to signing the Convention on December 17, 1997, can be seen to lie in the compromise enshrined in Section 3 of the Revised Recommendation, which ensured that criminalization measures would be enacted by April 1998, even if the negotiation of a binding instrument failed. This development is revealing of how the neglected period of pre-negotiations is much more important than usually assumed. In the social construction of problems, the decision to open treaty negotiations would suggest a high level of intersubjective agreement on the parameters of the problem. This is not to say that the negotiation of the binding treaty was not a difficult process. Metcalfe (2000) provides an elaborate account of the negotiation process itself and shows that the negotiation was an abrasive process, of which the participants were not 'enamored' (150). The main reason for that, however, was the last minute introduction by the United States of the divisive issue of criminalization of payments to foreign political parties (Metcalfe 2000). The particular issue did not make it into the final text, but criminalization as the 'strongest form of condemnation' (Abbott and Snidal 2002, 167) testified to the formal seriousness that OECD member states now attributed to the problem of corrupt payments.

The specific facet of corruption, defined as transnational bribery, enshrined in the OECD Convention and the Council Recommendations appeared as a threshold through which corruption arrived publicly on the intergovernmental and global agendas. This is also formally acknowledged in the explicit statement of influence or the discursive impact of the RBIBT and the OECD Convention on agreements reached in international organizations, such as the CoE, the EU, OAS and the UN (in particular Article 16 of UNCAC).[19] With the OECD, the OAS, the EU and CoE being on board with the anti-corruption agenda, the UN followed suit with the Global Program Against Corruption in March 1999. Elaboration on a potential global instrument commenced the following year with the UN General Assembly Resolution 55/61. The final version of the UN Convention Against Corruption was ready by the end of 2003 and entered into force on December 14, 2005.

A few elements contributed to the re-introduction of the topic of corrupt payments to the UN in a different tone. The most important one was that the UNCTC was abolished in 1992 under a US-inspired financial restructuring of the organization and the work on the Code of Conduct was suspended. Following the adoption of the two OECD Recommendations in December 1996, the US Department of State sponsored the UN Declaration Against Corruption and Bribery in International Commercial Transactions (Department of State 1997). The Declaration 51/191 closely followed the language of the RBIBT urging states to criminalize corruption and bribery of foreign public officials and to proscribe the tax deductibility of bribes. A year earlier on December 20, 1995, Resolution 50/106 was adopted, which in Article 6 urged ECOSOC to decide on a time frame for the UN Draft Agreement on Illicit Payments developed

[19] As it was noted earlier, the RBIBT of 1994 which led to the resurgence of the negotiations at the OECD was paralleled by the recommendations of the 19th Conference of European Ministers of Justice in Valletta in 1994 that prepared the ground for the 'Programme of Action against Corruption' adopted by the Committee of Ministers of the CoE in November 1996. Resolution 1, adopted by the European Ministers of Justice at their 21st Conference in Prague in 1997, followed the adoption of the revised OECD Recommendation and urged for the implementation of the Program. In the EU, the Common Position 97/661/JHA from October 6, 1997, defined by the Council on negotiations in the CoE and the OECD relating to corruption, also established a formal link between the adoption of the RBIBT, the OECD Anti-Bribery Convention and the subsequent Criminal and Civil Law Conventions on Corruption adopted in 1999.

under the auspices of the eponymous commission (A/RES/51/191).[20] The Draft Agreement on Illicit Payments from 1978 (UNTERM 2014) was based on the FCPA. Boswell (1997) argued that the UN Declaration against Corruption and Bribery from 1996 was indicative of the expanding political will to approach globally the question of corruption and bribery in particular. In 1999, however, when the UN Secretary-General was launching the Global Compact at the World Economic Forum, he was still reluctant to talk about anti-corruption provisions (Vogl 2012). Despite the Declaration from December 1996, anti-corruption legislation was slower to emerge at the UN. Vogl (2012) credits the fact that other regional organizations came to develop anti-corruption instruments, as well as the mounting pressure from the Clinton Administration to investigate bribery and kickbacks in the Oil-for-Food Program, as incentives for anti-corruption work at the UN in the late 1990s.

Following the Global Program Against Corruption in March 1999 and after the inclusion of provisions on corruption in the United Nations Convention against Transnational Organized Crime (UNTOC) in December 2000, the decision to work toward an international legal instrument against corruption was taken by the General Assembly (A/RES/55/61). The Ad Hoc Committee for the Negotiation of the Convention against Corruption met over seven sessions in the period from January 2002 to October 2003. As the declassification period of the UN documents is 20 years, records and minutes from the pre-negotiation talks and the negotiation of the UNCAC Treaty are not yet made available. The former chairman of the Ad Hoc Committee for the negotiation of a Convention against Corruption, Dr. M. Touq, has elaborated that while criminalization was seen as the sensible way forward by all states, UN members were 'bitterly divided over the definition of corruption' (Touq 2013). Another source of initial controversy was that the G77 and China wanted to include illegal transfer of funds, which led to the provision on asset recovery (Vlassis 2004).

The final text of the Convention had significantly broadened the type of covered practices, such as trading in influence and private sector corruption (UNODC 2014). The point of view had shifted, however, and as the next chapter shows, this cannot be entirely explained with the end of the Cold War and the natural waning of ideological controversies.

[20]This line of work was carried out in accordance with the UN Crime Prevention Congresses and was discussed in Chapter 6.

Furthermore, by the time the UNCAC was negotiated, it was seen as the cumulative work on top of a number of intersecting legal regimes that had already been put into place in regional organizations (Touq 2013). From a constructivist vantage point, the agreements reached in regional organizations and the OECD discursively shaped the parameters of debate for the UN as well. Although 'UNCAC expands past definitions of corruption' (Eicher 2012, 120), the question of corrupt payments in the UN in the 1990s had lost its radical potential in comparison with the talks in the 1970s. The UN debates on corruption were no longer challenging the rules of the international economic system and the power of multinational corporations to shape politics. The global anti-corruption campaign had shifted its focus from corporate to government abuse of power, and this dramatic change is given further attention in the final chapter.

References

Abbott, Kenneth W., and Duncan Snidal. 2002. "Values and Interests: International Legalization in the Fight Against Corruption." *Journal of Legal Studies* 31 (1): 141–178.

Adonis, Andrew, and Andrew Jack. 1995. "OECD to Press for Anti-Corruption Laws." *Financial Times*, March 21. Copy in the OECD Archives.

Alldridge, P. W. 2012. "The U.K. Bribery Act: 'The Caffeinated Younger Sibling of the FCPA'." *Ohio State Law Journal* 73 (5): 1181–1216.

Ashe, Daniel Patrick. 2005. "The Lengthening Anti-Bribery Lasso of the United States: The Recent Extraterritorial Application of the U.S. Foreign Corrupt Practices Act." *The Fordham Law Review* 73 (6): 2897.

Baumgartner, Frank, and Bryan Jones. 2009. *Agendas and Instability in American Politics*. 2nd ed. Chicago and London: Chicago University Press.

Bean, Bruce W. 2012. "Further to Professor Alldridge's 'Caffeinated' Article: What 'Stuff' Did the Professor Have in Mind?" Working Paper, Social Science Research Network.

Blum, Jack. 2009. "Testimony on the Problem of Curbing Grand Scale Global Corruption Before the Committee on Financial Services, U.S. House of Representatives." 111th Congress, 1st Session, May 19.

Blustein, Paul. 1997. "Fight Looms over Foreign Bribery: France, Germany Blocking Efforts to Outlaw Practice, U.S. Officials Say." *Washington Post*, May 9. Copy in OECD Archives.

Boswell, Nancy Zucker. 1997. "Emerging Consensus on Controlling Corruption." *Journal of International Law* 18 (4): 44–69.

Business Anti-Corruption Portal. 2014. "Compliance Resources." Accessed October 22, 2014. http://www.business-anti-corruption.com/.

C(94)75/FINAL. 1994. *Recommendation of the Council on Bribery in International Business Transactions, Adopted by the Council on 27 1994 at Its 829th Session* (July 11). OECD Archives, Paris Headquarters.

C(96)27/FINAL. 1996. *Recommendation of the Council on the Tax Deductibility of Bribes to Foreign Public Officials, Adopted by the Council on 11 April 1996 at Its 873rd Session* (April 17). OECD Archives, Paris Headquarters.

C(97)123/FINAL. 1997. *Revised Recommendation of the Council on Bribery in International Business Transactions, Adopted by the Council at Its 901st Session on 23 May 1997* (May 30). OECD Archives, Paris Headquarters.

Carreño, Edmundo Vargas. 2000. "The Inter-American Convention Against Corruption." Paper Presented at the Conference for Transparency and Development in Latin America and the Caribbean, Lima, Peru, February 8–10.

Coburn, Sara. 1995. "OECD Symposium Against Bribery." *BBC TV1*, March 13. Copy of transcript in the OECD Archives.

Common Position 97/661/JHA. 1997. "Common Position Drawn Up on the Basis of Article K.3 of the Treaty on European Union on Negotiations in the Council of Europe and the OECD Relating to Corruption." *Official Journal L* 279 (October 6): 1–2.

Conference of European Ministers of Justice. 1995. *Administrative, Civil, and Penal Aspects, Including the Role of the Judiciary, of the Fight against Corruption. Proceedings, 19th Conference of European Ministers of Justice CM(94)117, June 14–15, 1994, Valletta, Malta.* Strasbourg: Council of Europe Publishing.

Council of Europe. 1999a. *Criminal Law Convention on Corruption = Convention Pénale Sur La Corruption.* Strasbourg: Council of Europe Publication.

———. 1999b. *Civil Law Convention on Corruption: And Explanatory Report.* Strasbourg: Council of Europe Publishing.

DAFFE/IME/PI(91)1. *Agenda.* Ad Hoc Group on Illicit Payments (June 13, 1991). OECD Archives, Paris Headquarters.

———(91)2. *Feasibility Study on Available International Means for Dealing with Illicit Payments in International Commercial Transactions.* Ad Hoc Group on Illicit Payments, Note by the Secretariat (June 13, 1991). OECD Archives, Paris Headquarters.

———(91)2/REV1. *Feasibility Study on Available International Means for Dealing with Illicit Payments in International Commercial Transactions.* Ad Hoc Group on Illicit Payments, Note by the Secretariat (September 30, 1991). OECD Archives, Paris Headquarters.

———(91)3. *Summary Record of the Meeting Held 13–14 June 1991.* Ad Hoc Group on Illicit Payments (September 23, 1991). OECD Archives, Paris Headquarters.

———(91)4. *Agenda.* Ad Hoc Group on Illicit Payments (September 23, 1991). OECD Archives, Paris Headquarters.

———(91)5. *Illicit Payments in International Commercial Transactions: Question of Future Work in OECD.* Ad Hoc Group on Illicit Payments, Note by the Secretariat (October 2, 1991). OECD Archives, Paris Headquarters.
———(91)5/ANN2. *Annex 2.* Ad Hoc Group on Illicit Payments (October 2, 1991). OECD Archives, Paris Headquarters.
———(91)7. *Illicit Payments In International Commercial Transactions.* Report by the Ad Hoc Group on Illicit Payments (November 21, 1991). OECD Archives, Paris Headquarters.
———(91)7/ANN1. *Annex 1: Feasibility Study on Available International Means for Dealing with Illicit Payments in International Commercial Transactions* (November 21, 1991). OECD Archives, Paris Headquarters.
———(91)7/ANN2. *Annex 2: Observations by the Italian Delegation* (November 21, 1991). OECD Archives, Paris Headquarters.
———(92)2. *Agenda.* Ad Hoc Group on Illicit Payments (June 16, 1992). OECD Archives, Paris Headquarters.
———(92)3. *Illicit Payments in International Commercial Transactions.* Ad Hoc Group on Illicit Payments, Note by the Secretariat (June 18, 1992). OECD Archives, Paris Headquarters.
———(92)3/ANN. *Annex: Substantive Elements to be Considered Together with Procedural Options* (June 18, 1992). OECD Archives, Paris Headquarters.
DAFFE/IME/PI(92)3/REV1. *Illicit Payments in International Commercial Transactions.* Ad Hoc Group on Illicit Payments (October 9, 1992). OECD Archives, Paris Headquarters.
———(92)3/REV2. *Feasibility Study on Illicit Payments in International Commercial Transactions.* Ad Hoc Group on Illicit Payments (December 4, 1992). OECD Archives, Paris Headquarters.
———(92)3/REV3. *Feasibility Study on Illicit Payments in International Commercial Transactions.* Ad Hoc Group on Illicit Payments (December 17, 1992). OECD Archives, Paris Headquarters.
DAFFE/IME(93)11. *Private Business Practices.* Note by the Secretariat (April 14, 1993). OECD Archives, Paris Headquarters.
———(93)17. *Programme of Work 1994.* Note by the Secretariat (April 7, 1993). OECD Archives, Paris Headquarters.
———(93)21. Illicit Payments, Note by the Secretariat (April 15, 1993) OECD Archives, Paris Headquarters.
DAFFE/IME/PI(93)1. *Elements of Recommendation—General Considerations.* Ad Hoc Group on Illicit Payments, Notes by the Netherlands Delegation (August 23, 1993). OECD Archives, Paris Headquarters.
———(93)2. *Elements of Recommendation—Definition and Domestic Action.* Ad Hoc Group on Illicit Payments, Notes by the Italian Delegation (August 23, 1993). OECD Archives, Paris Headquarters.

———(93)3. *Elements of Recommendation—International Cooperation*. Ad Hoc Group on Illicit Payments, Notes by the United States Delegation (August 23, 1993). OECD Archives, Paris Headquarters.

———(93)5. *Assimilation*. Ad Hoc Group on Illicit Payments, Note by the German Delegation (August 23, 1993). OECD Archives, Paris Headquarters.

———(93)6. *Tax Treatment of Illicit Payments*. Note by the Secreatriat (August 27, 1993). OECD Archives, Paris Headquarters.

———(93)9. *Report on the OECD Recommendation on the Bribery of Foreign Public Officials*. Report to the CIME (October 26, 1993). OECD Archives, Paris Headquarters.

———(93)10. *Draft Recommendation of the Council on the Bribery of Foreign Public Officials*. Ad Hoc Group on Illicit Payments, Note by the Unites States Delegation (December 7, 1993). OECD Archives, Paris Headquarters.

———(93)11. *Report on the OECD Recommendation on Bribery in International Business Transactions*. Draft Report to the CIME, Ad Hoc Group on Illicit Payments, Note by the United States Delegation (December 27, 1993). OECD Archives, Paris Headquarters.

DAFFE/IME/BR/RD(95)1. *Criminalisation of Bribery of Foreign Public Officials*. Working Group on Bribery in International Business Transactions (October 11, 1995). OECD Archives, Paris Headquarters.

DAFFE/IME/BR(96)2. *Implementation of the Recommendation on Bribery in International Business Transactions*. Draft Report of the CIME to the 1996 Meeting of the Council at Ministerial Level (March 27, 1996). OECD Archives, Paris Headquarters.

DAFFE/IME/BR/A(96)6/REV1. *Agenda*. Working Group on Bribery in International Business Transactions (November 6, 1996). OECD Archives, Paris Headquarters.

Della Porta, Donatella, and Yves Mény, eds. 1997. *Democracy and Corruption in Europe*. London: Pinter.

Department of State. 1997. "Promoting the Model Business Principles." Department of State Publication 104846. Accessed August 20, 2016. http://library.law.columbia.edu/urlmirror/4/PromotingtheModel-BusinessPrinciples.htm.

Eicher, Sharon. 2012. *Corruption in International Business: The Challenge of Cultural and Legal Diversity*. Farnham: Gower Publishing.

Eigen, Peter. 2013. "International Corruption: Organized Civil Society for Better Global Governance." *Social Research: An International Quarterly* 80 (4): 1287–1308.

Elliott, Kimberly Ann. 1997. "Corruption as an International Policy Problem: Overview and Recommendations." In *Corruption and the Global Economy*, edited by Kimberley A. Elliott, 175–233. Washington, DC: Peterson Institute for International Economics.

Ervin, Carolyn, fax to M. Pieth. September 23, 1996. OECD Archives, Paris Headquarters.
European Union. 1998. "Convention Drawn Up on the Basis of Article K.3 (2) (C) of the Treaty on European Union on the Fight Against Corruption Involving Officials of the European Communities or Officials of Member States of the European Union: (May 26, 1997)." *International Legal Materials: Current Documents* 37: 12–21.
FCPA Enforcement. 2018. The FCPA Top Ten List. Accessed June 10, 2018. http://www.fcpablog.com/blog/2018/6/7/socgen-replaces-total-sa-on-the-top-ten-list.html.
Feinberg, Richard E. 1997. *Summitry in the Americas: A Progress Report.* Washington, DC: Peterson Institute.
Galtung, Fredrik, and Jeremy Pope. 1999. "The Global Coalition Against Corruption: Evaluating Transparency International." In *The Self-Restraining State: Power and Accountability in New Democracies*, edited by Andreas Schedler, Marc Plattner, and Larry Jay Diamond, 257–285. Boulder, CO: Lynne Rienner Publishers.
Glynn, Patrick, Stephen Kobrin, and Moises Naim. 1997. "The Globalization of Corruption." In *Corruption and the Global Economy*, edited by Kimberly Ann Elliott, 7–31. Washington, DC: Peterson Institute.
Harris, Robert. 2003. *Political Corruption: In and Beyond the Nation State.* London: Routledge.
Heimann, Fritz. 1996a. "Will There Be a Tipping Point in the Fight Against International Bribery: The Synergy Between Government and Business Measures to Curb Corruption." Presented at Meeting of OECD Working Group on Bribery in International Business Transactions, Paris, France, November 6.
———. 1996b. "The Role of the ICC in Combating Extortion and Bribery." Presented at Meeting of OECD Working Group on Bribery in International Business Transactions, Paris, France, November 6.
International Trade Commission. 1997. *Operation of the Trade Agreements Program, the Year in Trade, 49th Report.* Collingdale, PA: Diane Publishing.
Larson, Alan. 1997. "US Policy on Corruption." In *Corruption and the Global Economy*, edited by Kimberly Ann Elliott, 237–241. Washington, DC: Peterson Institute.
Manfroni, Carlos A., and Richard S. Werksman. 2003. *The Inter-American Convention Against Corruption: Annotated with Commentary.* Lanham, MD: Lexington Books.
Metcalfe, D. 2000. "The OECD Agreement to Criminalize Bribery: A Negotiation Analytic Perspective." *International Negotiation* 5 (1): 129–155.
Mills, C. Wright. 1959. *The Sociological Imagination.* New York: Oxford University Press.

Pieth, Mark. 1999. "International Efforts to Combat Corruption." Paper Presented at the 9th International Anti-Corruption Conference (IACC), Durban, South Africa, October 10–15.

———. 2013. "Introduction." In *The OECD Convention on Bribery: A Commentary*, edited by Mark Pieth Lucinda A. Low, and Nicola Bonucci, 3–56. 2nd ed. Cambridge: Cambridge University Press.

———. 2018. "Bribing Foreign Officials: The OECD Anticorruption Instruments." In *Confronting Corruption: Past Concerns, Present Challenges, and Future Strategies*, edited by Fritz Heimann and Mark Pieth, 75–101. New York: Oxford University Press.

Pope, Jeremy. 2011. "Getting Integrity Reforms Adopted Internationally." In *Delivering Policy Reform: Anchoring Significant Reforms in Turbulent Times*, edited by Evert A. Lindquist, Sam Vincent, and John Wanna, 145–167. Canberra: ANU Press.

Spector, Malcolm, and John Kitsuse. 2009. *Constructing Social Problems*. 4th ed. Rutgers, NJ: Transaction Publishers.

Symposium on Corruption and Good Governance. 1996. OECD Working Papers (34) 4, OECD Archives, Paris Headquarters.

Szarek-Mason, Patrycja. 2010. *The European Union's Fight Against Corruption: The Evolving Policy Towards Member States and Candidate Countries*. Cambridge: Cambridge University Press.

Tanzi, Vito. 1998. "Corruption Around the World: Causes, Consequences, Scope, and Cures." *IMF Staff Papers* 45 (1): 559–594.

TI Press Release. 1998. "G 7 Summit holds Key to Global Anti-Bribery Treaty: Canada, France, Italy and UK Must take First Step." Accessed September 20, 2014. http://www.transparency.org/news/pressrelease/g_7_summit_holds_key_to_global_anti_bribery_treaty.

The White House. 2014. "Summit of the Eight: The Sherpas." Accessed October 22. http://clinton5.nara.gov/WH/New/Eight/sherpa.html.

Touq, Muhyieddeen. 2013. "UNCAC is the Fastest Convention in History." TI Deutschland. Accessed August 6, 2015. http://www.transparency.de/UNCAC-is-the-fastest-conventio.2414.0.html.

UNCTAD. 2002. "UNCTC Evolution: United Nations Center on Transnational Corporations." Accessed August 2, 2014. http://unctc.unctad.org/aspx/UNCTCEvolution.aspx.

UNTERM. 2014. "Draft International Agreement on Illicit Payments." Accessed October 10. http://unterm.un.org/dgaacs/unterm.nsf/8fa942046ff7601c85256983007ca4d8/52f9e4bc389a5e61852569fa00003a47?OpenDocument.

UN Economic and Social Council. 1996. 86th Session. "Resolution 51/191 [Declaration Against Corruption and Bribery in International Commercial Transactions]." December 16 (A/RES/51/191), New York.

U.N. General Assembly. 2000. 55th Session (81st Plenary Meeting). "An Effective International Legal Instrument Against Corruption." December 4 (A/RES/55/61), New York.

Vlassis, Dimitri. 2004. "The United Nations Convention Against Corruption: Origins and Negotiation Process." *Resource Material Series* (66).

Vogl, Frank. 2012. *Waging War on Corruption: Inside the Movement Fighting the Abuse of Power*. Lanham, MD: Rowman & Littlefield.

Washington Embassy, Telegram to Foreign and Commonwealth Office (UK). May 21, 1997. RefN 1160. OECD Archives, Paris Headquarters.

Washington G7 Meeting of Ministers and Central Bank Governors. "Communiqué" (April 27, 1997). Accessed October 22, 2013. http://www.g8.utoronto.ca/finance/fm970427.htm.

World Bank Group. 1992. "Report to the Development Committee and Guidelines on the Treatment of Foreign Direct Investment." In *Legal Framework for the Treatment of Foreign Investment*. Vol. II. Washington, DC: World Bank Group.

CHAPTER 8

Global Anti-Corruption Talks in the 1970s and 1990s: The Story of Two Utopias

This chapter compares global anti-corruption debates in the 1970s and 1990s in order to provide the big picture in the development of a global corruption problem. The chapter suggests that anti-corruption rhetoric was indeed neoliberalized in the 1990s, but the link between anti-corruption, as part of a broader agenda to regulate multinationals, and neoliberalism, as an agenda for deregulation, could be more complex than previously assumed. Anti-corruption debates in the early 1970s concentrated on the impact of big business, and in particular, multinational corporations on politics, democracy and equitable development. Allende called this role 'corruptive' in 1972, while the neoliberal counterrevolution, which engulfed his country in 1973, aimed to prove that this role was universally beneficial. The genealogical root of global corruption can be traced back to the divisive topic of the pursuit of corporate profit and the public interest in the global political economy. If the historical root of these debates is to be revisited, the concern at the time was that multinational corporations are growing in power and attempting to subvert politics to their own benefit. This concern was provoked by the revelations of the role of the ITT Corporation in the political life of Chile. The elegant neoliberal solution to these concerns was to reinstate a harmony of interest between the pursuit of private (corporate) profit and the public interest. There was no need for further government intervention, and especially international regulation of multinational corporations, because the best way to achieve economic growth and serve the

E. Katzarova, *The Social Construction of Global Corruption*,
Political Corruption and Governance,
https://doi.org/10.1007/978-3-319-98569-5_8

public interest simultaneously was to remove obstacles from the free market, rather than creating new ones.

Scholars have long criticized the subversion of anti-corruption policies to a global neoliberal agenda (Brown and Cloke 2004; Krastev 2004). This chapter suggests that, to some extent, neoliberal restructuring can be seen as a radical answer to the fundamental question about the role of multinational corporations in global social progress. The presumed attempt of multinational corporations to subvert the political process to their own benefit was what initially came to be labeled as 'corrupt' influence in global forums, such as the UN. The answer to this problem was not to negate altogether the positive effect that corporations play in the global economy, but to establish common rules to mitigate the potential conflicts between private (corporate) and public interests. This study of the role of transnational corporations and the public interest was the major task of the UNCTC (Hamdani and Ruffing 2015). Already in the 1980s, it was becoming increasingly difficult to stick to the task of working on common rules for multinationals in the global economy because the advent of neoliberalism was challenging the very legitimacy of this goal. While examining the complex reasons for the neoliberal turn of the 1970s and 1980s is beyond the scope of this study, this chapter briefly tackles some of the factors discussed in the literature in order to suggest that an anti-corruption agenda and an anti-neoliberal agenda could be connected in more than one way.

Fake Empires: Corporate Abuse of Political Power

The story of global anti-corruption efforts is wrought with meaningful ironies. For one, a debate that started in the G77 found its resolution in the G7 more than twenty years later. Nowadays, even to students of IR, the G77 sounds like a knockoff of the G7 despite there being good reason to believe the exact opposite. When the first official meeting at Rambouillet took place in November of 1975, the most pressing issue on the agenda of the then six most developed countries in the world was to temper the rambunctiousness of oil-exporting states. As G77 and OPEC members were unionizing in the early 1970s, so were countries in the Global North. The UN General Assembly might have appeared like a good place to start democratizing global political and economic structures in the post-colonial era, but it was simply more efficient to work in a small group of states. The US anti-bribery initiative bore testimony to that. Not that the United States could impose its agenda with ease, even when it was holding the moral high ground in trying to clean up global exchanges from what appeared to be widespread corporate bribery. If anything, the protracted story of the global anti-bribery agreement shows that the United States was not imposing its will on anybody without having to put a very long fight. OECD members proved to be just as formidable a challenge as developing nations were in the UN. The switch between the major venue for anti-corruption talks from the UN in the 1970s to the OECD in the 1990s constituted another way for the leader of the free world to claim ownership of global anti-corruption efforts. Despite the strong European opposition to US demands, OECD members shared similar interests in trying to defend the legitimacy of the multinational corporation.

In addition to the venue switches, the biggest transformation was in terms of content. Corruption was transformed from corporate abuse of power in the 1970s to government abuse of power in the 1990s. The trope of the corrupt corporation came to be supplanted by the tropes of the corrupt politician, corrupt public official and corrupt country. In the process, the blame for corruption was shifted from developed countries (and their corporations) to the developing countries (and their governments). Today, we automatically assume that the locus of corruption is government. This appears to be caused by an extraneous event, such as the rise of the neoliberal tide from the 1970s onward. The transformation of anti-corruption from a call for more regulation into a call for less regulation, however, puts the separation of the two processes into question. With the transformation of corruption from a corporate into a government problem, the content of anti-corruption shifted from more state in the economy to less state in the economy. With the locus of corruption in government, it made sense that government abuse of power should be checked with limiting the opportunities for corrupt behavior by politicians and public officials. Government was not the solution, government was the problem, as Reagan eloquently put it in his inaugural address in January 1981.

Given that the United States tried to initiate an intergovernmental ban on foreign bribery both in 1975 and in 1989, what made the latter attempt successful? There are some differences in the US approach that were independent of the big changes in the global political landscape, and which concerned the strategy of the US executive and the level of certainty within which this strategy operated. The former means that while in the 1970s the United States developed a problem with foreign corporate payments, by the 1990s the United States had a problem with the FCPA. Capitalizing on past mistakes, the US executive could develop a systematic strategy to internationalize the FCPA through lobbying, public diplomacy and the art of summitry. Essential in the process of internationalizing the FCPA were the couple of Latin American countries that the United States engaged with prior to and during the Miami Summit in 1994 and the couple of EU countries the United States engaged with prior to and during the G7 Summit in 1997. Working on global problems through summitry was light years away from debating issues in the General Assembly of the UN. The strategic shift in venues and the instrumental use of publicity were already given due attention in Chapter 7. What made this coordinated US campaign in the 1990s possible was that the FCPA was providing a very clear mandate for the US executive, and also that achieving agreement at regional organizations and the OECD was not conditional this time on an agreement at the UN.

The latter factor listed above concerns the certainty within which the US strategy operated. In 1975, the US executive operated within an environment of uncertainty as to what the fate of the anti-bribery response is going to be at home. As Chapter 5 showed, the American legislator was worried that the executive is trying to circumvent real reform by getting involved in complex intergovernmental talks that would ultimately be ineffective at proscribing foreign payments by American corporations. The push to form a national legislative response to foreign bribery in the two-year period between 1975 and 1977 also operated within a climate of uncertainty as to whether a disclosure or criminal approach would be chosen. The US executive was clearly in favor of a disclosure approach and so were SEC and Senator Church, so when the criminalization approach sponsored by Senator Proxmire prevailed and was signed into law by the next president, the conditions for the multilateral negotiations changed drastically as well. The United States went from arguing that something be done in the line of disclosure to the very specific mandate of trying to internationalize the FCPA in a little over two years.

Another notable difference between the 1970s and the 1990s lies in the demands of the Global South. The draft agreement on illicit payments produced in the UN in 1979 was mostly based on the FCPA. This means that even in the 1970s, the United States was successful at influencing a draft agreement at the UN that served the purpose of internationalizing the FCPA. There was one notable addition to the draft agreement however, and this was the inclusion of an article on the payments made to the apartheid regime in South Africa. As noted previously, the inclusion of such payments under the umbrella of illicit payments was consistent with developing nations claims that it was the political consequences of corporate action that made such behavior illicit or corrupt. A couple of months prior to President Carter signing the FCPA into law, the UN report on the final session of the Working Group on the Problem of Corrupt Practices[1] presented the US position on payments to South Africa as counterproductive:

> The underlying basic political problem is that the U.S. which (partly for reasons of domestic–i.e. presidential/congressional–policy) is pushing hard for a treaty on bribery and illicit payments, is not, at present at least willing to pay the price asked for it by the African countries, i.e., a corresponding criminalization of the payments of royalties and taxes to the illegal minority regimes in southern Africa. Moreover, many developed countries other than the U.S. are indifferent to the idea of setting up elaborate standards for reporting and disclosure of illicit payments. (UNCTC Inter-office memorandum 1977, 1)

The claims on payments to the apartheid regime were also supported by the G77. The position of the Global South was that the Code of Conduct on Transnational Corporations was more important in trying to solve the problem of corporate influence than was the US limited preoccupation with corporate bribery. This is why conditioning the adoption of the agreement on illicit payments on the adoption of the Code of Conduct was consistent with the developing nations demands to bound corporate behavior in a legal framework of collectively agreed-upon rules. Both of these demands were gone by the 1990s. The apartheid issue was no longer part of the parcel and the UNCTC was abolished after a US-inspired restructuring of the UN. The relative ease with which the United States managed to orchestrate the OAS Convention could appear to support the argument that after the end of the Cold War attempts to internationally regulate multinationals and the task of managing the complex interplay between political and economic goals in the

[1]The Working Group on the Problem of Corrupt Practices was superseded by the Committee on an International Agreement on Illicit Payments.

public interest simply dissipated with the end of ideological warfare. The US success in the 1990s can be attributed also to the change in attitude of developing nations toward FDI and their readily incorporation into the line of thinking that informed the 'Washington Consensus.'

There are two major, albeit simplified, ways to explain the developing nations' change of heart. The first is the 'battle of ideas' thesis. Under Soviet influence, developing nations entertained some misguided ideas about the role of the state in development and the need to regulate multinationals. These ideas collapsed by themselves and were replaced by what in 1989 came to be called 'The Washington Consensus' (Williamson 2008). This was a strictly intellectual battlefield, and the ideas of the Washington Consensus prevailed because they were simply better at describing how economies actually work, and how they should work. With the collapse of the already bankrupt Soviet enterprise, the theoretical and practical prowess of the set of ideas of the Washington Consensus became self-evident. There simply was no alternative, as Thatcher had said a decade earlier.

The second explanation is more sinister. US-backed dictatorships in Latin America—from Brazil to Chile—swept the elites of these countries, who were entertaining the wrong ideas. The recycling of petrodollars from the 1970s oil crises fueled oil-importing developing nations' debts through US and European banks' lending. When the Volker shock happened in 1979, and interest rates soared, Latin America could no longer service its debt. The conditionality attached to IMF and World Bank dealings with debtor developing nations finished what the military coups of the previous decades had started. The world was ready for a particular brand of capitalism, now called neoliberalism.

Similarly, when analyzing external factors to the success of the US delegation to internationalize the FCPA in the 1990s, and the failure, especially in the late 1970s, we can go in two major directions. The first one is to stress the role of agency, and in particular the new agents, who were not present in the 1970s. The coalition-building role of TI and the leadership of Mark Pieth would come to the forefront of such agency-based explanations. The second aspect of US success can, on the contrary, be pinned down to structural changes. With the end of the Cold War, controversies, like the ones in the 1970s, simply dissipated. It was easier for the United States to convince developing countries of the necessity to internationalize the FCPA in the 1990s because they were speaking the same language of free market entrepreneurism and FDI. If we are to entertain the 'battle of ideas' thesis, this explanation makes a lot of sense. If we are to look into the second option above, once again things start to look more sinister. It is that the ideas developing nations entertained about regulating multinationals and actively guiding their own development were purged out of the Third World in the 1970s and 1980s, sometimes with the help of violent dictatorships and debt politics. There was nothing natural about the confluence of thought that emerged after the Cold War; the neoliberal project took decades of forceful persuasion tactics.

To speculate about the possibility of a link between the Third-World resurgence in the 1970s, and in particular the calls to regulate multinationals, and the US turn to neoliberalism would be that; just a speculation. Still, when we turn to function and not the study of motivation, it is difficult to not see that the basic tenets of neoliberalism ticked a lot of boxes. To give some substance to this argument, it would suffice to look at the two major ideas of regulating multinationals in the public interest and the self-regulating market. The problem of corporations and the public interest emerged as a central aspect of the work of UNCTC. This was not part of some poorly disguised communist propaganda, as critics would have it. According to Hamdani and Ruffing (2015), the task of aligning the corporate with the public interest was an inherently American agenda, which was supposed to strengthen the free market enterprise. The conflicts of interest between multinationals and the public were not insurmountable, of course, but were judged to require some government intervention and international regulation. This is where the idea of the self-regulating market comes into play. The self-regulating market made the attempt to regulate multinationals in the public interest redundant. The basic idea was that there was no conflict between the interests of multinational corporations and the public interest. The self-regulating market was in the best interest of everybody. Yet, neoliberal thinking on the public interest remained fuzzy. Four albeit schematic basic arguments could be distinguished: (1) the 'trickle down' argument; (2) the 'corporations are people too' thesis; (3) 'the road to dictatorship' argument; and (4) the 'there is no society' thesis. The first one is an extension of the 'trickle down' thesis that is usually used to justify cuts in taxes. If corporations are left to flourish in a market free of government constraints, they will eventually benefit the rest of society through job creation and investment. The second argument is that corporations are people too. There is no fundamental difference between individuals and conglomerations of individuals, such as multinational corporations.

Accordingly, to limit corporate freedom would mean to limit personal freedom. The third argument is 'the road to dictatorship' thesis. State intervention is a slippery slope, which increases government oppression of businesses and individuals alike, and is a one-way ticket to a Soviet-style dictatorship. If all else fails, the fourth argument is the 'there is no society' thesis. There is no public interest, there are only individual interests and it would be impossible and dangerous to run after some vague public interest, that incompetent government officials would only try to use to their benefit.

How did this business-friendly ideology become the new economic science has been the central subject of many books (Offer and Söderberg 2016; Stedman Jones 2014; Harvey 2007; Klein 2007; Duggan 2003). This book suggested that one of the unexplored avenues for the neoliberal turn could be found in the rise of the Global South in the 1970s and the international attempts to regulate multinationals in order to curb corporate power. The threat that the Third-World resurgence in the 1970s posed to the international order of things could easily be underestimated had it been an isolated case. Calls to regulate multinationals were not a project solely of the Third World, however. Trade unions had also attempted it in the ILO in the late 1960s (Petrini 2017). Globally, international trade unions and Third-World countries were challenging the power of corporations in world affairs. In the United States, the public interest movement was also threatening to provoke a renewed regulatory vigor on corporate affairs and so were other social movements. Altogether, according to Harvey (2007), a turn to the left was looking more likely as the preferred choice for tackling the crisis of Keynesianism. The future of the global economic system appeared to be holding more regulation and some of it international, rather than less.

If we do not subscribe to the battle of ideas thesis without accounting for strategic human agency, what happened was that the 1970s witnessed a period of intensive business mobilization. Posed with threats on multiple fronts, businesses for the first time realized that they had common interests, which they could more effectively defend collectively. Paradoxically, it was in the period after the FCPA was signed into law that business managed to 'turn the tide' (Vogel 2003, 148). Vogel shows that the political influence of business in the United States started to increase in the period 1977–1980, at the expense of organized labor and the public interest movement. These fluctuations in the relative power of the labor and consumer movements against the power of organized business should not have been a cause of concern, had this inequality in interest representation not become a permanent feature of the political landscape. Gilens and Page (2014) find that in the period from 1981 to 2002 organized business interests have come to dominate politics at the expense of democratic electorates. Globally as well, the power of business was in no way matched by an increase in the bargaining power of labor and global consumer movements. In the 1970s, even proponents of the free market system expected that global consumer movements, intergovernmental accords and international labor unions will keep rising corporate power under check (Bock and Fuccillo 1975).

Legal lobbying can be more consequential than bribery when it comes to influencing public policy, as Campos and Giovannoni (2007) find. In studying, what they call 'legal corruption' Kaufmann and Vicente (2011) argue that a significant amount of channels and transactions to achieve influence have remained legal (especially in transnational context). This allows corporate actors to achieve gentle forms of state capture in developed and developing countries alike. Putting the stress on influence raises the question of how to distinguish between benevolent and malevolent forms of influence. After all, anti-corruption protestors who topple a government are also exerting influence. In addition, not all corporate influence is necessarily against the public good. The answer is perhaps in what Heidenheimer and Johnston (2011) call public-interest-centered definitions of corruption. In the public-interest-centered definition, the role of public officials is to guard the public interest and not give way to special interests, which might attempt to capture the political agenda. As difficult as it may be to define the public interest, the relevant question is, if a given policy or the rules of the game benefit the majority of the population or a select few. When special interests manage to subvert the rules of the game, a mild or more acute form of state capture may occur (Hellman et al. 2003). The efforts of companies to shape the institutional, legal and political framework within which they operate may not be the result of illegal action, but once again, if the stress is placed on influence rather than the means through which influence is achieved, the decisive factor would be whether corporate influence on policy serves the public at large or only special interests. When the influence of special interests over the political agenda is high, policy makers may be seen as being more responsive toward the demands of corporate actors to the detriment of the public interest.

Arguably, at the same time that corporate bribery was being tackled, organized business interests were finding less conspicuous modes of political influence. This effort can be captured partly by the concept of 'legal corruption' (Kaufmann and Vicente 2011). Legal corruption may be present in a collusive relationship between business and government elites, which can manifest through legal lobbying, legal campaign funding or revolving door practices. As Della Porta and Vannucci (1999) have shown, the commodities of the corruption market are two: (1) influence over political decision-making and (2) access to privileged or restricted information (39–45). Influence on regulatory oversight is another aspect of legal corruption. Kaufmann (2008) refers to a meeting that took place on April 28, 2004, between representatives of the SEC and representatives of the five largest investment banks. The meeting led to amendments to the net capital rules, which have been in place since 1975. Despite being contested as the source of the global financial crisis, the relaxation of the net capital rules can be seen as a relevant example of corporate influence over regulatory institutions without any payments or other monetizable awards. If the SEC changes are to be credited, at least to some extent, as having contributed to the global financial crisis of 2008, the role of the federal government agency as protector of the public interest had been compromised. At the same time, Kaufmann (2008) does not imply in any way that there were inappropriate or illegal exchanges between investment bank representatives and SEC representatives. Rather, it is the economic power of the largest investment banks that is readily convertible into political influence.

Even prior to the bailouts of 2008, following the Emergency Economic Stabilization Act of 2008, political connectedness appeared to be central to government financial assistance. Faccio et al. (2006) find in a study of companies across 35 countries in the period 1997–2002 that politically connected companies are much more likely to be bailed out in periods of economic turmoil. Political connectedness, however, is also not illegal and it is difficult to segregate due from undue influence. Kaufmann's (2005) definition of corruption as 'the extent to which many powerful private firms engage in undue influence, to shape state policies, laws and regulations, for their own benefit' (82) is more in line with the Chilean legacy of understanding corruption in the global economy. Kaufmann (2010), who also happens to be a Chilean national, calls for a re-formulation of the problem and redefines corruption as a form of collusion between government officials and business actors which has remained outside the grip of the law. This collusion may start with legal forms of influence peddling and lead to a subtle form of state capture.

Corruption as corporate capture of democracy is not far from Allende's framing of the ITT affair. The neoliberal counterrevolution offers legitimacy to this corporate capture. Systemic corruption is not unrelated to payments, of course, but it could be understood better through the imprecise concepts of 'money in politics,' revolving door politics, but above all as coming from the underlying principle that there is a natural alignment of business and public interests. This underlying philosophy may present the relaxation of regulatory oversight as being in the public interest because more profit for business means more benefits for society. At the same time, this logic can be seen to institutionalize undue corporate influence on politics. It is not difficult to imagine that the corporate-backed military dictatorship of Pinochet, which swiftly turned to neoliberalism, would have constituted the epitome of corruption for Allende. In fact, understood as corporate capture, corruption has only intensified around the globe since the early 1970s. The mobilization of business interests witnessed in this decade has led to better tactics of corporate influence on politics. Business as a philosophy of governance has also exerted powerful influence over public institutions. The underlying philosophy of neoliberalism itself has transformed politics into managerialism, while the marketization of everything—from education through health care to environmental protection—has led to radical transformations of societies and natural habitats. Economic calculus has started to dominate so many aspects of the public sphere that the complete corporatization of government is starting to look within reach.

Corporations and the Public Interest

It is not difficult to see that corruption as undue corporate influence on politics is not compatible with a neoliberal agenda of deregulation and privatization. In fact, neoliberalism—understood as the disproportionate influence of corporations and business thinking on politics—can be seen as a form of political corruption. This argument is not purely conceptual, but is based on global anti-corruption debates in the 1970s, which concentrated on corporate abuse of power and the way market prerogatives can overrun political and democratic objectives. Contemporary concerns over the influence of corporate money on national elections and public policies illustrate the enduring relevance of corruption as undue business influence on politics. The successful framing of a global corruption problem in the mid-1990s channeled an ascendant neoliberal narrative emphasizing the merits of the free market and the shortcomings of politics. Corruption was redefined (and operationalized in academic research) as a problem not of broader corporate and business influence on politics but primarily of bribery. This chapter suggests there might be new avenues for research on the links between corruption and neoliberalism.

What would an anti-corruption agenda that is also a movement against neoliberalism look like? An anti-corruption agenda in the legacy of Allende would study the private (corporate) abuse of the political power. The fundamental anti-corruption goals from that vantage point would be to revisit the premise that there is no fundamental clash between corporate and public interests, and then regulate on behalf of the public in the cases when such clashes are seen as significant. Such an agenda would put into question revolving door practices that are based on the same assumption—that there is no fundamental conflict of interest between governmental and corporate positions of power.

The task of studying and regulating the corporate abuse of power encounters a couple of fundamental questions about whether corporations should at all pursue the public interest, whether government regulation in that respect would do more harm than good, and whether corporations are indeed persons (see *Citizens United vs FEC* 558 US 310 [2010]). The answers some neoliberal thinkers give to these questions are quite emphatic. Hayek (1944) famously argued that not only is government intervention in the economy inefficient, but it also leads to the concentration of power in government, which over the long run leads to a severe limitation of personal freedom in the form of totalitarianism. Regarding the question about the role of corporations in serving the public interest, Friedman (1970) remarked that the only responsibility of business is to increase its profit and that the notion of corporate social responsibility 'involves the acceptance of the socialist view that political mechanisms, not market mechanisms, are the appropriate way to determine the allocation of scarce resources to alternative uses.' The attempt to disembed business from most social and political constraints can be seen as a major goal of the neoliberal agenda.

The disembedding of the market economy (Polanyi 2001) is particularly stark when corporations start to share the proverbial international anarchy of nation states. The attempt to regulate the conduct of corporations internationally, which was evident in the UN effort to finalize a binding Code of Conduct, can be seen as an attempt to put multinational corporations under some political and social constraints that are negotiated internationally. That the Code of Conduct would have faced significant implementation problems was a fact, but more important was perhaps the spirit of such attempts to bind the global market by political means that temper the extremes of profit maximization at a global scale. Neoliberalism successfully delegitimized this attempt with the assertion that market economies, nationally or globally, should not be contaminated with politics. Neoliberalism constituted a counterrevolution against what at the time was perceived as a swing to the left. In asserting the moral bankruptcy of any opposition to the reinvented free market dogma, the neoliberals took Hayek (1944) a step further and managed to establish a confluence between state intervention in the economy and totalitarianism. In the process, Developmentalism and Keynesianism became Stalinism. The irony of the early neoliberal experiments in Latin America, of course, was that it took a dictatorship in Chile to set the market free.

Neoliberals admit indeed to a conflict of interest between political and economic objectives, but only because governments are trying to regulate against the interests of corporations in the pursuit of a vague (and actually nonexistent) public interest. The job of governing should actually be to create the right conditions for businesses to pursue their interest and the market would take care of the rest. The neoliberal counterrevolution of the 1970s and 1980s amounted to nothing less than a war between politics and economics as the best way to organize and manage societies. The radicalization of free market proponents should also be seen as reactionary. Hayek was reactionary to Keynes, and the 'Chicago boys' were reactionary to a more active state in the developing world. Early anti-corruption debates about the role of multinational corporations in societies showed concern about business interests becoming too enmeshed in politics. Neoliberalism provided a blunt answer to such concerns: There was nothing to be feared.

Corruption, from a question about the impact of corporate power on democracy and politics, became a question of limiting the impact of government on the economy. That inversion was quite revolutionary in itself, but the neoliberal transformation of society went even further. It went to demand government to transform in the image of a business, to adopt the same governance mechanisms, the same goals, the same language. Anti-corruption rhetoric and practice also went to contribute toward the goal of making government look and act more like a business. First, as noted before, the locus of corruption was government, and government officials were no different than any other market actor—they were interested in the pursuit of their own interest. Public officials' abuse of power was the question to be tackled, and not corporate abuse of power. To downsize government and privatize most of its former prerogatives was a natural and efficient way to fight government abuse of power and hand more services to the impartial free market.

Critics of neoliberalism often lament the excessive marketization and managerialization of metaphoric and actual public spaces (Webb 2009). The words of Margaret Thatcher from her 1987 interview for 'Woman's Own' that there is no society, just individuals and their families are often referenced as a signifier for this new annihilation of the very concept of the social that was ushered by the neoliberal era. Perhaps, lesser known are her words from a 1981 interview for 'Sunday Times' that: 'Economics are the method; the object is to change the heart and soul' (271). It is quite possibly in 'changing the heart and soul' of individuals that the major success of neoliberalism lays. It is in the assertion that individuals and conglomerations of individuals, such as corporations, should relentlessly pursue their private interest and somehow, by the mysterious grace of the market, the common good would still be within reach. While in the 1970s the inherent contradictions of the excessive pursuit of private (corporate) profit and the public interest were still in the center of debates, by the 1990s these conflicts of private and public interest seemed to have been all but forgotten.

The Career of Global Corruption and Problem Definition

The process through which corruption came to be understood and defined as a global problem holds some relevance for academic debates and purely conceptual musings on what constitutes corruption. The Senturia (1931) definition 'misuse of public power for private profit' (448) is truly versatile in its simplicity and can accommodate more than one meaning. To understand corruption as corporate abuse of political or public power for private profit would be one way to accommodate the lost debates of the 1970s. As noted previously, if corruption is to be understood in that tradition, as disproportionate business influence on politics, this has implications for the locus of corruption.

Despite minor alterations in the wording, the contemporary understanding of corruption revolves closely around the institution of the public office. In both grand and petty corruption, it is public officials at different levels of government, who fail to observe the public interest and become focal point of concern. Heidenheimer and Johnston (2011) argue that in relation to the referential frame for the misuse, four definitional variants exist; a 'public-office-centered,' a 'public-interest-centered,' a 'market-centered' and a 'public-opinion-centered' (3–12). It is the way in which the Senturia definition is applied, that implies the locus of corruption is in government and public authorities. As is well known, political corruption and administrative corruption are also 'grand' and 'petty'; the former implicates political decision makers, while the latter is concerned with lower-level bureaucrats. Furthermore, systemic corruption vertically cuts through petty and grand corruption and 'implicates an entire bureaucratic hierarchy, electoral system or overall governmental structure from top to bottom' (Rose-Ackerman 2007, xvii). Once again, when it comes to notions of 'systemic corruption,' the locus of corruption is firmly rooted in government and politics. The systemic understanding of corruption from the vantage point of developing countries in the 1970s had a very different meaning. The lack of global rules on corporate conduct was contributing to the corruptive influence that multinationals could, in certain cases, exert on political institutions for their own benefit. The major concern in this sort of systemic corruption was the lack of accountability and the impunity with which multinational corporations operate in the global economy.

The international counterpart to the corrupt politician and the corrupt public official is, of course, the corrupt country. This development has been due mostly to the charms of corruption rankings, a neat way to rank countries based on their level of perceived corruption, which generates headlines and keeps governments accountable. One of the consequences of conceptualizing corruption as a 'transaction,' and in particular, as bribery, was that corruption becomes measurable. Selecting a piece of the puzzle such as illicit monetized payments between private and public agents makes corruption quantifiable and was done for the purposes of economic analysis (Rose-Ackerman 2007). Quantification of the perception of corruption in the CPI index is, nonetheless, not limited to bribery of public officials, but includes public procurement kickbacks and embezzlement of public resources. All of these also seem to be understood in relation to government.

Should we then move the locus of corruption to the private sector? The notion of corruption as corrupt payment implies that corruption is a transaction. The idea of a business—government interaction is already present in the notion of transaction, but is not exhausted by it. It is not difficult to accommodate the idea that there is something wrong in the interaction between business and politics. As noted previously, this moves the locus of corruption not from politics to business, but to the space of interaction that defines the relationship between the two. In this way, we escape both the trope of the corrupt politician and the trope of corrupt businessman.

What is happening in the interaction between business and politics? It is not difficult to discern a neoliberal argument in the enduring tropes of the corrupt public official, the corrupt politician and the corrupt country. The politics of placing the locus of corruption in government is quite straightforward. It implies that we should be wary of increasing the power of government, and in particular its regulatory capacities, leading directly to the argument of the 'lean' state as the best way to minimize corruption. As noted previously, the idea of corporate actors as the source of corruption led to debates on the pursuit of private (corporate) profit and the protection of the public interest. The discursive construction of the corrupt politician can be seen as a direct response to the corrupt corporation. Every time we automatically resort to the trope of the corrupt politician, who takes an envelope under the table, we become part of the neoliberal narrative. This is in no way a justification for government abuse of power, but simply a recognition that the tropes of the corrupt politician, corrupt public official and the corrupt country are charged with ideological connotations. Furthermore, from a constructivist point of view, the neoliberal transformation of society and politics creates, as much as it describes, the political villain that we are now so used to. It is characteristic that public choice easily turns from descriptive into prescriptive theory, when arguing that the self-serving politician is preferable to the public interest fanatics.

In an interview for the New York Times, entitled appropriately 'The Bribe Busters,' Stanley Sporkin, who was central to the SEC's work on bribery at the time said: 'I really think we're dealing with corruption of the process. There has been a lack of attention to the way corporations are managed in this country (…). Capitalism is the greatest thing going, but unchecked it's its own undoing' (Kohlmeier 1976). It was under the banner of 'saving capitalism' that the 1970s attempts to regulate multinational corporations should be understood and evaluated. The uneasy relationship between business and democracy was exacerbated by globalization because a global market without regulatory oversight offers ample ground for a lot of reckless behavior. Although neoliberalism was marketed as 'the alternative' to communism in the post-Cold War era, in the 1970s the battle of ideas was between the two strands of economic liberalism: the radicalized free market version that came to be known as neoliberalism and the more moderate version, characteristic of the postwar compromise. As a utopian project neoliberalism is self-perpetuating, with every crisis, more market distortions have to be overcome by removing regulatory barriers and public institutions have to be disciplined with more austerity. The free market trope found a powerful ally in the trope of the corrupt politician. The weakness of politics in front of the capacity of business and technologies to shape the future seemed like a welcome deliverance from the presumed incompetence of government. Without politics in the way, we had moved into a utopian future beyond conflict of interest between employees, consumers and employers. This harmony of interests was also extended to the Third World. The new ideology was offering deliverance to the wary governments of the Global South, who only had to surrender to the free market dogma to join the prosperous North.

The radicalization of the Global South discussed in this book was, of course, also a utopian project. Developing nations perhaps took their independence a bit too literally. Their assertiveness in the 1970s showed that they thought they could choose and mix approaches. Despite the Cold War rhetoric, this 'mix and match' approach was seen by the economist of the South, Raul Prebisch, as progressive capitalism (Margulis 2017). The communist threat was perhaps not the major function of adopting a tough stance against unruly governments, such as the one of Allende. The uncertainty of expropriation was multiplied by the chance that the Allende model might become widespread. On Allende's agenda, the question was if what was good for General Motors was also good for Chile. Nixon's answer would have been an emphatic 'yes.' In fact, his successor, Gerald Ford, also believed that what happened in

Chile was in the interest not just of the American, but also the Chilean people (Ford 1974).[2] What was good for General Motors was good for everybody.

The Road not Traveled

In the second half of the 1990s, there was an explosion of anti-corruption treaties and initiatives. The world, it appeared, was finally ready to tackle the perennial problem of political corruption. This book offered a critical appraisal of the 'corruption eruption' that seemed to have captured the imagination of global policy makers and ordinary citizens. The book showed how the framing of global corruption at the time promoted a narrative on the merits of the free market and the deficiencies of politics that was decisively neoliberal. Global anti-corruption initiatives first had to frame a global corruption problem and transform business–state relations in the process. From being understood as a problem of corporate influence on politics, corruption became redefined—and operationalized in academic research—as the much more limited offense of bribery. The locus of corruption shifted from the private to the public sector, and our understanding of corruption came to be dominated by the image of the greedy politician. Globally, the idea of a 'corrupt country' captured the public imagination through the spread of perception-based country rankings. Everybody is an anti-corruptionist now, but anti-corruption discourse and practice are not as neutral, technocratic and devoid of struggles for power as we would assume. The direction and content of global anti-corruption efforts have been shaped by one country, more than any other—the United States. This book offered the story of how this happened.

Academic literature so far has neglected the way in which definitions of corruption have been shaped within and between international organizations, such as the OECD, the UN, the CoE, OAS and the EU since the 1970s. This book distinguished between American and Chilean legacies in international organizations. The American legacy took root in

[2] It should be noted that in the context of the conference, President Ford was suggesting that the US involvement in Chile was limited to supporting the opposition and the media outlets friendly to the opposition, because President Allende was presumably trying to silence them. It is probably in this context of supporting freedom of speech that Ford's utterance should be understood.

the OECD and defined corruption as bribery. The Chilean legacy took root in the UN, in particular, in the UNCTAD, the UNCTC and the G77, and defined corruption as corporate influence. Without adumbrating the definitions of corruption, promoted by these two legacies, and the impact they had on countries in the Global South and the Global North, the institutional interplay that allowed the emergence of a global corruption problem in the 1990s looks incomplete. The American legacy prevailed in the 1990s and corruption globally became to be widely accepted as transnational *quid pro quo*, as well as a limited single-actor offense. The Chilean legacy was promoting a rather radical critique of the global economic system by conceptualizing of corruption as corporate influence over politics. The cure for corruption, according to this perspective, was establishing commonly agreed rules to regulate corporate conduct internationally. This understanding of corruption and its policy implications became largely delegitimized, starting in the 1980s, with the onslaught of policies of deregulation and privatization. The American conceptualization of corruption, as the more limited offense of bribery, and as an individual failing, rather than a systemic problem, was more resonant with the policy mood of the 1980s and prevailed in the 1990s. The Chilean and American legacies, however, are still relevant for current debates on anti-corruption policies and definitions of corruption as a global problem.

The title of this section makes reference to the widely known, and equally widely misunderstood, poem by Robert Frost 'The Road Not Taken.' In the poem, a traveler finds two paths in the woods and decides which one to take. The irony of the poem is that even though the traveler would later justify her choice as inevitable, the two roads were rather similar. In hindsight, we all want to believe we took the right decision, and we would go out of our way to justify the road taken as meaningful and even inevitable. To the more critical among us, the opposite might apply however. We would imagine the alternatives to the chosen course of action and might sincerely believe that if only we had taken the other road, most or all of our current calamities would not have happened. Both positions are equally alluring and deceptive. The 'road not taken' will always appeal to critical analysts, but as its practical implications have never been tested, that road might not have led us to a better outcome. Still, imagining alternative roads, utopian counterfactuals to our current predicaments, might not be entirely without merit.

This book touched upon the way in which, in the 1970s, states found themselves at a similar crossroad—faced with two diverging ways to organize the global economy. One entailed more state intervention in the global market and preserving the position of nation states (especially democratic nation states) as the guardians of the public interest. This road was corruption as corporate influence over politics. During the 1980s, the opposite view prevailed. Rather than regulating corporate conduct internationally, a movement for deregulation and privatization swept the globe. The problem was not so much private to public influence, as the developing nations claimed, but public to private influence, because governments should not interfere in the workings of the market. With the locus of corruption in government, the corrupt corporation was supplanted by the corrupt politician and the corrupt country. Propped by the ascendant neoliberal narrative, the anti-corruption debate had been reversed at 180 degrees and became safe for export in the new millennium.

References

Bock, P. G., and Vincent J. Fuccillo. 1975. "Transnational Corporations as International Political Actors." *Studies in Comparative International Development* 10 (2): 51–77.

Brown, Ed, and Jonathan Cloke. 2004. "Neoliberal Reform, Governance and Corruption in the South: Assessing the International Anti-corruption Crusade." *Antipode* 36 (2): 272–294.

Campos, Nauro, and Francesco Giovannoni. 2007. "Lobbying, Corruption and Political Influence." *Public Choice* 131 (1): 1–21.

Della Porta, Donatella, and Alberto Vannucci. 1999. *Corrupt Exchanges: Actors, Resources, and Mechanisms of Political Corruption.* New York: Aldine de Gruyter.

Duggan, Lisa. 2003. *The Twilight of Equality?: Neoliberalism, Cultural Politics, and the Attack on Democracy.* Boston: Beacon Press.

Faccio, Mara, Ronald W. Masulis, and John McConnell. 2006. "Political Connections and Corporate Bailouts." *The Journal of Finance* 61 (6): 2597–2635.

Ford, Gerald. 1974. "The President's New Conference." September 16. Accessed October 22, 2017. http://www.presidency.ucsb.edu/ws/index.php?pid=4717.

Friedman, Milton. 1970. "The Social Responsibility of Business Is to Increase Its Profits." *The New York Times Magazine*, September 13. Accessed October 22,

2017. https://www.colorado.edu/studentgroups/libertarians/issues/friedman-soc-resp-business.html.
Gilens, Martin, and Benjamin Page. 2014. "Testing Theories of American Politics: Elites, Interest Groups, and Average Citizens." *Perspectives on Politics* 12 (3): 564–581.
Hamdani, K., and L. Ruffing. 2015. *United Nations Centre on Transnational Corporations: Corporate Conduct and the Public Interest.* London and New York: Routledge.
Harvey, David. 2007. *A Brief History of Neoliberalism.* Oxford: Oxford University Press.
Hayek, Friedrich A. 1944. *The Road to Serfdom.* New York and London: George Routledge and Sons.
Heidenheimer, Arnold J., and Michael Johnston. 2011. *Political Corruption: Concepts and Contexts.* Rutgers, NJ: Transaction.
Hellman, Joel, Geraint Jones, and Daniel Kaufmann. 2003. "Seize the State, Seize the Day: State Capture and Influence in Transition Economies." *Journal of Comparative Economics* 31 (4): 751–773.
Kaufmann, Daniel. 2005. "Myths and Realities of Governance and Corruption." In *The World Economic Forum, Global Competitiveness Report 2005–2006*, edited by Augusto Lopez-Carlos, Michael E. Porter, and Klaus Schwab, 81–98. New York: Palgrave Macmillan.
———. 2008. *Daniel Kaufmann's Farewell Lecture: Governance, Crisis, and the Longer View: Unorthodox Reflections on the New Reality.* Washington, DC: World Bank.
———. 2010. "Daniel Kaufmann on State Capture." *World Policy Journal* 27 (1): 3–4.
Kaufmann, Daniel, and Pedro C. Vicente. 2011. "Legal Corruption." *Economics & Politics* 23 (2): 195–219.
Klein, Naomi. 2007. *The Shock Doctrine: The Rise of Disaster Capitalism.* New York: Picador.
Kohlmeier, Louis. 1976. "The Bribe Busters." *New York Times*, September 26.
Krastev, Ivan. 2004. *Shifting Obsessions: Three Essays on the Politics of Anticorruption.* Budapest: Central European University Press.
Margulis, Matias. 2017. *The Global Political Economy of Raúl Prebisch.* London and New York: Taylor & Francis.
Offer, Avner, and Gabriel Söderberg. 2016. *The Nobel Factor: The Prize in Economics, Social Democracy, and the Market Turn.* Princeton: Princeton University Press.
Petrini, Francesco. 2017. "Capital Hits the Road: Regulating Multinational Corporations During the Long 1970s." In *Contesting Deregulation: Debates, Practices and Developments in the West Since the 1970s*, edited by Knud

Andresen and Stefan Müller, 185–199. New York and Oxford: Berghahn Books.

Polanyi, Karl. 2001. *The Great Transformation: The Political and Economic Origins of Our Time*. Boston: Beacon Press.

Rose-Ackerman, Susan. 2007. *International Handbook on the Economics of Corruption*. Northampton, MA: Edward Elgar.

Senturia, Joseph. 1931. "Corruption Political." In *Encyclopedia of the Social Sciences*, vol. 4, 448–452. New York: Macmillan.

Stedman Jones, Daniel. 2014. *Masters of the Universe: Hayek, Friedman, and the Birth of Neoliberal Politics—Updated Edition*. Reprint edition. Princeton and Oxford: Princeton University.

Thatcher, Margaret. 1981. "Interview for Sunday Times." May 1. Thatcher Archive. Accessed October 22, 2017. https://www.margaretthatcher.org/document/104475.

———. 1987. "Interview for Woman's Own," September 23, Thatcher Archive. Accessed October 22, 2017. https://www.margaretthatcher.org/document/106689.

UNCTC Inter-office Memorandum. 1977. "Final Session of the Working Group on the Problem of Corrupt Practices." July 7. Series 0897, Box 7, File 4, UN Archives, New York Headquarters.

Vogel, David. 2003. *Fluctuating Fortunes: The Political Power of Business in America*. Washington: Beard Books.

Webb, D. 2009. "Where's the Vision? The Concept of Utopia in Contemporary Educational Theory." *Oxford Review of Education* 35 (6): 743–760.

Williamson, John. 2008. "A Short History of the Washington Consensus." In *The Washington Consensus Reconsidered: Towards a New Global Governance*, edited by Narcís Serra and Joseph E. Stiglitz, 14–31. Oxford: Oxford University Press.

Index

E. Katzarova, *The Social Construction of Global Corruption*, Political Corruption and Governance,
https://doi.org/10.1007/978-3-319-98569-5

The manufacturer's authorised representative in the EU is Springer Nature Customer Service Centre GmbH, Europaplatz 3, 69115 Heidelberg, Germany. If you have any concerns regarding our products, please contact ProductSafety@springernature.com

Printed and bound by CPI Group (UK) Ltd, Croydon, CR0 4YY
30/09/2026
02225595-0005